Two in a Bed

Two in a Bed

THE SOCIAL SYSTEM
OF COUPLE BED SHARING

PAUL C. ROSENBLATT

STATE UNIVERSITY OF NEW YORK PRESS

Published by
STATE UNIVERSITY OF NEW YORK PRESS
ALBANY

© 2006 State University of New York

For information, address
State University of New York Press
194 Washington Avenue, Suite 305, Albany, NY 12210-2384

Production, Laurie Searl
Marketing, Fran Keneston

Library of Congress Cataloging-in-Publication Data

Rosenblatt, Paul C.
    Two in a bed : the social system of couple bed sharing / Paul C. Rosenblatt.
        p. cm.
    Includes bibliographical references and index.
    ISBN 0-7914-6829-1 (hardcover : alk. paper) — ISBN 0-7914-6830-5 (pbk. : alk. paper)
1. Sleep—Social aspects. 2. Sleeping customs. 3. Interpersonal relations. 4. Couples.
I. Title.

    GT3000.3.R67 2006
    306.4—dc22

                                                                                    2005026824

ISBN-13: 978-0-7914-6829-6 (hardcover : alk. paper)
ISBN-13: 978-0-7914-6830-2 (pbk. : alk. paper)

10   9   8   7   6   5   4   3   2

CONTENTS

ACKNOWLEDGMENTS   VII

1   INTRODUCTION   1

2   FORMING THE COUPLE SYSTEM:
    LEARNING TO SHARE A BED   13

3   THE BED   25

4   GOING TO BED   37

5   ACTIVITIES IN THE TRANSITION FROM AWAKE TO SLEEP   49

6   TEMPERATURE PREFERENCES   65

7   TALKING AND TOUCHING   77

8   ANGER AND THE COUPLE BED   93

9   ILLNESS AND INJURY   105

10 HOW CAN YOU SLEEP SO SOUNDLY
    WHEN I'M SO WIDE AWAKE?   113

11 OUTSIDE INTRUSIONS INTO COUPLE SLEEP   123

12   BATHROOM TRIPS, TOSSING AND TURNING, RESTLESS LEGS,
         SLEEP TALKING, GRINDING TEETH, AND NIGHTMARES   131

13   SNORING AND SLEEP APNEA   147

14   SAFETY, INTIMACY, AND WHY COUPLES SLEEP TOGETHER   161

15   WAKING UP IN THE MORNING   177

16   WEEKENDS   183

17   EVERYDAY LIFE AND THE COUPLE SYSTEM   189

     APPENDIX   199

     REFERENCES   203

     NAME INDEX   213

     SUBJECT INDEX   217

ACKNOWLEDGMENTS

This book has benefited from conversations with many people. I must not list the names of the people I interviewed, because that would violate our confidentiality agreement, but what they had to say is absolutely central to this book. Among people who provided timely and insightful conversation that was most helpful, I want to especially thank Martha Rueter and Sara Wright. I doubt that I would have carried out this research and written this book if they had not provided supportive and stimulating conversation as I edged up toward beginning the project. I want to thank Wanda Olson and Ira Rosenblatt for helping me to think about the issues. In the academic world in which I work, there have been dozens of people who offered interesting, stimulating, and supportive comments about this project. My thanks to all of them. Finally, I want to thank the people with whom I shared a household as I worked on this project, Sara Wright and Emily Wright-Rosenblatt. This is not the kind of work that could have been done without strong and affirming support from them. So thanks. Thanks to everyone.

ONE

Introduction

ALMOST EVERYTHING THAT has been published in the social and behavioral sciences and in medicine about adult sleep has looked at adult sleep as an individual phenomenon. Yet millions of adults sleep with another adult. For them, sleep is a complicated, changing, and often challenging social experience. The events of couple bed sharing are quite remarkable once we learn what couples who share a bed have to say. Based on intensive interviews with adults who share a bed, this book explores the challenges, achievements, routines, patterning, and context of couple sleeping This book is written primarily for researchers and practitioners who focus on couples (for example, family scientists, couple therapists, family sociologists, family psychologists, family social workers, family educators, and others who focus on close relationships). I hope that this book will help readers see how shared sleeping is central to couple relationships and that there is much of great value to learn by looking at how couples experience and deal with the wide range of issues connected to couple sleeping.

THE IMPORTANCE OF STUDYING EVERYDAY LIFE

Everyday life should not be taken for granted. It is at the core of what goes on in people's lives. The term *everyday life* can be used in ways that are mystifying and ambiguous (Sandywell, 2004). I do not want to claim more by my usage of the term than that I am studying recurring events that people take as ordinary in their own lives. By everyday life I mean the ordinary things (often treated as unremarkable) that happen day in and day out and are so commonplace that they hardly merit attention (Berger, 1997, pp. 20–27, citing Braudel, 1981, and

1

Lefebvre, 1971). In studying everyday life, the focus is on what occurs in concrete, natural settings, as opposed to settings created by researchers (Douglas, 1980, p. 1). Everyday life is mundane and routinized in ways that make it taken-for-granted (Weigert, 1981, p. 36) and hence easy for anyone, including scholars, to ignore.

Everyday life can seem to lack drama and importance. But in everyday life people find meaning (Weigert, 1981, p. 36), nourishment, safety, and renewal. Everyday life also has value and meaning because it is linked by many threads to the deepest, most-close-to-ultimate meanings (Berger, 1997, p. 6). For example, the act of sleeping is linked to the value of life itself, to the religious meanings touched by bedtime prayer, to the unconscious that boils up in dreams, to the ways that death is thought of as "going to sleep," to the power of love, and to the daily choices that keep one healthy and alive. The act of sharing a bed is linked to the discomfort of being alone and the awesome power of being close to another human being, the religious meanings that many people impute to the couple bed, and the many meanings of sexual acts. In sleeping, and for most people sleep occurs at night, there are links to the power of nighttime and darkness, to what is frightening and unknowable, to vulnerabilities, human limitations, and a darkness that can give desired privacy. Perhaps, for most people, the bed evokes some level of awareness of those meanings and is considered a place for dealing with or distancing themselves from those meanings.

The couple bed can be a place to turn away from and ignore dangers, with the banalities of the everyday bed routine used as an aid to avoiding what could be quite threatening (Lefebvre, 1971, p. 24, cited in Berger, 1997, p. 23). Some of the people I interviewed were clear that they used routines centered on the couple bed to distract them from what was upsetting, painful, worrisome, or frightening.

> CINDY: There's nights where I'm really upset about life or whatever, and I tell him, "I am not gonna be able to go to sleep unless you come up there and go to bed with me." And I tell him, "I want you to read to me. I want you to talk to me. Just do anything to get me to stop thinking about everything's that got me upset."

For many people the shared bed is a nest, a place of great safety, comfort, security, and trust (Dunkel, 1977, p. 138) in another human and perhaps in God.

It is easy to take everyday life for granted because it is often automated, obvious, what everybody else seems to be doing, and something of a background for what is unusual or counted as important. But that does not mean that everyday life lacks significance. In fact, many scholars have emphasized how meaning-laden, important, interesting, and revealing the study of everyday life is (e.g., Berger, 1997; Braudel, 1981; Douglas, 1980; Smith, 1987). There are deeper meanings in everyday life, perhaps deeper than participants and observers may realize. These meanings are revealed when things go wrong, when people are confronted by paradox or change, when people lose some aspect of their everyday life, or when people find themselves in intimate relationship with someone whose view of or action in everyday life differs substantially from their own.

From another angle, some scholars (e.g., Berger, 1997) say that when we look closely at everyday life, we see that it is very much about the human relationship to objects. It is not the life of free-standing humans but of humans using and relating to things. This book is no exception to that perspective. It is not only about the deep meanings and fears that may appear in the couple bed. It is also about the everyday life of couples as they relate to beds, bedding, bed clothes, thermostats, books, television sets, lights, window shades, alarm clocks, medications, electric fans, and bedside tables.

COUPLE SLEEPING IS A NEGLECTED TOPIC

Most of the thousands of research reports and clinical articles on sleep are written as though people sleep alone. In *PsycInfo*, the American Psychological Association compendium of abstracts from the psychological literature, there were, on May 19, 2005, 7,334 works listed on human sleep, 9,198 on couples, and 16,022 on marriage and marriage counseling, but only nine abstracts among all those thousands dealt with couple or married couple sleep. In the *Medline* compendium of abstracts in medicine, there were, on May 19, 2005, 40,214 entries dealing with human sleep, 34,295 dealing with couples, and 19,162 dealing with marriage and marriage therapy; but only fifteen abstracts dealt with couple or married couple sleep. On May 19, 2005, the web-based version of *Sociological Abstracts* contained 17,659 abstracts on couples or marriage, 514 on sleep or sleeping, and only one on couple or married couple sleep or sleeping.

Despite the neglect of the topic, it is clear from published writings in the psychological, medical, and sociological literature that the sleep problems of one partner in a couple can create sleep problems for the other (for example, Armstrong, Wallace, & Marais, 1999; Beninati, Harris, Herold, & Shepard, 1999; Mitropoulos et al., 2002; Parish & Lyng, 2003; Shvartzman et al., 2001; Scott, Ah-See, Richardson, & Wilson, 2003; Ulfberg, Carter, Talback, & Edling, 2000). Physicians who treat sleep disorders hear daily from patients and their partners about couple effects. In fact, for certain sleep disorders, it is the partner of a sleeper more than the sleeper herself or himself who can describe the disorder (Aldrich, 1999, pp. 102–103; Bonekat & Krumpe, 1990; Chokroverty, 1994;

Walsh, Harman, & Kowall, 1994). Nonetheless, in the psychological, medical, and sociological literature, sleep has, for the most part, been written about as though it is an individual matter.

Then there is the self-help sleep literature. There are dozens of books in print about how to solve individual sleep problems, but none that I know of that focuses on the couple. The self-help sleep literature seems, like the research and clinical literature dealing with sleep, almost entirely focused on individuals. Self-help sleep books seem to be about how the individual can fall asleep more easily, stay asleep, and have a restful and restorative sleep. The central message of this literature is that sleep problems are individual and are solved by the individual.

Despite the individual focus of psychological, medical, sociological, and self-help sleep writings, for many adults, sleep is a couple experience. The lifetime of most adults will include thousands of nights of shared sleeping with another adult, and often the challenges of sleeping are very much about the couple relationship. To understand sleep we must look at the social aspects of it.

Daly (2003) has written about the "negative spaces" in family theory and research, areas that family scholars ignore but that are central to the lives of couples and families. Couple sleep is one of those "negative space" areas. It is time to look at couple sleep, to begin to fill that negative space with research and theory.

PIONEERS IN THE STUDY OF ADULT SLEEP AS A SOCIAL PHENOMENON

There have been scattered voices in sociology arguing for the importance of studying adult sleep as a social phenomenon. Aubert and White (1959a, 1959b) asserted that sleep is an appropriate sociological concern and an important social event. They pointed out that it is legitimate to analyze preparation for sleep and sleeping itself as role behavior and rule governed. Gleichmann (1980) pointed out that research on sleep has consistently viewed sleep as individual, ignoring social aspects, although from an historical perspective, sleep has been social for many centuries. In Gleichmann's analysis, sleep is a sociological phenomenon in part because it is regulated by societal rules. For example, there are rules about when to sleep and when to be awake—sleep at night, be awake during the day—and where to sleep—sleep in privacy or semiprivacy in a bed; do not sleep in public places.

One can extend the idea of rules for sleeping to look at relationship rules among people who sleep together (Schwartz, 1970). Perhaps without realizing it, a couple who sleeps together will have worked out hundreds of rules about going to sleep, sleeping, and waking up. Consider, for example, rules concerning waking up (Schwartz, 1970). Those rules will almost certainly deal with how and when partners might verbally interact during the minutes or perhaps even hours following waking up.

Taylor (1993) argued that sleep research has ignored the social aspects of sleep while sociology has systematically ignored sleep as a topic for study and theorizing, and yet sleep is obviously defined socioculturally and is likely to be patterned according to social class, gender, age, and other sociological categories. Taylor also pointed out that sleep is socially defined and that the way it is socially defined has consequences for how people "do" sleep.

Williams (2001), in advocating that a sociology of the human body should pay more attention to sleep, emphasized that sleep is socially conceptualized and organized. In focusing on the association of health and sleep, Williams (2002) again emphasized the neglect of the social aspects of sleep, and pointed to the social patterning of sleep, the social role of the sleeper, and the "colonization" of sleep by medical experts. Hislop and Arber (2003b), citing Williams, laid out a strong case for the idea that there is much more to sleep than can be framed and analyzed from the perspective of medical knowledge about the functioning of the individual body.

Although none of these pioneers seems to have carried out couple interviews focused on sleep, their writings make clear how valuable it is to look at sleep as a social phenomenon.

THE STUDY

I interviewed eighty-eight adults, forty-two couples and four individuals who were in a couple bed sharing relationship. Although with the last of the eighty-eight I was still hearing things I had not heard in earlier interviews, the eighty-eight provided a great deal of commonality about the main themes in this book. I stopped interviewing when I thought I had a book's worth of material, not when I thought I had learned all there was to learn about couple sleeping. All of the eighty-eight were residents of the thirteen county Minneapolis-St. Paul metropolitan area (including two counties in Wisconsin). Three of the forty-two couples were lesbian and three were heterosexual and not married. Three of the four people who were interviewed as individuals were not married but had current bed sharing relationships; the other person who was interviewed as an individual was married. I did not ask people about race/ethnicity, but I believe one person would self-identify as African American, one as Latina, and one as Afro-Caribbean.

Most interviewees volunteered after learning about the research from television, newspaper, or radio reports. Although some responded to a neutral description of the study as about the experience of sharing a bed with another adult, others responded to a more sensational description voiced by television anchors who decided to announce the study in that way. The more sensational descriptions called for volunteers for research dealing with "bed hogs" or "snoring." That might mean that the people who were interviewed had more sleep problems than the normal population. Although there is reason to think that sleep problems occur for most people in the "normal" population (Fietze & Diefenbach, 2003), this is a study of volunteers, not of a representative sample.

Most interviews were carried out in people's homes; a few were carried out in my university office; and one was carried out at an interviewee's place of business. All interviews were carried out in complete privacy.

There was an interview schedule covering a wide range of experiences related to sharing a bed, which contained a core set of questions that was asked of everyone. (The interview schedule is in the Appendix of this book, as is some basic information about the people interviewed.) Each interview flowed with the narratives, situations, and enthusiasms of the interviewee(s). As a result, much of what was talked about and the sequence of what was talked about was up to the person or couple being interviewed. In addition, some questions were only asked of some people. Sometimes this was because the questions obviously did not apply—for example, only people who had children were asked about the effects of children. There were some matters not on the interview schedule that had to be asked because of people's situations (for example, a specific health problem).

The typical interview lasted close to two hours. Interviews were tape recorded and then transcribed word for word. In three cases I botched the audiotaping. When that happened, I wrote extensive notes about the interview as soon as I could after the interview had ended. Interview transcriptions retained most of the linguistic complexity and nuance that could be heard on the tape. So the transcriptions include laughter, pauses (with an estimate of how long the pause lasted), slurs, repetitions, stutters, throat clearings, heavy breathing, sighs, tears, emphases, and records of one partner talking while the other talked. To facilitate reading, most of this complexity has been edited out of the quotes in this book, but I paid attention to it in trying to make sense of what people said.

In the spirit of grounded theory research (Strauss & Corbin, 1998), the data analysis was carried out partly as each interview went on. I thought about what might be implied by what people said and what theoretically might fit what they said, and that often guided my next questions, as I asked for clarification, elaboration, or for a partner's view on something that I was thinking about analyzing in a certain way. This continuing data analysis also meant that, to some extent, the interview schedule evolved over the course of the study as it became clear that some issues that seemed important before the study began were not so valuable to explore, whereas others deserved more textured, deeper-digging questions. Also, I was making interview transcriptions constantly after the study began, and that led me to think all along about the data analysis and about how to be a better questioner about certain issues during upcoming interviews.

Data analysis focused on themes. In analyzing the data, I read through several transcriptions to make a preliminary outline of bed sharing/sleeping themes that seemed to be significant in the relationship of at least some couples. Then I used the outline as a basis for analyzing the other transcriptions and the interview notes. The analysis involved frequent outline revision and returning to previously coded transcriptions as each succeeding transcription analysis led to questioning and sharpening previous analyses. The coding process also involved frequent challenges and checks—anything from checking the context of a quote or the next words that somebody said to tabulating something for all cases to be sure that the trends in the interviews were characterized accurately. The frequency checks were facilitated by the transcriptions having been created in WordPerfect 5.1, which has a powerful key word search capability. An important dimension of the coding was the effort to retain interviewees' realities and the sense they gave of what they wanted the interviewer to know and understand. For me, this is a matter of ethics as well as of research validity. I intend to respect interviewees' realities and not privilege my own to the extent of obscuring theirs.

The interviewees ranged in age from twenty-one to seventy-seven. All but one had at least a high school education; fifty-one had a college degree; twenty-five had education beyond the bachelor's degree. The couples had been sleeping together as little as six months and as long as fifty-one years. The homes I saw ranged from a small public housing unit and a one room apartment to several very large homes in wealthy suburbs. Some people not only talked about sleeping with their current partner but also about sleeping with past partners, particularly previous spouses. Nobody talked about having more than one current sleeping partner.

I promised all who were interviewed that I would quote them in a way that masked their identity so that nobody who knew them would know who it was I was quoting. That means that I have changed names and other identifying information. Also, I have simplified the quotes—cutting out repetition, most sounds that aren't words, and most instances of "you know," "I mean," "well," "kind of," and "like." At many places I have quoted words that seem to be at the heart of a point being made but cut out the words that do not seem to me to be central to the point. Wherever I have omitted material from a quote, I indicate the omission with ellipsis dots. The words one person said while another was talking I have put in parentheses.

STUDYING WHAT IS BACKSTAGE

As Goffman (1959) described social life, we have backstages where we can be out of the character(s) that we present to our publics and can rehearse future performances. We share backstage regions with those with whom we jointly put on performances, and we agree with them to keep confidential whatever goes on backstage. For a couple, the privacy of the couple bed is almost certainly a backstage region. There they can express feelings and ideas they do not dare to express in public. It is there that things can happen in their relationship they would not want others to know.

I tried to respect what I thought might be the deepest secrets by not asking much about sexuality and asking nothing about violence in bed, but some people did talk about those matters. Also, there were many instances in the interviews when people said that they were revealing things to me they had not revealed to anyone else. I am sure secrets were withheld from me, but much was revealed that makes sense, is interesting and important, and is consistent with what others who were interviewed said.

THE COUPLE SLEEPING SYSTEM

For couples who share a bed, sleep is a relationship system. It is the interplay of the physiology, behavior, psychology, needs, preferences, previous learning, beliefs, fantasy life, and so on of the two people that makes the phenomena of sleep happen for them. As a system (e.g., Minuchin, 1974; Rosenblatt, 1994), whatever emerges comes from the interaction of the individuals involved. The whole is not the sum of what A does plus what B does. It comes from their interaction. This book is an extended development of ideas about how couple sleeping systems come into being, how they operate, what influences them, what maintains them, and what changes them.

The system of sleep is not merely a couple phenomenon. It occurs in a system of larger systems (Maddock, 1993; Richardson, Fowers, & Guignon, 1999). It interacts with these larger systems, although in terms of leverage, power, resources to make things happen, larger systems typically have much more influence on couple sleeping than the reverse. For example, the system of jobs means that often the demands, involvements, insecurities, and harmful effects of the job will come home to the couple bed.

I SIT THERE AND WATCH YOU SLEEP

Often a person with whom one shares a bed can tell one how one sleeps—for example, the tossing and turning, the snoring, and the sleep talking. In fact, even actions one might presumably have to be awake to perform during the night, like going to the bathroom or getting up to close a window, one might not have any memory of doing and only know one did because of the report of one's sleeping partner. We could simply take this as an interesting fact, that people learn about their sleeping from the reports of the partner with whom they share a bed.

KRISTEN: Sometimes I sit there and I watch you sleep.

MONICA: There are a lot of mornings when he'll go, "I didn't sleep at all last night," and I was like awake all night with worrying about something or not feeling well or whatever, and he slept the whole night as far as I could see. And snoring on top of it.

JOHN: She's like, it's this little pah. . . . She doesn't really wake up. I've watched her do this. It wakes her up just enough so she's not in really deep sleep (sounding amused). It's very cute. . . . I can watch it for hours. Yeah, I'm always awake in the morning before she is.

An obvious point about one partner observing the other sleeping is that this book is built partly out of partner reports of what the other does while sleeping, just as the couple sleep system is. It arises in part from what a couple does with one partner's observations about the sleep of the other.

IT'S MOST OF OUR TIME TOGETHER

For many people in the United States, life has become extraordinarily rushed (Robinson & Godbey, 1997). Most of the couples I interviewed said that most of their time together was the time they were in bed. And for some it was when they were going to bed and in bed that they did most of their talking together.

DAN: The majority of our relationship is spent sleeping together. (KRISTEN: Yeah) 'Cause I come home from work and you'll go to sleep an hour after I get home, so we spend more time together sleeping than we do anything else.

MIKE: She works two jobs, and about the only time that we get alone is that bed time.

LIZ: That's like the only time that we're even by each other.

So bedtime is not just about sleep. It is about renewing and maintaining the couple relationship. It can be the one time when partners learn what has been going on with one another, plan, make decisions, deal with disagreements, solve problems, provide necessary information, and put words to their realities. Bedtime contact seemed crucial to maintaining the relationship of many couples I interviewed, as a symbol of their being a couple, in their meeting one another's needs, and in the information exchanges that enabled them to coordinate with and know one another.

Sleeping takes up a quarter to a third of most lives. That is far too much of a couple's time together for those of us interested in couple relationships to ignore. Some people who were interviewed had similar notions, that there was so much togetherness time in and around couple sleeping that it was important to pay attention to that time.

> JOSH: Sex is ten minutes, and you got eight hours in bed. (MARGARET: Yeah, most of the time it's just sleeping.) It's one third of your life, so what goes on during that time?

With sleep so much of a person's life and with so many couples having little time together except in their bed sharing, understanding couple experiences in bed is central to understanding couples. The content and quality of that time can tell a great deal about a couple's life. Many couples spoke of how important the connection that centers on sleeping together was for them. It was a time for connection, intimacy, pleasure, and feeling comfortable together. For some couples, the time in bed together was not only about their life as a couple. It was their crucial human contact. If it were not for that, they could feel quite alone. Maria and Vic had shared a bed for 14 years.

> MARIA: We don't really know a lot of people here, so (laughing) we only have each other, and it just means a lot to . . . go to bed, to end the day close, and then to start out with, I mean, we often talk about it as the best part of our day. (VIC: It is.) Going to bed and waking up together.

For couples who lose their time together, there can be a feeling of threat to the relationship, perhaps particularly for younger couples.

> ZACK: My dad was a minister in a small country church, and then he talked to different people at different times, and then sometimes Mom and Dad would be talkin' about it afterwards and us kids, we had elephant ears. And he said, "If a young couple quit sleeping together that's often the end of the marriage." That's what he said. "But," he said, "if

it's an old couple, they sometimes have to sleep in their own beds because they can't stand each other anymore because of the snoring or the getting up at night frequently and disturbing each other. They slept better that way. They had more rest." And so I guess that's sort of, probably it wasn't too far from right. It's not wrong.

Modern life, with its work demands, its commuting, the busy-ness of being a consumer, the fact that the typical adult in the United States reports watching roughly two hours of television each day (Pew Research Center for the People and the Press, 2005), the separation of partners by their personal spheres of work (and perhaps school, organizations, and peer groups), makes it difficult for a couple to have much contact. These days heterosexual couples may have even less opportunity to talk than in the past because increasing numbers of married women are in the work force (MSN.Encarta, 2005). Thus, modern life has made the sleeping situation more important, more imperative. On most days, it is in the sleep situation that the couple connection is symbolized, forged, enacted, and maintained.

Arguably there is some minimum amount of talk necessary to maintain a shared view of key realities (Berger & Kellner, 1964; Rosenblatt & Wright, 1984; Wiley, 1994). Perhaps most couples have learned how to carry out their relationship together so that, on most days, a few minutes of verbal contact suffices. For many of the couples I interviewed, that verbal contact often occurs each night when they are first in bed together.

THE PATHS THIS BOOK FOLLOWS

This book takes the reader along two related paths. One path is to develop the notion of the couple system with regard to sharing a bed and sleeping together. It is based on family systems theory and elaborates on that theory by developing, chapter after chapter, details about the systemic context, processes, and challenges of bed sharing and sleeping together.

The other path follows couples through the process of getting to bed and to sleep, sleeping, and awakening. It starts with the bed, then addresses the processes of going to bed, then what goes on as people reach the bed and get into it. It then addresses issues that can be present at bedtime that affect what goes on during particular nights—anger, sexual intercourse, illness and injury, and how work and children may intrude into couple sleeping. Then, assuming at least one of the partners is asleep, it addresses issues related to difficulties falling asleep, including light sleepers (versus heavy sleepers), tossing and turning, and restless legs. The book then addresses problems that can come up during the night—snoring, sleep apnea, sleep talking, tooth grinding, and nightmares. It then moves to waking up times. Finally, there is an analysis of what happens to sleeping and the couple relationship on the nonstandard nights—weekends and times when the partners sleep apart.

TWO

Forming the Couple System: Learning to Share a Bed

COUPLES HAVE TO LEARN to sleep together. Routines of sleeping together can only be established through substantial amounts of learning, and it is not just a matter of learning one or two things. Sleeping together is an achievement of coordination on many dimensions—where to locate one's head, body, arms, and legs, where to put one's pillow, how to relate to the blankets, when to talk and not talk, when to touch the other and when not, how to touch the other, what ways of expressing displeasure with the other are acceptable and work, how free one is to toss and turn, what to do when the other makes noise, what to do and not do if one awakens during the night.

The learning is not a matter of each partner learning independently of the other. It is the two partners learning together. That complicates the learning of each and, in a sense, makes for moving targets. As partner A learns, she or he changes, and that makes things change regarding partner B's learning. Furthermore, people change, life situations change, the sleeping environment changes, and the couple relationship changes. Even reality changes in that one or both partners may come to a different sense than before about, for example, what is healthful or what it means to come to bed when not tired. So the learning involved in sharing a bed never ends because new demands for learning emerge over the course of the couple relationship. An injury is, in a sense, a metaphor for all the changes in body, life situation, and couple relationship that will come up over the years a couple is together. Consider the time when Karen and Richard had to learn that they could not snuggle together as they had in the past.

KAREN: When I first had the injury, snuggling just wasn't even possible, because we just couldn't get comfortable. Or I couldn't get

comfortable with (RICHARD: Right) the different positions that you
had to get into to be able to snuggle.

The learning a couple does in order to sleep together can be framed in
terms of sociological ideas about sleep as a role and rule system and a system
of rights and obligations (Aubert & White, 1959a, 1959b; Schwartz, 1970). If
sleep were simply a biological act, like digesting food, there would be no need
for learning. But since there is a social system to sleeping, people have repeated
demands to learn together as they work out how to carry out their shared
sleeping.

The learning a couple does in order to sleep well enough together can be
framed in the context of family development theory (Aldous, 1996). That theory talks about the developmental tasks that are part of the career of a couple
and family. As far as I know, no writings in the family development tradition
have addressed the issue of sharing a bed. But it is consistent with the theory
to acknowledge that it is part of a couple coming together and staying together
that the partners successfully navigate developmental challenges concerning
sleep. If a couple shares a bed, they must master the tasks of bed sharing. Doing
so means that they will have enough sleep to engage adequately in the rest of
their daily activities and that their bed sharing will not undermine the commitment of one or both partners to continue in the relationship. At the
extreme, a failure to work out an adequate and tolerable couple sleeping
arrangement can end the couple relationship. In chapter 5, I quote what Brenda
said about how her ex-husband's insistence on watching television in the bedroom was a factor in their divorce.

A couple's learning to sleep together can also be framed in terms of family systems theory (e.g., Rosenblatt, 1994). A couple system comes into existence as soon as the couple begins to have a relationship. But family systems
theory does not focus merely on the fact that a relationship exists. Family systems theory is about recurrent patterns of interaction, about the development,
evolution, and maintenance of relationship rules and roles, about communication patterns, and more. So the learning a couple does regarding sleep is part of
the process of building, evolving, and maintaining their couple system.

FIRST LEARNING TOGETHER

The first learning that couples do may be essential to their continuing to have
a relationship. Without some success in their first learning they may feel that
the relationship has no future. Each partner can, in a sense, take the first learning situations as compatibility tests. Also, that first learning begins to establish

the bases of the relationship, their degree of good will, what forms of power are legitimate to use, how, if at all, they compromise, what their standards are for learning ("barely good enough," for example, versus, "as good as is humanly possible"), and what their rules of engagement are in areas of difference, disagreement, and upsetness with one another. The first learning, even about minor matters, sets precedents that may conceivably affect the couple relationship for all the couple's time together. But people are not necessarily beginners when they come together in a new couple relationship. Many have had prior learning experiences sharing a bed.

Some people enter a new relationship having been in other marital, romantic, or sexual bed sharing relationships. Those experiences may be relevant to how couples approach various issues, perhaps particularly how they approach issues of conflict and anger concerning bed sharing (see chapter 8). Even if neither partner has ever shared a bed with a romantic partner, they may have had childhood experiences of sharing a bed with a family member, and that experience may have taught them valuable lessons. Thirty-three of the eighty-eight people I interviewed had experience sharing a bed as children, typically with a sibling or grandmother. To the extent that sleeping with someone else is governed by a social rule system that one has to learn (Aubert & White, 1959a, 1959b), having learned to share a bed previously could make it easier to learn to share a bed with someone else. In fact, some of the people I interviewed who had shared a bed with a sibling or grandmother said the previous experience made their current couple bed sharing easier. Monica, for example, did not think that she and Don had problems sharing a bed when they first started sleeping together.

> MONICA: I slept with my sister most of my childhood. So I was used to having somebody there.

What might people learn from having shared a bed with others? Among many possibilities, sharing a bed with anyone may teach one to sleep parallel to the long side of the bed and to hang on to one's blankets and pillow. Carol talked about learning rules concerning bed territory, touching, and what to do when rules were violated.

> ME: Do you think that having shared a bed as a kid has affected how you sleep as an adult?
>
> CAROL: Yeah, I do. I think I'm much better at staying on my own side of the bed, and draw the line down the middle of the bed (in complaining childish voice:), "She's touching me. She's on my side of the bed," (chuckling) and all that kind of stuff. When we first moved into

the house that my dad just sold this year, it was just a little cabin. . . .
I was gonna be twelve that fall. My sister was gonna be ten. My
brother was gonna be eight. And we slept crosswise, the three of us,
on the bed, until we started having growth spurts and we hung over
the edges, and then my brother moved out on the couch, and my sister and I shared it. So I always slept with somebody . . . so I think I'm
much more able to accommodate to do that.

I also suspect that the early experience teach self-control, even in sleep, so
that one is unlikely to violate the rules.

BEGINNERS WITH EACH OTHER

It could seem from what Monica and Carol said that they needed no new
learning when they started sleeping with their current partners. However, there
is always learning to be done when one is with a new bedmate. See, for example, what Carol and her partner had to say about cold feet and cold bodies and
about anger in the bed (in chapters 6 and 8). A few couples said that they slept
together effortlessly from the very beginning, but all of them also talked about
problems they had to learn to deal with in their bed sharing.

What does it mean that couples would say sleeping together was effortless
and yet they had problems? I think some couples might remember how joyous
and comfortable their first time sleeping together was and focus so much on
the joy and comfort that the challenges they had in learning to sleep together
are masked. Remembering what was good makes what was difficult less salient,
and the couple relationship might well have been wonderfully rewarding at
first. The challenges that required learning might have become apparent only at
a later date. Consider Nick, remembering the first time he slept with Sarah
three and a half years prior to the interview.

ME: Do you feel like you had to learn how to sleep with each other?

NICK: Actually it felt really natural and (SARAH: Umhm, right) one
time we just went out on a date, [and] I took her up to Duluth for the
weekend (SARAH: [that was our] first time), and we were going to do
all this stuff. Instead we stayed in the room and we fell asleep, and we
missed our dinner reservation. We just were so relaxed around each
other that (SARAH: Umhm) we slept for I think (both laughing)
twelve, thirteen hours. That was almost sort of the whole vacation
there. And I don't even think I was that tired, but it was very relaxing
and just very comfortable.

But then, in the discussion of territory in the bed (chapter 3), Sarah talks about having to jab Nick when he moves to her side in his sleep. So it has not been easy all of the time for them. She had to learn what to do about his invasion of her territory, and he had to learn what to do when she jabbed him.

Even if two people are experienced at bed sharing when they first share a bed with each other, they are beginners with each other. The prior learning may even be a problem if it sets up patterns and expectations that may be inappropriate in the new relationship. I think every couple must do considerable learning in order to accommodate their differences and to arrange their bodies in relation to each other.

An additional challenge the first nights a couple sleeps together is that neither partner knows what will happen. They may be very attracted to each other and may imagine a delightful future together. Even if they know each other very well from other situations, in the bed for the first time, they are strangers. Because of this, although some people move effortlessly through their first nights of sharing a bed, others are stiff, apprehensive, filled with self-doubt, concerned about the impression they will give the other and perhaps even their safety, and not able to sleep easily with the other.

> ME: Do you remember the first night you slept together?
>
> CAROLINE: Yeah. . . . It was our first date, yeah. (Ben laughs) And it's kind of embarrassing (chuckles), 'cause (imitating a shocked, critical voice:) "You're sleeping together on your first date!" We weren't *sleeping* together, but we slept together.
>
> BEN: It's funny, 'cause she was all stiff as a board. CAROLINE: (chuckling) Yeah, yeah. . . . And we weren't cuddling. . . .
>
> ME: And that stiffness was . . . about?
>
> CAROLINE: It was more self conscious. . . . It was . . . like, "Okay, what did I just get myself into?" 'Cause I'd never slept with anybody before. . . . I'm like, "God, this guy has just (chuckling) got his arm around me (laughing). What is he doing?"

TEACHING THE PARTNER WHAT ONE NEEDS AND WANTS

An important part of learning how to sleep together, both at first and over the years, is for the partners to teach one another what they need and want in order to sleep comfortably. A person may be able to say even before getting into bed for the first time what some of that is. But often one does not know what one will need or want until something happens that is uncomfortable, annoying, or frustrating. Many couples will say how important it is to work out how to sleep together through gentle and respectful communication, but some can also look back at their learning to sleep together as a process that included complaint. Their teaching or complaint could be about many things, for example, what form and timing of touch is tolerable, what is done with the covers, or the partner not crossing the midline of the bed.

> ANGELA: I remember just being vocal about I don't like the arm draped across my chest or my stomach area because it feels heavy when I breathe. . . . And yeah, learning where your head fits on his shoulder, and I guess we never really made an issue out of it. It's just kind of, "Okay, this is comfortable, rest here in this position."

> ME: It sounds like you somehow learned to swing your elbows less in bed . . . and contain your knees more. . . .

> VIC: Not "somehow." There's no "somehow" (chuckling). It's her telling me, "That hurt!" (laughs) Or "Don't do that!" Or "Watch where you're swinging that elbow."

LEARNING FROM SORE SHOULDERS AND ARMS THAT FALL ASLEEP

Not only does instruction come from one's partner, it comes from one's body. For example, it is not uncommon that couples in their first nights together sleep entwined in ways that give one or both of them sore shoulders or arms that have fallen asleep. Nobody I interviewed could tolerate such discomfort night after night. Such discomfort strongly motivates people to figure out how to sleep in ways that are more comfortable.

> JOE: When we got married, for about three or four months, I was having pains . . . especially in this shoulder. . . . I couldn't even raise my arm. . . . I finally realized that I'd been . . . sleeping right next to her, and it sort of pushed my arm in. . . . When I finally figured out what it was, I'd leave a little room, and then after that it went away.

> DONNA: When you're first married, you're just starting to sleep with each other, you have this . . . notion that you have to sleep . . . intertwined or spooning. . . . [But] we learned . . . that it was really okay for us not to do that. . . . We didn't have to be touching. . . . We could spread apart. Because he had his arm under my head, and I'd get a kink in my neck from having his arm there, or cuddling, you have one arm up and it falls asleep.

SANDRA: I used to always sleep on his arm, without a pillow even, and that's how we started. Do you remember? Your arm would go to sleep.

LEARNING TO DEAL WITH DIFFERENCE

Much of the learning that goes on in couple sleeping concerns differences in what the two partners prefer or need. Perhaps many couples start their relationship assuming that they are more similar than they are. So getting along while sharing a bed is partly a matter of becoming aware of differences and then dealing with them.

ANGELA: Before we got together I would normally fall asleep with the TV on, and he did not do that at all, and so when we moved in together, that was something that we had to overcome. . . . It made him uncomfortable and he couldn't sleep so I was sympathetic to that need. And so I've taught myself to go to sleep without it.

MOLLY: He was just recently out of the military and still had the military mentality that the appropriate time to wake up in the morning was 5:30, and I did my best to disabuse him of that notion as soon as possible (laughs), because I have never been a morning person.

THOMAS: And it took me some time to appreciate her need to sleep.

MOLLY: He just denied it. I mean it was just like I was being lazy, and I physically need more sleep than he does.

KAREN: When we first got married, why he was so shy, he'd go change in the bathroom. . . . "Wait a minute. We're married, and you're gonna change. Wait a minute. Get this straight here." So I needed to learn how to be a little bit more sensitive to his shyness, and he's come around to being a lot more comfortable with the hugging and that sort of thing.

RICHARD: Yeah, I was not a toucher before I got married.

Compromise in sharing a bed can be difficult. People may not want to give up what previously made sleep easy and rewarding. For example, they may resist giving up their freedom to use the whole bed, to have the precise bedroom temperature they want, or to have the covers the way they have slept with them for years.

LINDA: When we were first married . . . it just was hard for him to get used to sleeping with somebody, 'cause he never had somebody all night long, day after day after (chuckle) or night after n- (laughing), "I wish she'd go away" (chuckles).

ME: It sounds like you had to do some learning to sleep together. . . .

CHARLES: You learn habits when you're young, sleeping and not having anybody touch you while you're sleeping for . . . twenty-three years, and all of a sudden you're in a situation where it's totally the opposite. So it makes it tough.

LEARNING TO ACCEPT A SLEEP PATTERN THAT IS NOT IDEAL

Some couples come together with an ideal image of bed sharing, something like the bedroom version of a movie scene in which a couple runs hand-in-hand slow motion through a field of wildflowers. For them, part of the early learning may be to accept the reality that what they have is not ideal.

ME: Do you remember the first times you got in bed, "How are we gonna do this?" and "Where's my arm gonna be?"

HANK: No, it wasn't that. It was more the joke of when you get in the bed you turn away from each other.

BARBARA: Yeah, that's what was funny is we found out that, like he said, you'd cuddle. We don't. We cannot touch when we're sleeping. So when we first were married, we'd lay in bed and talk. Or maybe we'd cuddle. "Well, good night." And then we'd both turn away from each other. . . . I said, "Why don't we cuddle . . . ?" And we realized we can't.

For many reasons a couple's routines in a bed sharing relationship might fall short of their ideal. To some extent, failures to achieve the ideal lie in irrational expectations and in the realities of characteristics of the partners and their situation that are unlikely ever to change. To some extent, failures to achieve the ideal lie in personal inflexibility, lack of economic or housing resources, the expectation that if something is wrong in the relationship it is the partner who should change, and failures of imagination. So accepting a sleep pattern that is not ideal may represent a great deal of wisdom about oneself, one's partner, and the couple situation—for example, an understanding that there are not the economic or housing resources to achieve the ideal.

LEARNING WHILE ASLEEP

If every night is potentially a new learning experience for a couple, one of the great challenges is that some of the learning must be done while asleep. Although there is some reason to think that certain kinds of learning may go on during sleep (Eich, 1990), it seems, based on my interviews, that most people cannot easily tune in to what they do while asleep and may ordinarily consider it impossible to control those things. But a concerned or annoyed partner may motivate one to tune in to what one does and to change.

> ERIC: She hears me. I say "Hey, did I just do that?" So then I start telling myself, "Okay, don't breathe like that." And I start to try to breathe out of my nose, and just try to redirect my breathing.

I think the key to the sleep learning people talked about is that it is not actually learning while asleep. People did not stay fully asleep when a partner tried to make them change. Partner A's nudge or complaint could bring partner B close enough to wakefulness for partner B to be aware of what the problem was and to make an appropriate change.

LEARNING TOLERANCE

If one part of learning to sleep comfortably together is a process of complaint and correction, another part is to learn to accept and live with things as they are without being annoyed, upset, or even awakened. In fact, as is shown throughout this book, perhaps the most common change people made in learning how to sleep together was learning how to accommodate what the partner did.

> JEFF: My legs, if they get too hot, the only way I can describe it is being chained up in a ball and having like a six pack of Jolt and not be able to do anything about it. There's just so much energy in my legs. . . . If you notice, my leg's going, shaking all the time (DONNA: They do that all night). . . . Especially the hotter I am. So when it's time to sleep, we usually (chuckles) go to our own ends of the bed.
>
> ME: When his leg is moving like that, does it make it hard for you to sleep?
>
> DONNA: In the beginning it did. It took me a while, 'cause it felt like the bed was just vibrating. . . . And when we first got married he would jerk his arms. He's not a very still sleeper. He kind of jerks his arms and kicks his legs and rolls over a lot, and it took me a while to get used to him doing that and not wake up.

Sometimes achieving tolerance required learning to think differently about what the partner did. If, for example, one initially thought that the partner was intentionally stealing covers, that made it difficult to be tolerant. Or if one thought that some moral, motivational, or character defect of the partner was creating a sleeping problem (for example, "If he weren't so selfish he wouldn't snore so much") it might be difficult to be tolerant. In fact, people often moved to greater tolerance by changing their view of the partner and what the partner was doing. This does not mean that at the time of the interview everybody had achieved tolerance or only had benign thoughts about their partner. In fact, as is shown at many places in this book, some people were far from tolerant or from a benign view of their partner on this or that issue.

What happens when people do not learn to tolerate something their partner does? There may be hard feelings, recurrent conflict, and ongoing struggles to make the partner change in some way. Some couples may start spending some nights or parts of some nights sleeping in separate beds.

THE DEVELOPMENT OF BED SHARING ROUTINES

All couples who were interviewed seem to have developed bed sharing routines. A working definition of "routine" in this context is a daily (or nightly) course of action, a predictable process adhered to by both partners. There were routines for how couples got to bed, what they did once both were in bed, how they fell asleep, how they slept, and how they woke up. For example, the routine of getting to bed might include watching the evening news together. When the news was over one person checked to see that the outside doors were locked while the other started the dishwasher. One of them might check on pets and children and turn out lights everywhere but the bedroom and the bathroom. They both went to the bathroom, brushed teeth, undressed, and, if they intended to wear something to bed, put on whatever that was. They almost always got into bed on the same side of the bed in the same way. One of them set the alarm clock. One of them turned out the bedroom lights. They snuggled and talked, and then fell asleep. Even when both were asleep they continued their routine, for example, both of them facing away from the middle of the bed and staying apart, or spooning and rolling over in synchrony.

Routine helps most couples to fall sleep easily and to sleep well. Indeed, people may think of bedtime routine as very important in their getting to sleep (Hislop & Arber, 2003b).

Routine makes it unnecessary to think very much, to decide very much, or to negotiate with one's partner about when and how to move toward, initiate, and carry out sleep. That is, automating what is done makes for efficient action uncluttered by individual decision points or couple discussion, argument, and negotiation (see Berger, 1997, p. 19). A couple's routines may work so well that the two partners might not pay much attention to them.

LAURA: After all these years (laughs) things just come so automatically, you don't think.

A couple's routines provide comfort and reassurance (Berger, 1997, p. 19) in that the routines keep them on familiar, predictable grounds with a sense that the chaos and threats of the outside world can be distanced because one is on a path that is known well and that has led to security and safety on many previous occasions.

THE COUPLE SYSTEM

Much of this book is about the sleeping routines and arrangements people have arrived at and the learning that has gone on in the various domains of couple bed sharing. Many of the chapters that follow this one deal with the learning process in specific areas of bed sharing. What do couples do when one of the partners is injured, starts working the night shift, starts snoring, or has to go to the bathroom often each night? What happens when somebody important to the couple is critically ill or when work stress disrupts a person's sleep? If the learning a couple does regarding sleep is part of the process of at first building and then evolving their couple system, this book is about the process of creating the couple system, the contents of that system, how the system is maintained, and how it evolves.

THREE

The Bed

TWO PEOPLE DIFFER in many ways, so it is not surprising that some couples differ substantially about the ideal bed, how to use the bed during waking hours, and what the bed means. What one partner prefers in terms of comfort, aesthetics, and the function and use of the bed might be far from what the other prefers or can even tolerate. For example, a comforter that looks and feels pleasing to one may be repulsive to the other. How do couples achieve a bed that satisfies both partners? To probe the couple politics of arriving at a bed suitable for both partners, this chapter looks at couple issues concerning the size of the bed, territoriality in the bed, the purchase of bedding, the making of the bed, what can be done during waking hours on a bed that is made, and determining who sleeps on which side of the bed.

WE NEED A BIGGER BED

I forgot to ask a few couples how big their bed was, but at least 78 percent of the couples shared a queen or king size bed. Why do so many couples sleep on queen or king size beds? For some it was a way to guarantee that partners who each wanted a substantial sleeping space had it, and that when they would rather not touch each other, that could happen. So some people purchased larger beds in order to solve problems in sharing a bed.

> ME: How did you decide to buy a king?
>
> AMY: He has started kicking. . . . He doesn't get any physical exercise, and it seems to be when it's stress. But (laughs) he doesn't really get too involved in himself. So kinda like it's, well, "You're not gonna go

to the doctor and try to do something; then we need a bigger bed." . . .
It was either get a king or separate bedrooms. . . . I can't sleep when
he's dancing.

ME: How did you come to decide to have a king size bed?

JIM: . . . I like to sprawl, so I like to cover as much bed as possible, and
I tend to lay on my back and just stretch (chuckles). We had a queen
size bed before and it wasn't big enough. . . . King size was . . . the way
to go.

As Amy and Jim said, moving to a bigger bed can be a way to deal with
problems of physical movement or sprawling. It also can be a way to deal with
an increase in physical size. Obesity peaks in the 45–64 age group, and that is
when people in the United States are often considerably heavier than they were
when in their twenties (National Center for Health Statistics, 2005). As partners increase in size, a bigger bed allows them to continue to feel that they have
enough room. A few people felt that they needed a bigger bed for that reason
but had not yet made the move to a bigger bed.

ME: You have a queen size bed?

MONICA: Yeah, queen, and I wish we had a king (chuckles),
because . . . as we get older we get heavier (laughs). . . . He's 6'4", 280
pounds. So he's got the big round face and the belly, so he can't help
but kind of touch. And that's okay, but I just think it'd be nice to have
more room.

It is possible that, for some people, the move to a bigger bed is not about
their physical size but about a general process of moving to bigger sizes in many
of the things they own (Busch, 1999, p. 116). One could take the move to big-
ness as a matter of status or higher quality of life, that one has higher status or
a higher quality of life if one has a bigger home, a bigger automobile, a bigger
bed, and so on.

STAY OUT OF MY SPACE

Some couples slept in physical contact part or even all of the night and were
pleased with this (see chapter 7 on snuggling, holding, and touching). Some people could not sleep if they were touching their partner, and typically they did
not want their partner crossing over to their half of the bed during the night.
That was one reason why many couples had larger beds, to minimize contact

when one or both partners did not want it. On the other hand, some people were good at defending their territory and moving an invading partner away.

ME: Do you ever have arguments about sleeping together?

SARAH: Just when his arm was on my side, and taking up too much room. (NICK: Yeah.)

ME: Then what did you do?

SARAH: I'm good at jabbing him now, and he moves. . . . I just have to jab.

NATALIE: We fight over the middle.

JOHN: Actually (chuckles), she's really good at pushing me right to the very edge of the bed.

For some people, the desire for distance or for maintenance of territory comes from not wanting to be pushed out of bed or to spend the night clinging to a few inches at the edge of the mattress.

BEN: She's always done that, where I end up on the edge of the bed (chuckles), and she's just (makes light snoring noise) (Caroline laughs) sprawled out all over the place, so then I kind of push her over and . . . say, "Hey, move over." (CAROLINE: "Move over." [laughs])

ME: Do you know when he's pushing you over?

CAROLINE: No. . . . I'm sure if I was even semiconscious when I was sleeping, I'd give him at least a foot of room (chuckling) . . . but, no, I have no idea.

Most people who had concerns about their partner invading their territory said they complained, nudged, or pushed to reestablish adequate distance and territory. Some talked about clinging unhappily to the side of the bed. One solved the problem of being pushed to the edge by getting out of bed and walking around to the now vacant other side of the bed.

STEVE: She tends to tell me that I'm hogging too much of the bed, and so she keeps pushing me over (she chuckles) and what will frequently happen, she'll keep pushing me over until the point where I'm so far off onto my side of the bed that I'll get up, walk around her, and come and sleep on the other side of the bed where there's more space (laughs).

I HAVEN'T GOTTEN ANYTHING TOO FLOWERY OR TOO PINK

The appearance, texture, weight, manufacturer, and softness of the sheets, pillows, pillow cases, blankets, bedspreads, comforters, and other bedding are
important to some people, women more often than men. In my interviews, the
most common pattern in heterosexual couples of resolving the problem of
picking bedding both partners found acceptable seemed to minimize power
battles about the bedding. It was that the woman picked out the bedding or
took the lead in picking it out but either consulted with the man or respected
the man's desire not to have bedding that was too "feminine." That way, the
bedding was acceptable to both partners.

> MOLLY: He has strong opinions about this, and I have made sure that
> I haven't gotten anything too flowery or too pink. Some of the sheets
> have a geometric design. The ones that do have flowers also have black
> and white stripes, so it's not a (THOMAS: Fluffy, fluffy) fluffy, fluffy,
> yeah (THOMAS: Flower, flower), because he would have a problem
> with that. (THOMAS: Yeah, perhaps) Yeah, you would. . . . Because
> early on you expressed those opinions about that. So don't just do this
> "women's role" thing, unun, no.

> HANK: She picked it out, and I said I liked it. And then she went and
> bought it.

> BARBARA: But I bought it with him in mind, knowing that he . . .
> wouldn't go for what I really wanted (both laugh).

> ME: What did you really want?

> BARBARA: Oh, I like a lot of florals in my bedroom.

The frequent leadership of women in heterosexual couples at picking out
bedding suggests a gender difference in something like nest building. One can
also take the gender difference as an extension of the workload of women in
many phases of the home life of the typical heterosexual couple in the United
States. If women, even women with full time jobs outside the home, carry out
an average of two-thirds of the household chores (Bianchi, Milkie, Sayer, &
Robinson, 2000), it is not surprising that they would be more likely to take
charge of picking out the bedding. Nor is it surprising that even though the
woman may do the majority of the work of picking out the bedding, the man
tends to get what he wants (relatively unfeminine bedding). From a related perspective, one could argue that if the household chores are more women's work,
she is judged more than a man by what the household looks like. In the eyes

of visitors to her home, it is a measure of her success at household work if the furnishings and arrangements, including what is in the bedroom, look appealing and appropriate. The household appearance is, in a sense, more her stage setting (Goffman, 1959) than it is her male partner's. From that perspective, the stakes may be higher for a woman in a heterosexual couple than for a man to make the bedroom look attractive. That may mean that she has more energy than he for shopping for bedding, learning about bedding options, and arguing for what she prefers.

FOR ME THE HOUSE IS JUST A PIT IF THE BED'S UNMADE

Most couple beds were made each morning. How did the couple decide who was going to make it? In some couples the rule was that the last one out of bed made it. But, generally speaking, in the heterosexual couples I interviewed, more women than men cared about whether and how the bed was made, and they made it. This is consistent with a vast literature that shows that women generally do more of the work around the house (e.g., Bianchi, Milkie, Sayer & Robinson, 2000; Rubin, 1976, pp. 100–105). However, one way in which what was said about bed making might not fit a simple assumption that women do more work because men want to do less work is that men were, on the average, not as invested as women in having a bed made, and men generally seemed to have lower standards for how the made bed should look. So it was not just that a man might shirk the task of bed making but that it was also that a woman might care more that the task be done and done well. This is consistent with the argument above in this chapter that the stakes are higher for women than for men concerning the appearance of the bedroom, because others will be inclined to take it as representative of the woman's standards and abilities more than the man's. It is also consistent with the notion that women are more invested than men in making a cozy and attractive nest. Nonetheless, even if a woman might care more, if she were the one making the bed she might still resent his not participating. However, routinizing who makes the bed seemed either to have minimized a woman's resentments or to routinize her resentments so they did not become the basis for a declaration of war.

> ME: Do you sometimes resent it that he's not invested in making the bed?
>
> SHANNON: Yeah, and for me the house is just a pit if the bed's unmade (chuckles). It always seems to me that half the housecleaning is done once the bed is made. There are times like, "(Grumbling noise) I wish he'd help" (small laugh).

A related gender difference is that more men than women disliked having the bedding tucked in at the foot of the bed and would, as part of settling into bed at night, untuck the bedding. Some people said that the man untucked the bedding because he was taller. So when he was in bed, his feet were closer to the end of the bed, and he felt more confined than she by tucked-in covers. Another factor was that more men than women said that they regulated warmth at night by moving feet or legs out from under the covers, and tucked in bedding would block them from doing that (for more on this, see chapter 6). Both partners might have feelings about the situation, with a man feeling annoyed that the covers were tucked in and a woman feeling annoyed that he untucked the covers on his side as soon as he got into bed. But, in the long run, couples in which the man was unwilling to sleep with tucked-in covers seemed to accept a routine of her tucking the covers in, him untucking them on his side of the bed, and both of them occasionally grumbling about the situation.

> DAN: When I get in bed, the first thing I do is kick my feet around and pull the sheets up (laughs).
>
> KRISTEN: And that makes me crazy, because I spent all that time making the bed, tucking the sheets under, and then he gets in bed and kicks 'em all out.
>
> DAN: When I lived by myself, I never made my bed. I didn't see any purpose in making a bed. I got up, went to work, came home, made dinner, watched TV, whatever I had to do around the house, went back to bed. Why make it? (both laugh) So now I come home and not every day, but I'd say four or five out of the seven days a week the bed's made. The sheets are all tucked in, and the first thing I gotta do is kick them out, 'cause my toes hang out the edge of the bed, and it drives me nuts. I can't straighten my toes up when I lay in bed. I have to lay with my legs to the side (laughing).

A few men had become accustomed to bedding tucked in at the bottom, perhaps because their partner continued to object to their untucking the bedding. And, just for the record, there were also women who did not like having the bedding tucked in.

SIT ON THE OTHER BED TO PUT YOUR SOCKS ON

In some couples, there were strong differences of opinion about whether a bed that was made could be used for this or that purpose. One partner, particularly the one who had made it, and that was often the woman in a heterosexual couple, might see the bed as an aesthetic display that should not be disturbed prior to going to bed. By contrast, the other partner might want to do things in the bed in addition to sleeping at night—watch television, read, wrestle with children, nap, or just sprawl. One way some couples resolved disagreements over the matter was to agree that the partner who mussed a bed before bedtime must remake it. Another resolution was to agree that the bed was to remain made until bedtime, so a partner who wanted to nap, wrestle with children, or read during the day must find another place to do those things.

> KRISTEN: It does aggravate me that we have this big fluffy down comforter, and the bed is this Martha Stewart bed (he snorts). And I pride myself on our bed. (DAN: Yeah.) It's a comforter and a duvet, and then we have our pillows, and then we have shams, and pillows.

> DAN: Pillows that can't be used as pillows. They're just decorative ones.

> KRISTEN: Right. They're decorative pillows. They're for the *look* (Dan laughs), the effect. And so altogether we have . . . eight pillows on our bed, four of which are just for show. And I'll get the bed all made and the comforter is all fluffy . . . and then he'll come in and sit down on it (laughing). And so I'll say, "You know what? That drives me crazy. If you're gonna sleep, then sleep. But if the bed is made and it's all fluffy . . . don't just go and sit on it. Go sit on the other bed to put your socks on."

> DAN: Usually . . . if I'm (chuckling) gonna take a nap . . . I go to the guest bedroom. . . . I don't mess the other bed. She gets upset if I take (she is laughing) a nap on the bed and I don't take the decorative pillows off the bed.

> KRISTEN: He just falls into them.

> DAN: It's just easier to go to the guest room than deal with the decorative pillow issue. . . . So me and the dog sleep together in the guest room.

WE HAVE OUR SIDES OF THE BED

In almost every couple I interviewed, each partner slept on the same side of the bed every night. Perhaps sleeping on the same side of the bed was part of having a predictable routine so things did not have to be negotiated or argued about at bedtime. But nobody I interviewed said that. In most couples one or both partners had one or more of eight specific reasons for sorting out the sides of the bed the way they did.

IT'S THE SIDE I SLEPT ON BEFORE WE WERE A COUPLE

Some partners chose a side of the bed based on which side he or she slept on before the couple got together. Some claims to a particular side of the bed were based on childhood sleeping arrangements.

> ZACK: I slept on that side of the bed when I slept with my brother when we were about so big. . . . And I slept on the inside. My side was up against the wall, so that I wouldn't fall out of the bed when I was real small. I was the little brother. And when I got older, why, it just stayed that way. And we roomed together when we were in the cities for a while, and he still slept on that side of the bed. . . . That's the side I slept on before I was married, so I suppose maybe that's what I liked afterwards.

Why should previous experience of sleeping on a certain side of the bed matter, either to the person claiming that as a reason to sleep on a certain side of the bed or to the person's partner? Perhaps the earlier experiences set a sleep routine in place that was too comfortable, familiar, and effective to drop. A break in the familiar pattern could make it difficult to fall asleep. It may also be that past experiences of sleeping on a certain side of the bed may represent certain things about a person's body—for example, a problem with a shoulder—so it is not really the past experience that is so important as the continuing limitation. Also, some couples started their bed sharing relationship when one of the partners stayed over night with the other. In those cases, the person whose bed it was always claimed her or his preferred side as something like a right of ownership—this is my bed and I'll sleep in it as I choose.

I GET CLAUSTROPHOBIC IF I'M NOT CLOSER TO THE DOOR

In some couples one partner said she or he had to be closer to the door (and away from the wall, if the bed was against the wall) because otherwise she or he felt trapped and claustrophobic.

> SHANNON: I tend to sleep on the outer, not up against the wall. . . . I just don't like being boxed in. So he gets the leftovers. . . .
>
> STEVE: If it had been up to me there'd be days I would sleep on the outside knowing that I get up earlier than she does, 'cause it's kind of a pain to crawl around her in the morning.

Why should feelings of being trapped or claustrophobic matter? Those feelings can be extremely strong and compelling. Some people who feel trapped or claustrophobic when sleeping farther from the door can be far too anxious to sleep or to sleep well.

I'M CLOSER TO THE DOOR TO PROTECT HER

Some men in heterosexual couples slept closer to the door to protect the woman, either because the man felt protective or because the woman wanted to feel protected by him.

> DAN: I just feel more comfortable sleeping by the door, kind of a protective thing. It doesn't matter where the bed is in the room, I have to sleep near the door.

> DIANA: I kind of like him by the door. . . . It makes me feel safer.

For more on this matter, see the discussion in the next chapter on bedtime security checks and in Chapter 14 on safety.

I WANT TO BE CLOSER TO THE BATHROOM

In some couples one of the partners wanted to be closer to the bathroom so that nighttime trips to the bathroom would be easier. In heterosexual couples where closeness to the bathroom was a factor, it was more often the woman who slept closer to the bathroom.

> GREG: I think historically it probably would go to which side of the bed had best access to the bathroom (CHERYL: Yeah, yeah.)

> ME: So who liked to be closer? You would like to be?

> CHERYL: Umhm. When we stay at motels or hotels I always sleep on the bathroom side.

It can be in the interests of both partners for the person who will make more night time bathroom trips to sleep closer to the bathroom. That way the person making the trips may get to the bathroom more easily and perhaps in a way that allows them not to come fully awake. For the partner who remains in bed, the shorter trip to the bathroom may minimize the noise and other potential interference to their sleeping as their partner finds her or his way to the bathroom.

It Depends on Who Gets Up First in the Morning

Some couples sorted out sides of the bed based on who got up first in the morning, with the person who got up first being closer to the alarm and/or the door. Or, if the bed was against a wall, the person who got up first would be more likely to sleep on the side away from the wall.

I'm Closer to the Door Because of the Kids

Some couples with young children chose sides of the bed based on who had primary responsibility for getting up to take care of the children or who they preferred to have deal with a child who wandered into the bedroom. In heterosexual couples, it was usually the mother who was closer to the door.

> LIZ: I'm the mom. I'm the protector of my children, and if something's going on I want to be able to be close to the door. . . . That's just always how I've been, because I had kids before I had a husband, and that's what I always did, so I could hear what was going on in the rest of the house.

It's Because of the Pain and Stiffness

Sometimes the choice of side of bed was based on body comfort and discomfort stemming from an injury or a chronic health problem. That might affect which side of the bed was easier to get in or out of or which side of the bed the person who had the body flexibility to turn off a reading lamp or an alarm clock would need to sleep on. Health problems might also affect preferences for side of the bed based on which side made it easier to sleep in the desired way regarding facing toward or away from the partner.

> CAROL: I can only sleep on my left side comfortably, 'cause my neck gets sore if I sleep on my right side. . . . If I sleep on the right hand side of the bed, then I'm facing her when I'm sleeping, and if I sleep on the left hand side, then my back is to her most of the time when I'm sleeping, and so I always sleep on the right hand side, and she sleeps on the left hand side.
>
> JANET: So we're facing each other.
>
> ME: You prefer sleeping face to face. (CAROL: Yeah.)

My Side Is Warmer

Occasionally the choice of side of the bed was related to which side of the bed was colder or warmer.

> DONNA: He sleeps on the side closest to the window because he likes to sleep with the window open.... He likes to sleep cooler than I do, and it's also the side with the air conditioner.

THE COUPLE SYSTEM

An important part of getting along with someone in a long term, intimate relationship is learning how to accommodate and tolerate. I assume that each relationship starts with both partners as beginners at accommodating to each other, even if they have had experience in previous relationships. So while two people are sorting out what to have on the bed, whether to make the bed, who makes the bed, which side of the bed to sleep on, and so on, they are also learning how to accommodate and tolerate. This is not to say that people necessarily achieve complete accommodation and tolerance. Some couples quoted in this chapter were still grumbling about issues concerning the bed years after they started sleeping together. Arguably, the grumbling represents a degree of accommodation and tolerance; still, it seems that some couples may struggle for all their time together with issues that one or both of them cannot bend about. And some people are undoubtedly less able and willing than others to learn to accommodate and tolerate. In a sense, the couple system comes in part out of the partners' separate dispositions to accommodate and tolerate. At one level, one can look at that as an issue of power and control. A person who is less accommodating and tolerating may be able to have her or his way more often. On another level, if there is not an adequate degree of accommodation and toleration, the couple system will have certain characteristics—perhaps a great deal of mutual dissatisfaction, perhaps considerable acrimonious wrangling, perhaps various attempts to get around rather than work with the partner.

The couple system is also created out of the personal histories the partners bring to the relationship and all the givens, shoulds, preferences, rules, and standards of the society from which they come. An obvious piece of what they bring to their developing couple relationship is their history of having shared a bed and of having slept on one side of the bed or the other. And those experiences are undoubtedly related to aspects of culture and social class. For example, some cultures are much more likely than others to give children the experience of sharing a bed (Whiting, 1964; Whiting & Whiting, 1975), and people who are not economically well off are probably more likely to give children years of experience at sharing a bed.

Another way in which the couple system is obviously built on the givens of the society or societies from which they come is reflected in the ways gender ideas intrude into couple practices concerning the bed. For example, there may be a relationship between societal patterns concerning who does what in the house and women's greater likelihood, in heterosexual couples, of being the decision maker about bedding and greater likelihood of making the bed and caring that it is made. Another way in which gender patterns in society seem to operate is in how some heterosexual couples choose sides of the bed on which to sleep based on which side better enables the man to protect the woman.

FOUR

going to Bed

FOR MANY COUPLES there are periods of months or even years when the going-to-bed process seems to run in a predictable and patterned routine. Nothing has to be debated. They are drawn along each night by the familiar routine.

I'LL SAY, "I'VE GOT TO GO TO BED"

Roughly half the couples I interviewed usually went to bed together in the sense that they routinely arrived in bed at the same time or within no more than fifteen minutes of each other. Some couples had an agreed time to go to bed—for example, 10:30, or after the weather report on the 10 PM news. But more couples had a signal that started them on the path to bed. Often the signal was simply that one of the partners announced, "I'm going to bed."

> TONY: I'd just say (laughing) she decides.
>
> MICHELLE: He usually is ready to go to bed before I am. And he says, "Come on." I'm usually on the computer on the internet at night. "It's time to go to bed."
>
> TONY: That's been forever. Wherever you were at, I have to go down and say it's time to come to bed (both chuckle), sometimes wondering if she'd ever come to bed if I didn't do that.

HE'LL HEAD OFF TO BED AND EVERY SINGLE LIGHT IS ON

Although roughly half the couples arrived in bed at the same time or close to it, the time the two partners in such couples started for bed might be

quite discrepant. In order to get to bed at close to the same time, one partner might have to head for bed much earlier than the other. In heterosexual
couples, there seemed to be a gender difference in this regard, with women
tending to use more time than men to prepare for bed. That meant that if
their bedtime was, say, 10:30, the woman might start getting ready for bed at
10:10, while the man started at 10:25. Even then, he might arrive in bed
before she did.

> DAN: She says she's going to go to bed. And I say, "Yeah, I'll come, I'll
> be in a couple of minutes." But when she says she's going to bed that
> means she has to straighten up the kitchen, put laundry away, what-
> ever, take a shower, and all that. So I'll have beaten her to bed by fif-
> teen minutes . . . so I'll lay in bed and read a magazine or something
> until she comes.

In Dan's brief quote is an interesting hint about gender and bedtimes. The
woman in a heterosexual couple might, like Dan's wife Kristen, take more time
to get to bed because she had more household tasks to finish—for example,
straightening the kitchen, starting the dishwasher, getting things ready for
breakfast, turning out lights around the house, and putting laundry away. Kristen was not alone among women in the heterosexual couples I interviewed in
feeling that her path to the bed took her through chores that her male partner
might conceivably have done but did not do.

> SHANNON: He'll say, "Shall we go to bed?" and he'll head off to bed,
> and every single light is on in the house, and so I get the job of lock-
> ing up and shutting lights off and trying to straighten the blankets or
> whatever. He's just laying there.

As part of their bedtime routine, the women I interviewed also tended to
spend more time on hygiene and appearance than the men, for example, remov-
ing makeup, combing out their hair, and applying creams or moisturizers.

This is not to say that men in heterosexual couples lacked areas of concern
at bedtime. A man might, for example, empty the dishwasher and let the dogs
out. Some couples talked about a bedtime security check of the house, to see
that the doors were locked, certain windows were closed, and the garage door
was down. More often, in heterosexual couples, it was the man who did the
security check.

> JEFF: I can't go to sleep at night, it's part of my compulsiveness, unless
> the door is dead bolted and has the chain lock on it.

ME: Do you feel that he's more on guard than you might be?

DONNA: As far as that goes, yeah. Even during the day, like if he goes in to take a shower, he dead bolts and locks the door. And normally at night he's the one that does it.

That some couples had a security check says something about life in the United States, and it also says something about what needs to be in place in order for people to sleep securely. If the bed is the nest, people need assurance that the nest is not likely to be invaded. That men are more likely to do the security check probably links to the way gender is conceived of in many heterosexual couples—man as household defender. Perhaps there is a bit of reality to that in that in most heterosexual couples I interviewed the man seemed physically larger. This may be one reason for his selection or self-selection as the couple security specialist.

I'LL JUST STAY UP LATE SO I CAN HAVE MY OWN TIME TO MYSELF

In many couples, the partners routinely went to bed at different times from each other. Typically, both partners seemed to feel good about that pattern. Perhaps one partner became sleepy earlier or had to get up earlier the next day. Or perhaps one partner was more of a night person, had more to do around the house before going to bed, or wanted to stay up to watch television, do something on the internet, read, play a computer game, or do school work.

For some, the central attraction of staying up later than the partner was having time by themselves. If one thinks of couple relationships as a matter of balancing togetherness and apartness (Rosenblatt & Titus, 1974), that both togetherness and apartness are needed, then moving toward discrepant bedtimes might be useful in achieving the balance. It is a solution to the problem of how to have time to oneself. Particularly in couples who spend considerable time together each day (for example, if both are retired or if they work together in a family business), one partner might want time alone after the other has gone to bed.

MARK: We spend a lot of time together . . . so if it just gets to be too much, we need a little space every now and then. I would say if that's the case, when it gets to be bedtime . . . one of us would probably stay up later and just, well, it's usually me. I'll just stay up a little later and watch some TV and . . . relax a little bit.

REBECCA: We usually do absolutely everything together. We drive to work together. All our hobbies and all our interests are the same. We never really go anywhere without each other. . . . We're the couple that always drags the other one along. . . . The only time that I really am without him is when I stay up late. And the only time he's really without me is when he gets up early. And we both kind of think that this is kind of a good thing because I get to do what I want during those couple hours.

The person who goes to bed first may also like the private time in bed.

> CINDY: I go to bed early and read, 'cause I'm sick of the TV and I'm sick of people on the phone, and I'm just sick of everything, and I just want to be alone, and I read, and I go to sleep, and then, I don't know when, (chuckles) I guess three or four hours later maybe, you come to bed.

Also, some couples had a routine of going to bed at different times because one of them had to get to sleep before the other one started to snore. (More about this in chapter 13.)

WHEN WE FIRST GOT MARRIED SHE WOULDN'T GO TO BED WITHOUT ME

Almost all couples who talked about the early days of their relationship said that they started out their relationship routinely going to bed at the same time. It was romantic and a symbol of their close relationship, commitment, and intimacy. I think they generally believed that was what couples should do, and in the early days of their relationship they may have had a busy sexual relationship. But as time passed, the routine of going to bed together might be discarded. Ed and Cindy started sharing a bed twenty-seven years prior to the interview. After twenty-seven years, they would often go to bed three or four hours apart.

> ED: When we first got married she wouldn't go to bed without me. So we were always going to bed about nine or ten o'clock, and that went for the first good two years.

HE SAYS HE CAN'T SLEEP AS WELL IF I'M NOT THERE

Some partners had strong feelings of disappointment with discrepant bedtimes.

> SUSAN: He does not like it if I don't go to bed when he does (chuckling). He says he can't sleep as well if I'm not there.

With discrepant bedtimes one might miss the talk, the physical contact, the feelings of safety and security, the sexual contact, the symbol of being a couple, the warmth of the partner, the change of the household to a silent, lights-off sleep mode, or the calming effect of the partner's breathing.

There were, however, couples who went to bed at different times who still were able to have many of the benefits of going to bed together. For example, they might go to bed at different times but routinely, when the second of them arrived in bed, touched and cuddled. Kathy and Mitch had another approach to having discrepant bedtimes but still having contact in bed at the beginning of the night. Their sleep routine was that at ten or even earlier she felt tired and started getting ready for bed. She would wash her face, take off her makeup, and so on, and then get in bed. She would watch television for a while or read. He would join her, and for a few minutes sit up in the bed, and they would snuggle. She fell asleep quickly and then he would get out of bed and watch television or do other things, maybe until midnight, when he went in bed. (For more on snuggling see chapter 7.)

MORNING PEOPLE AND NIGHT PEOPLE

Some people are consistently morning people, some consistently night people. A morning person wakes up easily and early and is almost immediately alert, energetic, and upbeat. At night, a morning person is generally emotionally and cognitively flat, without much energy. By contrast, a night person is emotionally and cognitively flat in the morning, ordinarily needing considerable time and caffeine to become fully awake and functional.

> CAROL: I'm not very talkative in the morning. I . . . get up and I'm pretty quiet until I'm awake awake. Morning is not . . . the best time to start a serious discussion. I'm just not very good.

It may not be until nighttime that a night person is fully energized. And because a night person feels so alive at night, she or he typically does not want to go to bed until rather late. When I asked people whether they were morning or night people, more than half found it easy to apply the concepts to themselves or their partner.

How do two people get along around issues of going to sleep and waking up when one is a morning person and one is not, or one is a night person and one is not? To some extent couples may select partners who match their circadian rhythm at the time they are exploring becoming partners (Hur, Bouchard, & Lykken, 1998). Often couples are mismatched, and there is some evidence

that partners who are mismatched in sleep/wake patterns get along less well
(Adams & Cromwell, 1978; Cromwell, Keeney, & Adams, 1976; Lange, Waterman, & Kerkhof, 1998; Larson, Crane, & Smith, 1991) and spend less time in
serious conversation and shared activities, including sexual encounters with
each other (Cromwell, Keeney, & Adams, 1976). A couple may become differ-
entiated as night person and morning person in order to achieve greater time
apart (Rosenblatt & Titus, 1976), but whatever the origins of their discrepant
sleep/wake pattern, being able to sleep well and maintain a comfortable relationship despite a discrepancy in sleep/wake pattern can be challenging.

BE QUIET; I WANT TO SLEEP

As might be expected, a person who is not a night person can be annoyed at
bedtime by the talkativeness and sounds of evening activities of a night person.
It can be a challenge for someone who is not a night person but who is part-
nered with one to fall asleep and get a good night's sleep in a way that is not
criticized by and offensive to the night person partner (Adams & Cromwell,
1978). A parallel challenge is for the night person to be able to get enough sleep
in the morning or to get the quiet, reflective, slow-to-get-going time she or he
needs in the morning if the partner is wide awake, perky, and busy then.

> JIM: I'm more high energy in the morning. At night she's kind of
> really energetic.
>
> ME: Do those differences ever irk you?
>
> MADELINE: A little bit. Once in a while.
>
> JIM: I'll try to get to sleep and she'll just be talking away (she laughs,
> then he).
>
> ME: And you don't dare fall asleep while she's talking.
>
> JIM: Oh, no (Madeline laughs). When I start to slowly kind of turn my
> back, she'll pick up on that and, "Okay, good night." (both laugh) So
> there're subtle ways to do that. In the morning . . . I kind of get up
> and sing and . . . so it's kind of opposites in the morning and at night.
>
> MADELINE: I like to be up early, but I like to have quiet time and just
> think things through and get ready for the day, and you're like I am at
> night (JIM: Yeah); you're just energetic, and all ready to go.

For some couples in which one was a morning person and the other a
night person, when they first started going together one of them tried to maintain the same schedule and pattern of energy that was natural for the other. It

was as though until the relationship was secure and committed, one of the partners forced herself or himself to keep up with the other. Some morning people, for example, would push themselves early in a relationship with a night person to stay up as late as the night person. But as the relationship matured and strengthened, the morning person felt more free to do what felt most comfortable and started going to bed and to sleep earlier than the night person.

ME: When you first were sharing a bed, was it annoying that he would prefer to stay up later?

MARK: I would say we stayed up later more often.

PATRICIA: I think so too. I think we went to bed at the same time a lot more than we do now. . . . We usually went to bed at the same time when we first started sharing a bed.

MARK: Yeah, but I think more of it was it was probably you staying up later than it was (PATRICIA: umhm) me going to bed earlier.

ME: So maybe you were forcing yourself to stay up.

PATRICIA: Right, so I could spend time with him (laughs).

I've Had to Try to Accommodate His Level of Energy

Night people can be irritated in the morning by a morning person's energy and cheerfulness. If they are going to be comfortable with the discrepant sleep/wakeful cycles it seems that they have to learn to tolerate the singing, chattiness, and so on, just as a morning person would have to learn to accommodate a night person's crabbiness and lack of energy in the morning.

DAN: I'm very chipper in the morning.

KRISTEN: I'm very not.

DAN: I'm up, ready to go, and she's walking around the house growling at everything.

KRISTEN: "Don't talk to me. Don't look at me. Don't ask me questions." Yeah.

ME: When you first realized that you had that difference, was that an issue?

KRISTEN: That was real challenging.

DAN: It's not really an issue for me. . . . It doesn't bother me, but it really bugs her that I'm up and chipper. . . .

KRISTEN: Yeah . . . he's up and talking and asking questions and singing songs and talking to the dog and . . . the cat, singing to me. And I just want quiet. I've really had to try to accommodate his level of energy . . . so that I'm not as irritable as I used to be.

ME: What do you do to be less irritable?

DAN: Turn the hair dryer on. . . . Close the bathroom door.

KRISTEN: Yeah. (Dan laughing) He can't not be cheerful. Just like I can't not be grumpy. It's just the way we are, so I just try to be more tolerant of his happiness.

Couples in which one was a night person and the other a morning person generally learned to accommodate to the difference. They went to bed at different times, awoke at different times, and learned to live with, be comfortable with, and work around one another's sleep and energy pattern.

ME: Is it a hassle for either of you that one of you is more a night person and one of you is more a morning person?

HANK: Not really. (BARBARA: No, not really.) We don't really have any problems. . . . We either go to sleep separately or (BARBARA: Get up separately) we get up separately. Yeah, that's not a big deal.

Among the challenges of a difference in sleep/wake patterns is how to accomplish the touching and conversation that couples with congruent sleep/wake patterns have (Adams & Cromwell, 1978). No couple with a discrepant pattern said that they had serious problems about finding time for touch and conversation. Many of them had worked out ways to achieve adequate contact despite their discrepant patterns.

JANET: When I came into the relationship (chuckles), I was even more Type A than I am now, and so the idea of (CAROL: Laying in bed in the morning was a very foreign concept for her) laying in bed in the morning was just not something, I didn't necessarily disapprove, I guess, but I had things to do, so (laughs) I'd say it probably took Carol seven years . . . to get me to enjoy (CAROL: It was like waking up with a . . . tornado [laughs]). She worked hard to get me to enjoy the idea of just chill out here and stay in bed. . . . I love it, absolutely love it, but it took her a long time to teach me how to do that (laughs). She was very patient.

Some people even learned to value the other's very different energy cycle. Walt, for example, who was not a morning person, claimed that he loved living with Lisa, who was a morning person. He said that her energy and enthusiasm motivated him to get going in the morning.

> WALT: When she wakes up in the morning she just hops right out, and it's very motivating (chuckles). I would miss that if I would sleep alone. "God, what's the point? I'll just stay here." So she lays that guilt trip on me (Lisa laughs). She gets up; she hops around; she's got tea going . . . and, "Well, I guess I better get up."

WHAT, IF ANYTHING, PEOPLE WEAR TO BED

The people I interviewed varied considerably in what they wore to bed. They might wear pajamas, nighties, t-shirts, sweat clothes, or underwear. In hot weather they might wear little to bed; in cold weather they might wear several layers of clothing and socks to bed. Nine of the eighty-eight people reported sleeping in the nude always or almost always. That so many did could be about the warmth the other person provided, but people who slept in the nude emphasized their feelings of freedom and the pleasures of skin contact.

> CAROL: She sleeps naked. (JANET: [laughs] Yeah. And that's because when we got together you thought it was a great idea.) We both sleep naked.
>
> JANET: Yeah. We do sleep naked, which is hilarious. . . . I think it's very liberating. (CAROL: Umhm) We both were married for a long time, and then when we came out at forty something it was like being a teenager all over again. . . .
>
> CAROL: I never slept with clothes on.
>
> JANET: . . . I'd always had a nightgown. . . .
>
> CAROL: I think it's really nice in that it's just that skin to skin touch. That's just very nice.

I Wish She'd Go to Bed Nude

As in other areas of sleeping, some couples did not agree on what to wear to bed. Even partners who had been together for years might still have their differences. Consider Vic and Maria, who had been together for well over a decade.

> VIC: I don't like the fact that you wear a nightie to bed, never have. I wish she'd go to bed nude. . . . That would feel closer, cozier. I feel like

that nightie is like this barrier. . . . It's not comfortable for me to be
not wearing anything and then rubbing up against some polar fleece
or some cotton. It feels unfair. . . . That would definitely make my life
more pleasant, without a nightie.

MARIA: (laughing) I'm sure it would.

It seems that the solution Vic and Maria had arrived at was to disagree
but not to make their disagreement a source of rancor or intense conflict. Vic
was wistful about what Maria wore to bed, not angry. In a sense, their solution was to see their disagreement as not personal but about the ways women
and men differ. His wanting her nude was, in that sense, just a guy thing for
them. He wanted sensual contact when he wanted it. Her wanting to be
clothed in bed was a woman thing for them, about being warm enough, perhaps about being modest, and also not giving Vic automatic permission to be
sexual with her.

Another couple who agreed to disagree labeled their difference of opinion a cultural matter, and that too made their disagreement less personal and
explosive than it might otherwise have been.

MOLLY: [He doesn't like to wear pajamas.] It was okay until we had
kids, or if there are . . . people . . . visiting. . . .

THOMAS: Why pajamas? (laughs) If it's a cold day . . . or maybe if we
have guests over, I have a robe, but I don't like to (MOLLY: You don't
sleep in it) . . . yeah, I don't like sleeping (chuckles) with pajamas. I
sleep in my underwear. . . . The cultural difference, yeah (MOLLY: is
that in my family it was okay for men not to wear shirts), whereas
(chuckling) in my family . . .

MOLLY: it's okay to run around in your underwear, but your chest
should be covered (laughs).

THOMAS: Yeah. Right. . . . Fruit of the Loom guy, yeah. . . . My kids
have seen me in my underwear, right. Whereas some people, "(gasp).
How could you?"

Aren't You Worried about the Kids?

As Thomas said and also as the interview excerpt below indicates, some couples struggled over what to wear to bed when children were in the house. The
struggle might be between the partners, but sometimes it was with what they
saw as family, community, or societal standards. A few parents had decided not

to let living with children stop them from going to bed scantily clad or nude. They had resolved their conflict with each other and with what they assumed were the standards of others.

> SUSAN: We never sleep with clothes on. We don't wear pajamas. We'll throw robes on when we leave our room, 'cause we have kids. . . . It's just our one little bit of freedom in life I think, just to be able to sleep nude. Don't you think? . . . My sister thinks we're just odd for doing that. . . . "Aren't you worried about the kids?" I said, "Oh, for crying out loud. We have blankets," and our kids are old enough now they figure out that we don't just sleep when we go to bed. Who cares? (chuckles) It's just our bodies. It's okay.

THE COUPLE SYSTEM

As couples work out their relationship and learn how to balance what it takes by their standards to be a couple with what they need as individuals, they crystalize their bedtime(s) and their bedtime routine. For many couples, considerable learning underlies the simple matter of going to bed at this time versus that. Bedtime can reveal a lot about the fundamental properties of the couple relationship. In learning about a couple's process of going to bed we can learn about division of labor by gender, how a couple does intimacy, what they do about balancing togetherness and apartness, and how they accommodate their differing needs and situations.

If one partner is a night person and one is not, their couple system concerning bedtime and sleeping could have been constructed to fit those differences. Alternatively, couple differences could arise or be magnified by dynamics in the relationship—perhaps interpersonal tensions that lead one or both partners to desire more time apart. There is evidence that couples in which one partner is a night person and one a morning person have a lower level of marital satisfaction, more arguments, less time in serious conversation, less time in shared activities, and less frequent sexual intercourse. However, I think that, without longitudinal study, it is difficult to interpret that evidence. Do the difficulties arise from the mismatch or do the difficulties cause the mismatch? Also, in light of the evidence summarized in this chapter, it seems that couples who are mismatched generally learn how to accommodate differences and still meet their basic needs.

It is easy to think of what people choose to wear to bed as matters of physical comfort, personal standards, couple standards, and standards of the larger community. However, it is also possible to think of what they wear as about the couple system. Clothing is a boundary between oneself and one's partner. Depending on the dynamics of the couple relationship and how the couple learns how to get along, one partner may want, while in bed, to welcome the other into closer contact or to keep the other at a distance. For example, a partner who is eager to make contact does not necessarily want to be held at bay by sleepwear that is heavy and that covers most of the body. A partner with whom one would welcome contact one might invite into contact by wearing little or nothing to bed. And the couple dance of contact and distancing might well be reflected in their similarities or differences in what they wear to bed.

From another angle, what a person wears to bed may reflect how temperature issues play out in the couple relationship. Differences in temperature preference will have led to certain couple actions regarding thermostat settings, windows being open or closed, and how many covers to have on the bed. And they may have led some people to need to wear heavier sleepwear and others to strip to bare skin.

The fact that other people's concerns about what a parent wears to bed were noted by some parents who slept with little or nothing on can be understood to say that even in the innermost privacy of the home, the couple system is not isolated from the outside world. There are concerns about what this relative or that friend or people in general might say. And even if the couple decides to ignore those concerns—for example, by sleeping nude though children are nearby—they will have defenses against outsider disapproval.

FIVE

Activities in the Transition from Awake to Asleep

MANY COUPLES DO NOT instantly move from wakefulness to sleep. For some, the bedtime routine includes transition activities. Among the most commonly mentioned ones were prayer, television watching, reading, and sexual intercourse. As we look at those activities, we learn interesting things about sleep and the couple system.

NIGHTTIME PRAYER

WE SAY OUR PRAYERS TOGETHER

For some people prayer was important in leaving the day's concerns behind and moving into a mental, spiritual, and physical state that made it easy to sleep.

BRAD: We say the same prayer for the last thirty-eight years.

TERESA: We say the Lord's prayer together. Then if we have anything else, oh, let's say, one day . . . I was having a party in the backyard (chuckles), so the night before we were having the party . . . I said, "Please, Lord, let it be sunny tomorrow." (both laugh) So that one I prayed, but I did say it out loud though. And he said, "I usually just say thanks for things." I said, "I'll do that tomorrow."

The prayer of some couples enabled them to share what they felt their blessings in life were and to go to sleep in a relatively upbeat mood. One example of that was the statement of thanks that Brad referred to. A similar example follows, prayer that includes a statement about the happiest moment of the day.

WILLIAM: Before we go to bed we say our prayers, and then we have this: "So?" And what that is the buzz word for, "So what was the happiest moment of your day?" (JULIA: Right) And so we do that every night. . . . We can't go to bed until we say something. (JULIA [laughs]: Yeah, you have to think of something that happens in your day.)

For Barbara and Hank, the shared bedtime prayer covered a wide range of matters, allowing them to communicate with each other while they communicate with God about what they have to be grateful for, what they hope for from God, and what they have done that merited confession.

BARBARA: We pray together, and we pray out loud.

ME: Does that follow a set pattern?

HANK: . . . Well, yeah, we have acknowledge, confess, thank, and (BARBARA: We talk at times) our petitions, or supplications.

BARBARA: We have a time of praise, a time of thanksgiving, a time we confess, and then we have like requests for God. . . . It's not (HANK: any topic), it's not repetition or rote prayers. (HANK: Right, right) It's just free form.

For Henry, who was concerned about his many friends who were not healthy, saying prayers with his wife was an act of caring about the friends and acknowledging his and his wife's own frailty. Their prayers were also for their children and for people throughout the world who were in difficult situations, which, among other things, was a way for Henry and his wife to communicate to each other about shared values.

HENRY: We usually say prayers. . . . We got many, many friends that are sick we think of. And many, many people throughout the world that we've tried to think of, especially those people in those third world countries, and we always say prayers and think of our children, and mention them by names . . . and many, many other. At our age in a community like this where we've lived all our life, we know almost everybody. So there's so many people that are sick and suffering and this and that.

PRIVATE PRAYER

For some people, prayer was a solitary bedtime routine. In heterosexual couples it was more often a woman than a man who spoke of engaging in solitary bedtime prayer.

MARTHA: I always say an act of contrition before I go to bed, and sometimes a full rosary.

LISA: I'll pray before I go to sleep, but it's usually when I'm feeling especially good and thankful and then I tend to pray, or if I'm worried about someone in the family I'll just think about them in a prayer form. But I don't have a routine where I fold my hands. . . . It's usually after we've hugged, and I turn over then. That's my routine, and snuggle into my pillow, and it's right before I fall asleep.

A few people said that their solitary prayer occurred in bed because that was where they might feel overwhelmed by worry.

Solitary prayer can require concentration and focus, so if something happens to disrupt the concentration and focus it can make it difficult to pray. Molly talked about such disruptions, saying that the ordinary touching by her husband Thomas at bedtime had undermined her silent praying.

MOLLY: When we first started sleeping together, he interfered with my spirituality because I would pray before I went to sleep every night. But I was not kneeling at the side of the bed. I would pray in my head as I was falling asleep, and if somebody is touching you, it just isn't conducive to prayer.

THOMAS: I never knew that.

MOLLY: Yeah, and (THOMAS: I didn't know she was praying) it has never fully recovered (laughs).

TELEVISION AT BEDTIME

Television has revolutionized family life in the United States. It has taken a substantial amount of time away from other free time activities (Robinson & Godbey, 1997, pp. 136–137), and it has made most U.S. homes television-centered (Kunstler, 1993, p. 167, cited in Robinson & Godbey, 1997, p. 138). So it should be no surprise that television watching had a prominent place in many people's accounts of going to bed.

Almost every interviewee talked about having at least one television set in a room other than the bedroom. One or both partners might watch that set as part of their process of unwinding and getting ready for bed. Before bedtime, some people fell asleep in front of that television set and had to wake up in order to go to bed. A television set in a room other than the bedroom allowed one partner to watch television while the other went to bed and to sleep. It might allow a person who could not fall asleep in bed, who could not fall back to sleep, or whose partner was making sleep impossible because of snoring or tossing and turning to have a place to which to flee.

A BEDROOM TELEVISION SET

The majority of the couples I interviewed had a bedroom television set. For some couples, television watching at bedtime was not a problem. They either had similar values and standards regarding television watching in the bedroom or they had ways to live with their differences. Many couples who had differences had agreements about watching television that were satisfactory for both partners—what to have on, when to turn it off, how loud to set the volume, and who controlled the remote. Some people arrived in bed so exhausted or had such powers of falling asleep that it did not matter whether a partner was watching television. But a few couples had ongoing hassles when one partner was in bed watching television while the other was trying to sleep.

Some people, including Brenda, hated having a television set in the bedroom. She said that dispute over television in the bedroom was one of the reasons she divorced her first husband. For her, a bedroom television set was not just an annoyance. It made her "crazy."

> BRENDA: I really hate television. That was one of the deciding factors in my divorce, 'cause he wanted the television in the bedroom, and it just made me crazy. It was on all the time.

Similarly, Kristen wanted the bedroom to be only for sleep, sex, and talking, not for television watching.

> KRISTEN: Our bedroom is used for sleeping, sex, talking. That's it. No TV, no phone. It's great. (laughs) So the mindset is, we're not going to go climb in bed and channel surf (DAN: Yeah, yeah).

Cindy and Ed no longer had a television set in the bedroom because it fed what Cindy considered their addiction, particularly Ed's, to television. A bedroom television set had cost them sleep and led Ed to spiral into the depths of what seemed to Cindy to be addiction. She felt the addiction had come to dominate his life and, because of that, hers.

> ME: Do you have a TV set in your bedroom?
>
> CINDY: No. And that's a big thing in our marriage (laughs). . . . (ED: She's not a television fan.) I am, but I already watch too much. Ever

since he was very, very, very young, he's been addicted to TV. I tell a lot of people there are men that are addicted to alcohol; there's men addicted to drugs, and then there's men addicted to TV. We've tried having TV in our bedroom. It does not work, because he continues to watch it after he comes to bed, and then I can't go to sleep, and it would even get so bad . . . that he would wake me up to say, "Hey, you gotta see what's on TV right now!" I was trying to sleep, so we finally said to stop all this fighting there's no more TV in our bedroom. Just to give you an example of how this guy likes TV, he has, would you say 3,000? (ED: No) No? (ED: About 2,500 maybe.) 2,500 or more VCR tapes.

When Are We Going to Talk?

Anything that blocks talking can be a problem for some couples, and one thing that can block talking is television (Gantz, 2001). As indicated in chapter 1, many couples had very little time for talking. Perhaps some of them would have had more time to talk if they had not watched television as much as they did, but none of the people I interviewed said that. In fact, some couples said that television watching helped them to connect, a connection of watching together, perhaps sitting close together, perhaps laughing together. No couple volunteered that they discussed what they watched on television.

To protect their talking time, some couples had worked out ways to talk despite watching television. For example, they might have an understanding that as they lay or sat in bed watching television they would talk during commercials or when what was on television did not engage either of them. Or they had an agreement that if either of them had something important to talk about that person could block the television set from being turned on or could insist that it be muted or turned off.

> JEFF: There's definitely those nights where you just have to talk (DONNA: Right) 'cause somethin's bothering you. . . . Those are the nights the television doesn't get turned on until we're done discussing what needs to be discussed. . . . When the television's on, we talk during commercials. (DONNA: We talk during the show sometimes too.) Sometimes we talk during the show, depending on what the show is and whether or not we've seen it.

> DONNA: It's one of those things that's used more to unwind and to fall asleep. . . . If one of us wants to talk . . . unless the sports are on the news (Jeff chuckles), then he ignores me, but after the sports is over then he's willing to talk.

Ana did not want television in her bedroom because it meant that her ex-husband (with whom she still slept on occasion) would not pay attention to her.

> ANA: He wants the TV in the room, and now I don't. "No. No TV, because before when you were here, you didn't listen. You heard me, but you didn't listen." . . . The room is for quiet time, to sleep, and if you're living together, you're sharing. If you have a TV, it's an interruption in the bedroom. And he gets like, "I can listen to a person," but he's like he's there and he's not there. . . . It's like a cellular phone. If you have a cellular phone on you on the street walking with somebody. . . . They're there, but it's like you're not there, 'cause they're walking and talking on the phone. . . . That's the way it is in the bedroom. . . . I could literally light a match to a blanket (chuckling) and he wouldn't know until he go in flame. . . . I don't allow TV in my room.

Perhaps Ana's ex-husband simply liked to watch television, but it is possible that for him television watching was a way to keep his distance from Ana. Where there is relationship tension, television set operation (whether the set is watched or is simply a source of sound and visual distraction) may be a way to keep the person with whom one might be uncomfortable at a distance (Rosenblatt & Cunningham, 1976). From that perspective, couples in which there was continued disagreement about television in the bedroom might be dealing with conflicting goals—using television to distance the other versus having the quiet and freedom from distraction to talk versus getting enough sleep versus actually watching something interesting.

I WANT THE TV ON TO HELP ME FALL ASLEEP

Consistent with a report by Gantz (2001), some couples who I interviewed who might generally be comfortable with having a bedroom television set squabbled when one of them wanted to sleep while the other wanted the set on. The one who wanted to sleep might want the sound off or might want the cuddling and other aspects of going-to-sleep interaction with her or his partner.

> MARIA: Sometimes there's tension, 'cause I want the TV on to help me fall asleep, and he wants it off. You need silence; you need no light.

Some couples had ways to minimize squabbles over television watching at such times—for example, using the closed caption option on the television set or an earphone. One couple worked out that television would be watched in the bedroom with the volume turned very low, and the partner who wanted to go to sleep would cover her ears with a pillow.

> MARGARET: I think we're pretty courteous of each other (JOSH: Yeah). If I have the TV on, I have it down real quiet. Or if he says, "Can I watch the TV?" "Sure, (JOSH: Yeah) that's fine." (JOSH: Turn it down real low.) I'll just throw a pillow over my head. We try to accommodate (JOSH: Yeah), 'cause we like each other.

Another solution that worked for some couples was to agree to ration television watching so the set was not on very long after one partner wanted to go to sleep. Some couples made use of the timer that was built into their television set to guarantee that the set would go off at an agreed upon time.

Some couples negotiated that both partners would try to stay awake until a certain point in a certain program, commonly until the end of the weather report on the 10 PM news, until the end of Jay Leno's or David Letterman's opening monologue, or until the end of a sitcom rerun that came on after the 10 PM news.

The solutions couples arrived at seemed tolerable to both partners but were not necessarily perfect. One woman, for example, complained that the arrangement she had with her partner to keep the bedroom television set sound turned low when he was falling asleep made it almost impossible for her to hear what was on television.

READING IN BED

Thirty-two of the eighty-eight people I interviewed said that they regularly read in bed before going to sleep. In a few couples, both partners were readers, but typically it was only one partner who read. In the heterosexual couples I interviewed, the bedtime reader was twice as likely to be the woman as the man.

People may read for entertainment, self-education, mental stimulation, as part of their work, or for the love of reading. They may read to fill the time while they are waiting for their partner to arrive in bed. They may read because they cannot fall asleep until they are warm, and reading in bed gives them the time they need to get warm. They may also read to unwind and relax and to distract themselves from what they might lie awake obsessing about if they did not read.

The partner of someone who reads after they are both in bed may not be bothered by the reading. He or she might find it easy to doze off.

ME: Can you fall asleep with her reading and the light on?

WILLIAM: No problem. Seriously, I just turn the other way, three, four breaths, pft, and I'm out.

What if one person's reading blocks or disrupts the sleep of the other? Reading is an interesting window into couple systems because it is generally a solitary activity but takes up social and psychological space in the couple relationship, and there is no compromise position that is part way between reading and not reading. The most common aspects of reading that bothered the nonreader were the light being on and the movements and sounds of page turning.

Some couples worked out a system in which the partner of the reader learned how to live with it, perhaps sleeping with a pillow or a blanket over his or her head. Alternatively, the partner of a reader might have learned to speak up in order to curtail the reading.

ME: Sometimes he's reading and you want to go to sleep?

MOLLY: Yeah. . . . I can't sleep with the lights on (chuckles).

ME: Do you say something to him?

MOLLY: Usually.

ME: What do you say?

MOLLY: "How much more do you have to go?" (chuckles)

But speaking up did not necessarily work. The reading did not necessarily stop. I did not interview anybody who felt very angry or who was thinking about divorce because of a partner's reading in bed. So one could say that every couple with differences concerning reading had found a way to cope with the differences. But for people like Steve, there were times of feeling that things could be better.

STEVE: There's been times when she'll be reading . . . and I go, "I gotta get some sleep; can you turn off your light?" She just keeps on doing her thing and ignores me (chuckles).

SHANNON: "No, I'm reading."

STEVE: Yeah. That's about it. (chuckles)

A few couples found a way for the reader to continue reading while minimizing what bothered the nonreader. Nancy, who wanted to read in bed until she was ready to stop, gave her partner Pam an eye mask to wear in bed, so Pam would not be bothered by the light.

NANCY: She has . . . (PAM: one of those masks). . . .

ME: Like from a long distance air flight? (PAM: Yeah)

NANCY: Yeah, if I'm going to stay reading longer, and I usually do, (PAM: And sometimes it bothers me more than others. . . .)

PAM: Probably about seventy-five percent of the time I'll wear that mask if she's reading beyond my desire to stay awake.

ME: Would you leave the mask on all night? (PAM: Yeah)

NANCY: . . . It did bother her, I think, that she wanted the lights to go out before I was ready to do that, and so I bought her that mask, so that I could continue to read if I so chose and she would be less disrupted.

Some couples resolved the power battle by agreeing that reading would only go on for a certain amount of time after both partners were in bed—perhaps until a page or a chapter was finished. Another way a couple might resolve the battle was to buy a bedroom reading lamp that concentrated its beams on the book. A few couples had agreed that reading was not for the bed, and so the person who wanted to read at night found another place in the house in which to do it.

Although the focus of most conflict over reading was on light and movements, Thomas spoke of a different focus that might be an unspoken aspect of dispute in other couples. It was that reading was a denial of intimacy and contact. He missed the touching and talk that was part of the going to sleep routine on nights when his wife, Molly, did not read. As Thomas voiced his objection to Molly's reading, he said he felt jealous of her reading because the books were getting attention that he was not.

SEXUAL INTERCOURSE

Some couples talked about their early experience of sharing a bed as much more about sexual intercourse than their current bed sharing experience. No couple said the opposite, that their early relationship was about sleep and now it was much more about sexual intercourse. Although there were couples who described their early relationship as not being very sexual, more couples said that there was a great deal of sexual energy in the beginning. As the sexual fires became more intermittent, more people found that they preferred to sleep out of physical contact. So initially some couples could sleep in a smaller bed, even a twin bed, but as was said in chapter 3, at the time of the interview more than three-fourths of the couples slept in a queen or king size bed. None was sleeping in a twin bed.

IF WE SLEEP TOGETHER WE CAN HAVE SEX MORE OFTEN

Some couples said that a reason they shared a bed was that it made it easier to have sexual encounters with each other. The other side of that is a person might move to a separate bed in order to avoid such encounters. One elderly heterosexual couple, for example, had recently stopped sleeping together on a regular basis because the woman, Grace, was tired of being awakened in the middle of the night to have intercourse. Grace said she no longer wanted sex, just a good night's sleep. Her husband, Sam, was not happy with the situation.

> ME: What do you miss now that you're sleeping apart most of the time?
>
> SAM: I like a nooky (chuckles).
>
> ME: Do you miss the company?
>
> SAM: Not that much. No. One track.

Another heterosexual couple who typically slept in separate rooms still had sexual intercourse at times, but the man was painfully aware that they had intercourse less often than they would if they were sleeping together.

> JACK: I had been used to having sex come out of sleeping together, as opposed to sort of planning some little tryst, although I did that too. Ninety percent of the times I was sexual it would come out of sleeping together. So ... [sleeping apart] really started to impact the amount of sex that I would have. And I've seen that with other partners as well, that when [we'd] sleep together, sexual relations would increase, and then when we'd go back into more of a kind of cohabitating [and not together] sleep, sex would kind of drop right out of the map.

WHEN PARTNERS GO TO BED AT DIFFERENT TIMES

For many couples, sexual intercourse was a regular part of the going-to-sleep routine. What happened to the sex life of couples who did not usually go to sleep at the same time? Some couples who went to bed at different times said that if either partner was interested in having intercourse they might plan together for a night of getting to bed and to sleep at the same time. It might be a matter of making a tryst, appointment, or date. Sometimes it was just a very casual signal of interest followed by a signal of agreement.

> WALT: Usually when we make love at night we've made a decision to go to bed together (LISA: Yeah). It isn't something that happened once we were in bed to decide, "Well, let's do it." (LISA: yeah).

LISA: Or we'll even sometimes be watching something . . . on television, and one or the other of us will say, "Do you want to go to bed together tonight? Rather than me going alone. Let me know." "Oh, yeah! Let's go have a nice night." We kind of plan for it.

The most common alternative for couples who went to bed at different times was for the partner who came to bed second to wake up the sleeping partner in order to have intercourse. However, the sleeping partner might not be happy to be awakened.

I'M TIRED

Making love at bedtime may be convenient for many reasons. There is nobody else in the bedroom, many distractions are out of the way, they are nude or wearing fewer layers of clothing than usual, and they might ordinarily fall asleep after having intercourse whether it was bedtime or not, so it is convenient to already be in bed. But many people said that they were so tired at bedtime that they rarely had the energy for a sexual encounter. Some couples who were aware that there was more sexual energy if they did not wait until bedtime tried to find times during the day, at least on weekends, for intercourse.

AMY: We make love sometimes in the evening before we fall asleep. . . . On a Saturday or Sunday afternoon if we make love [it might be] in the . . . afternoon, 'cause . . . that's another time that's stronger for . . . both of our sexual motivations than late at night.

WE WAIT UNTIL EVERYBODY IS ASLEEP

Aubert and White (1959a) pointed out that sleep is associated with nighttime and privacy in western culture. Consistent with that, most people I interviewed who lived with others in the house reserved sexual intercourse for nighttime privacy. Some people, women more than men, said they felt inhibited about having intercourse if others in the house might become aware of it.

ME: Do you ever get into hassles about sex?

SARAH: If someone's around.

NICK: Yeah. She'll get uncomfortable. Usually I won't care either way. . . . I'll still want to get sexual, and she'll be too nervous about [it].

SARAH: Yeah. [I don't want] the bed to make noise (laughs).

Quite a few parents were concerned about children who slept in nearby bedrooms becoming aware of the sounds of parent intercourse. With children nearby, many parents felt that it was difficult to have intercourse freely, frequently, and spontaneously.

> KAREN: When you're just a young couple and it's just the two of you, anything goes. Then you have the kids . . . and you gotta kind of work around the little kids and teach 'em how to knock on the door before they come in. . . . Then with the teenagers . . . then you might work around whether they're home or not home. . . . Teenagers . . . can be a real challenge. I can remember saying, "Sh-h-h." (laughs) Or trying to be quiet.

Among the reasons that couples said that they had intercourse when they were in bed for the night was that then they were more likely to have privacy from their children. But even with children seemingly asleep, fear of a child awakening or not yet being deeply asleep led some couples to wait until late in the night.

A noisy headboard is a challenge to a couple having intercourse if children or other family members are nearby. One couple disposed of their headboard once they realized that it vibrated loudly at the "drop of a pin." A newlywed couple who had moved in with the woman's mother and sisters had just learned that the sounds their headboard made revealed too much to the woman's mother and sisters.

> ROBERT: Her sisters are right there. They sleep really on the other side of this wall.

> ME: So if you're being romantic here in bed, you've gotta whisper and not make the bed make noise (ROBERT: Right). . . .

> EMMA: And we both are thinking about that the whole time, so it's kinda . . .

> ROBERT: Right, it's definitely distracting.

> EMMA: We try to hide it kind of.

> ROBERT: Right, and a lot of it's right after, too. I mean thinking, "Oh my goodness, we probably were really loud," when consciously the whole time we know we're being quiet. . . . [It] would be a huge help in our relationship . . . not being right next door to them.

> ME: Have they ever said anything?

ROBERT: No.

EMMA: Well, my mom made a comment. She didn't say she heard it, but she asked, "Are you guys going to keep the bed against that wall?"

With children inhibiting parent intercourse, a couple might move to a bigger house so that the children's bedrooms are farther from their own. Some couples rearranged how rooms in the house were used so that there would be no child sleeping close to the parent bedroom.

ME: Where's your bedroom in relation to the kids' bedrooms?

SUSAN: Ours is right there at the end of the hall, and all of our kids' bedrooms are downstairs.

ME: Do you feel like you have privacy from them?

SUSAN: Yeah (ADAM: Umhm). When all the kids were at home, the bedroom across the hall . . . two of our daughters had a bunk bed in that room, and it was okay, but it definitely got in the way of privacy.

ME: With them downstairs do you . . . have enough privacy to be snuggling or (SUSAN: umhm) kissing or (ADAM: umhm) making love? (SUSAN: Umhm).

ADAM: Yup.

SUSAN: Yup, definitely.

Some couples waited to have sexual intercourse until their children were away. A child's sleepover could do wonders for the parental love life. One couple talked about times of rather tense waiting until their teenage children left for school.

AL: Our sex life is hit and miss (they both laugh). More miss than hit. . . .

MARTHA: You have to have a sense of humor.

AL: Yeah, unless we're alone at the cabin, which isn't too often, we never really have sex at night. (MARTHA: No, it's during the day when the kids are gone.) It's in the morning. . . .

ME: After the kids have left for school?

MARTHA: Umhm. (AL: Yeah) So he hangs around the house (both laugh), until they're gone. He usually doesn't, so I know (Al laughs) when he hangs around the house what he wants.

For some couples who lived with children, part of the lovemaking routine was closing and locking the bedroom door. Locking the door was more about keeping the children out than about achieving auditory privacy.

> MARGARET: We keep our door open at night (JOSH: Yeah), and in the morning, before we make love, you get up and lock the door (JOSH: close it and lock it), because [our son] just comes in. He does-n't knock. There's no privacy.

Some couples enjoyed the increased sexual opportunity that came when their last child moved out of the house. Although they felt relief at their sexual freedom with the children living elsewhere, they might look back with humor to times when children were present and were too aware of parent sexual encounters.

> BRAD: Life begins when the dog dies and the kids leave home (they both laugh).
>
> TERESA: . . . We can close the windows and parade around the whole house now naked (both laugh) if we want too. One time when our son was seven. . . . I don't know if that's when we put the lock on the door after that (BRAD: It was [laughs]). We put a lock on the door. We were having intercourse, and, you know, women are a little loud, and he calls in and he says, "Mom, are you okay?" (all laugh) And I said, "I'm just fine" (laughing). And I think after that then we put a lock on the door (laughs). Yeah, when the daughter got married she said, "Don't come over without calling," and I said, "Well, don't come home without calling."

THE COUPLE SYSTEM

This chapter focuses on four activities that were commonly mentioned as part of the transition from wakefulness to sleep, prayer, television watching, reading, and sexual intercourse.

Shared prayer might strengthen the couple connection. It could be a way of expressing shared values, and it can connect the couple relationship with deep cultural and personal meanings. Shared prayer can nurture and enhance the spiritual side of the couple relationship while putting the couple on a path toward together winding down to a sleep of peace and security. In addition, making prayer a shared couple activity could be a powerful way of saying that, "We are in God's world together" and "We share hopes."

In a sense, shared prayer makes the couple system more than a dyad. It brings God into the couple relationship. Having God present may alter the couple relationship. For example, the presence of God may soften couple conflicts or make for easier ends to conflict (Butler, Gardner, & Bird, 1998).

Although prayer was part of the bedtime routine of some couples, many more couples said that television watching was part of their bedtime routine. I do not think that one necessarily precludes the other, but nobody who talked about prayer at bedtime talked about television watching at bedtime. Perhaps prayer and television watching at bedtime involve different kinds of winding down. Both may allow some distance from the stresses of the day, and both may bring a greater readiness to relax and sleep, but more often prayer may be about feeling safe, centered, at peace, and connected with God. Television watching may be more often about distraction.

Compromise seemed to work for most issues that most couples had concerning television—including where the set was located, what was watched, who controlled the remote (Walker, 1996), how loud the sound was, how late it could be watched, and when to talk to each other while it was on. That some couples, even those who had been together for years, still had not worked out a system that would enable both partners to feel good about the television set does not mean their learning process had broken down. Television watching is a challenging topic for learning. Not only is acceptable television usage entangled in ever-changing issues of differing sleep needs, it is also complicated by the changing nature of what is broadcast and the changing technology of television.

The television set is not simply something to help a person wind down, to entertain, and perhaps to inform. In a sense, the television set is part of the couple system in that the partners often focus on it together. Television can be part of the system, almost like another person, in that some people will listen so closely to and value the words of television personalities and performers so much that they will not turn away from them, turn them off, or speak over what they are saying. Certain television personalities—for example, Leno or Letterman—are treated as valued figures by some people and are brought into the couple bedtime routine, almost as though an interesting third party were present. Some people may use television watching to obtain emotional distance from a partner with whom they are uncomfortable. So the bedroom television set not only impacts the interactions of couples. In a sense, it can be another player in the couple system.

Although partner reading may, as Thomas said, involve an unwelcome withdrawal of partner attention, most people who had problems with a partner reading seemed more concerned about the lights being on or the bed moving as the partner turned pages. I think that puts reading in bed in the couple systems area of compromise and tolerance. The challenge of couple reading to most couples is, I think, to work out a pattern that is tolerable to both partners.

In the bookstore down the street there are no self-help books on couple sleeping, but there are over one hundred different titles on couple sexuality. But, as this chapter makes clear, the two areas are not independent. If a couple has certain sleeping issues, they have certain sexuality issues. A couple who does not sleep together is likely to have less sexual contact. Some couples who went to bed at discrepant times found that even though they had ways to deal with how the discrepant bedtimes interfered with sexual contact they still had less frequent sexual contact than if they went to bed at the same time. But even then, so many people were typically very tired at bedtime that the need for sleep often made sexual interaction less interesting than sleep. And then, just as couple sleeping is vulnerable to intrusion from others in the house, so is couple sexuality. Putting all of this together, I wonder whether the bookstore down the street would find that it could do a brisk business in books that deal jointly with couple sleep and couple sexuality.

SIX

Temperature Preferences

DIFFERENCES MAY BE essential to what draws two people to each other. Differences can also be frustrating, uncomfortable, even infuriating. In couple bed sharing, one of the most common and challenging areas of difference is temperature. Often a bedroom that is too warm for one person is too cold for the other, and the covers that are too warm for one are inadequate for the other. If they want to cuddle, how do they do it when one person has icy feet or one person's body feels as hot as an oven to the other? Temperature differences are not all bad. A person can find it rewarding, even joyous, to snuggle up to a warm partner on a cold night. In fact, that is probably why there is more bed sharing in cold climates (Whiting, 1964; Whiting & Whiting, 1975). But still, for many couples I interviewed, there were temperature differences to be dealt with.

HE'S USUALLY WARMER

In seventy-five percent of the heterosexual couples who said one of them was usually warmer than the other, it was the man who was warmer. Particularly in the years prior to menopause, he was warmer when they first climbed into bed; he generated more heat; his feet were more likely to be warm; he warmed up faster in bed; he preferred a cooler bedroom; and he generally wanted fewer blankets. This pattern is consistent with the findings of physiological research that shows that cold temperature stress reduces women's cutaneous blood flow more than it does men's (Cankar & Finderle, 2003; Cankar, Finderle, & Strucl, 2000) and that women report greater pain than men when cold-stressed (Keogh & Herdenfeldt, 2002).

I ALWAYS HAVE MORE COVERS THAN HE DOES

When two people differ in preferred temperature, how do they make the bedroom and bed comfortable for both of them? One way to deal with the issue
is an approach to bed sharing that enables one partner to cool off or warm up
independently of the other. For example, some people, men more than women,
said that they dangled feet out from under the covers part of the night in order
to cool off. That way one partner could be cooling off while the other
remained snug and warm under the covers.

Some people, women more than men, said that they slept with extra covers, while other people, men more than women, pushed covers off at night.

REBECCA: I always have more covers than he does. He's always
warm. He's hardly ever cold. I'm always cold. So it's kind of easily
solved. He kicks the covers off, and I take them.

Electric blankets with dual controls provide another solution to the challenge of one partner needing more warmth than the other.

ME: How do you compromise about the blankets?

CYNTHIA: I put an extra blanket on my side of the bed and not on
his, and the electric blanket is a dual control. He keeps his side off, and
I keep mine usually on 8.

Some people, women more than men, said that they slept with more or
heavier night clothes.

KRISTEN: Sometimes it's really too warm for him, and sometimes it's
too cold for me. . . . But I just put on sweats and a sweatshirt, and
wooly socks, 'cause I can always put on more clothes and still be
(laughing) (DAN: warm) warm. But he can only take off so much.

THERMOSTAT WARS

In heterosexual couples, if there were differences about household thermostat
settings, typically the woman wanted the thermostat set at a higher temperature than did the man.

MIKE: Every woman I've ever been with, I'm not saying I've been
with a lot of women, but women always like it warmer. . . . I keep the
thermostat around, at night, sixty-two, sixty-three, whereas she can

have it at seventy-two, seventy-five, and still have all these goddamn blankets on. My ex-wife is the same way. And it'd just be so god-damned hot that I would just have a sheet and maybe a light blanket.

In a few couples the difference led to what might be called a thermostat war, with each partner repeatedly sneaking to the thermostat to counteract how the other set it.

ME: Do you ever have arguments about setting the thermostat?

ADAM: I just move it.

SUSAN: It's like a cat and mouse game (laughs). I see him, he doesn't think I see him walk by casually set back the thermostat, and I don't say anything because if I do I know he'll be watching my next move. I act like I don't notice. Then when I walk by, I just kinda look to see what it's on, and I'll turn it back (chuckling) to what I want it, and we kinda do that without really saying anything.

Some couples, however, had agreed that one partner had control of the thermostat setting.

ME: How does the thermostat get set for nighttimes in cold weather?

WALT: . . . I would tend to keep it cooler, and I think she tends more to turn it up. . . . When she's been cold she just goes and changes it. We don't have a big conversation about it or anything like that. (LISA: yeah) It's not an issue.

Other couples ended the thermostat war by agreeing to a thermostat setting that both could live with. For example, one couple had agreed to leave the thermostat set at seventy in cold weather. That temperature was too cool for her and too warm for him, but they had made their peace.

WINDOW WARS

A few couples said that they argued about bedroom windows being open or closed. In warmer weather the argument often focused on fresh air or air movement, but in winter it was about temperature. That was when the battle over the window resembled battles over thermostats. With window wars, as with thermostat wars, some couples said that they had worked out a peace agreement. They either had agreed on a setting for the windows that both could tolerate, or they had agreed that one partner would always have her or his way.

With bedroom windows it can also help for the person who wants the window open in cooler weather to sleep closer to the window. Then she or he is the one who feels the full force of arctic air, and her or his body and body heat can help to protect the partner from the chill.

BRR! YOUR FEET ARE COLD

In cold weather, as the body works to conserve heat, it seems to abandon the feet. Even on a day when the temperature of the surrounding air is comfortable, feet may be the coldest part of the body and feel quite cold to a partner. So it is no surprise that roughly two-thirds of the couples said that on some nights, particularly in cold weather, they confronted the issue of what to do with cold feet. Some couples said that they worked at keeping apart, or at least keeping their feet apart, until their feet were warm enough.

> ME: She must have cold feet some of the time. What do you do about that?
>
> MIKE: I think everybody does, and until the feet get warmed up, you just (chuckles) keep 'em to yourself (laughs). . . . I usually curl 'em up under myself to get 'em warm. It has never been a big issue, but it has happened. It just scares the hell out of someone, just startles somebody.

Some couples had agreed that one partner had the right to warm her (and in heterosexual couples it was usually "her") cold feet by putting them on the other partner. That did not mean that the partner providing the warmth was entirely comfortable doing that.

> ME: What do you do about your cold feet?
>
> JULIA: (laughing) Warm them up on him (laughing).
>
> WILLIAM: She sticks them right on my feet. . . . (JULIA: Right, because you're so warm). . . . I'm her personal heater (JULIA: Yes), I'm her P.H. If she's cold, her feet come right on me, and boy, after about a minute, she's comfortable, and my thermostat just dropped . . . from ninety-eight to sixty.

> LINDA: He can't stand when I put my cold feet on him.
>
> ME: Where do you put them?
>
> CHARLES: Right on my legs.

ME: On the lower part of your legs.

CHARLES: Yes. . . .

LINDA: It's like, "Oh! God, your feet are cold!" . . . But he is warm, very nice.

ME: Do you feel like you're doing a good deed when she's warming herself?

CHARLES: Yeah, I'm earning my points to heaven.

In a few couples, a partner with cold feet warmed her or his feet by some wonder of modern technology. Two couples said that they used a bag of dried rice heated in a microwave oven.

ME: Are his feet ever cold for you?

MARY: . . . Once in a great while . . .

ME: Then do you want to stay away from him and not have his feet touch you?

MARY: No, I give him the rice bag (chuckles).

ME: I don't know what a rice bag is.

MARY: Oh. I'll show you. (she gets up) . . . You put rice in here. You put it in the microwave for three, four minutes, and it gets real hot.

ME: It's just regular white rice?

MARY: Yeah.

MATT: Yeah. Oh, it's wonderful.

Some women said that wearing socks to bed sufficed to warm their feet.

CHRISTINE: If my feet are really cold, I'll just have socks on when I get into bed. I think that's very rude to put your cold feet on somebody else (laughing) [who is] gettin' ready to doze off.

Warming cold feet on a partner can be taken as a symbol of couple intimacy and caring. When one partner is in need it is a sign of intimacy and caring for the other partner to help out. And the helped partner can also express intimacy and caring by trying to minimize the burden on the helper. For example, in some cases the partner with cold feet warned the other partner before putting cold feet on him, and most people with cold feet did not often put them on a more sensitive part of the partner's body.

IT'S NOT JUST FEET

For some people it was not just feet that were cold, but hands, ears, perhaps everything. That could make the cold partner heat-seeking, cuddling up to the warmer partner, possibly even without being awake. But having a cold partner cuddle up to one can be unpleasant. The partner who is used as a heat source might simply learn to tolerate the chilly contact. But some warmer partners also pulled extra covers over the colder partner.

> CAROL: She warms up (JANET: I'm a furnace) when she sleeps. And I get cold. My temperature . . . drops I think markedly when I'm asleep, so I tend to get cold, and I'm not very good about when I'm cold waking up and figuring that out, so (laughs) I tend to just snuggle over and (Janet laughs) curl up. And that's been problematic on some occasions.
>
> JANET: Once I figured out what was going on, that you were cold, because you kinda bump into me in a funny way, and it isn't like you wake up enough to, I mean it doesn't look particularly affectionate. It's very much (chuckles) she's looking for heat (both chuckle). . . . So I'd wake up and then I'd pull the other cover up on her and tuck her in.

Chapter 7 deals with the array of needs, the situational challenges, and individual difference factors that affect couple snuggling. Here I want to say that what may seems obvious from the quote immediately above and from what other people have been quoted as saying about warmth and cold in bed, that snuggling is not necessarily only or even primarily about affection. It can be about warming a cold body. In cases where the partner providing the warmth might be chilled by the partner seeking heat, a couple might work out a pattern that minimizes the cold shock the warmer partner receives during cuddling.

> SUSAN: He's like a human furnace, so I'll just back up to him (chuckles) and absorb his body heat. . . . I usually plaster my back right to his to get the full body heat. Then I'll turn over like I'm roasting a weenie. I'll turn over and heat up the front half of my body. My feet I very carefully sort of glide them along his feet and get them warm. If I stuck them right on him he would be like out in the street 'cause he would have flown through the front window. . . . They're usually like ice in the wintertime.

Some people who willingly provided warmth to a cold partner protected themselves from cold shock by wearing socks or additional bed clothing for the first minutes the couple was in bed.

IT'S PART OF THE HOT FLASH TYPE THING

Around the time of menopause some women feel warmer, at least periodically, with hot flashes and night sweats (Avis et al., 2001; Voda, 1982). In the heterosexual couples I interviewed, all but one of the women who felt warmer than her male partner was over forty, and most were fifty or older. Sometimes, with the older couples I interviewed, the challenge may have been not only to deal with the temperature difference but to make sense out of and adjust to the woman's physical changes. Being able to attach a label like "premenopause" or "postmenopause" seemed to make what was going on easier to make sense of and deal with.

> MONICA: I turn on our ceiling fan now because I probably have that premenopausal sweat during the night. I seem to get hot, and I wake up hot. . . . I used to always have cold hands and feet. They were icebergs. So I'd get in the bed, put my feet in between his thighs (laughs) to warm 'em up, but a while back that changed. And my hands and feet are always warm now. . . . I don't wear socks to bed anymore.

SUMMERTIME

Summer in the Twin Cities area can be uncomfortably hot and humid. Many couples said that in hot weather they made various accommodations, turning on air conditioning, sleeping on a lower and cooler floor of the house, or turning on a fan. Some couples also moved farther apart in bed or even slept in separate beds. Neither wanted the partner's body heat to add to their sense of already being too hot.

For couples with air conditioning, the pattern of temperature preferences they had in winter often carried over to summer. That is, the person who needed less bed clothing and a lower thermostat setting in winter often needed a cooler air conditioning setting in summer. So the thermostat wars and window wars that might go on in winter can also go on in summer. In hot, humid summer weather, air conditioner thermostats may be repeatedly turned down and up and windows closed and opened. But as with winter adjustments, many couples had learned to accommodate to their differences. For example, they might give one partner control of the air conditioner thermostat, or they might agree on an air conditioner setting so that both could tolerate the situation.

GIVE ME MY COVERS BACK

The television family sitcom image of couples sleeping together is often of two people lying quietly under neatly arranged covers. Their shared covers symbolize their togetherness and unity. But the reality is that many people pull, tug, roll up in, and throw off covers as they sleep. If we watched a couple sleep together, what we saw might look like a battle to be covered or uncovered, to hold on to covers or to get rid of covers, and to claim a fair share of the covers. At times the action of one partner would uncover the other, pile the other high with covers, or move the covers to a place far from the partner. A couple's blanket wars can be difficult to resolve, partly because what people do in their sleep is not easy for them to monitor and control.

LIZ: He grabs all the covers.

ME: Then what do you do?

LIZ: Either grab them back or just have the sheet.

ANDY: She thinks I do it on purpose, but . . .

LIZ: I don't think you do it on purpose. I just know that you do (ANDY: subconscious) it all the time.

KARL: I don't have enough covers (AMY: Yeah) most of the time.

AMY: But he's actually the one that's most aggressive about the covers . . .

KARL: (laughing) As far as I know she takes 'em, and I have to get 'em back (both laughing). And I'll take that to my grave. (AMY: [laughing] Yeah)

AMY: . . . He doesn't notice that the whole pile is right by him (chuckling). He just starts pulling (both laugh).

CHRISTINE: We start out with one blanket on top of the other, and invariably by the morning each of us has a blanket, because he's a crazy man with the blankets (George guffaws). . . . I've seen him roll it up in his sleep and put it on my head (George laughs uproariously) . . .

GEORGE: Sometimes I'll take a pillow (chuckles), and it'll end up half way across the room or on top of her or it won't be by my head anymore. And I don't know why I do that.

Another problem is that if one partner arrives in bed after the other has gone to sleep, the other may be sleeping on top of the covers in a way that makes it hard for the partner who has just come to bed to get properly covered.

CHRISTINE: If he's gone to bed before me, he might claim a lot of territory (GEORGE: Umhm), and maybe he fell asleep on top of the covers instead of underneath, and it's very difficult to get him to move.

CHRISTINE: . . . I'll just take whatever I can get, and just wait (George laughs) until he rolls over and then (chuckling) just grab whatever I can (George laughing). Occasionally I may come out here and just wait for a little while and then try again.

Trying to take enough covers back from a partner who has captured them may draw strong protests from the partner.

MARTHA: He cocoons (laughs). . . . He sticks it underneath him, and (AL: No, I *don't*). Yes you do.

AL: (sounding irritated and long suffering) You throw yours over on me, and I'll lay on 'em (MARTHA: Yeah sometimes) (chuckles) . . .

MARTHA: Usually they're kind of tucked in to him, and then if I get cold during the middle of the night I have to grab a corner. . . . He'll yell, "What do you want?! The whole blanket?" And I have this little corner.

One strategy that some people used in holding their own in the covers tug-of-war was to tuck the covers in, either under the mattress or under the body, so the partner had trouble moving them. Another strategy was to make the bed so that the partner who was more at risk of having covers pulled away had more of the covers to begin with.

Note that in every quote so far in this chapter, even though people expressed strong feelings about getting a fair share of the covers and even though tugs-of-war over covers took a toll on the amount and quality of their sleep, most people chuckled or laughed about their problems with covers. I think the chuckles and laughter represent affection, acknowledgement and acceptance of human imperfection, and a desire not to blow the cover battles into a change-or-we-divorce showdown. It seems that many couples had learned that humor and laughter are constructive in dealing with problems with blankets and other bed sharing problems. Humor and laughter may be an important element of the couple system in dealing with differences that are resistant to effective problem solving. They may also be important in dealing with problem solutions that may be optimal but still leave one or both partners uncomfortable. For example, as can be seen in the discussion of cold feet, many people who allow themselves to be used as a partner's foot warmer joked and laughed about it as they talked. I take that to mean that there is real discomfort for the partner providing the warmth, and the humor and laughter are ways of acknowledging the discomfort without allowing it to become a basis of conflict or of ending the foot warming relationship.

WE NEED DIFFERENT COVERS

Many couples start out each night under exactly the same covers. That may be part of the blanket war problem, because one person may need fewer or more covers than the partner. Even in couples who need roughly the same number and weight of covers to keep warm, one partner may want a covering or more covering all the time, even in warm weather, perhaps because of body modesty or feeling more secure when covered. So if the person's partner kicks the cover off, the other will struggle to keep covered, but not necessarily for warmth.

Some couples eventually agreed to have separate covers even though they slept in the same bed. Having separate covers is a defense against one partner pulling blankets off the other. But the move to separate covers may have meanings to the couple that the partners feel bad about, perhaps that they are not as intimate as they used to be or should be. However, a partner who does not like moving to separate covers because it seems to mean the relationship is not so intimate can get used to the new arrangement, particularly if the couple works out ways to interact that mean to them that they are still intimate.

> VIC: She likes just one single big blanket for both of us. And I really prefer to have my own.
>
> MARIA: It's fine for me that we don't now.
>
> VIC: But it wasn't there for a while.
>
> MARIA: Yeah. . . . If it was up to me our bodies would be touching all night long. So I didn't like, you know, it means then that you're not so affectionate. I didn't like that. But it's fine now, just because you do move around a lot at night. . . . It doesn't seem to be an issue now. So in the morning . . . one of us will go under the other person's blanket.

In couples in which one partner puts on or takes off large amounts of weight, it becomes clear that body weight is insulation because a person who loses weight may need more covers and a person who gains weight may need fewer covers.

> CHERYL: Part of the reason why he needs so many covers now is that he has less (laughs) to keep him warm. (GREG: Less insulation) Yeah.
>
> GREG: Diminution of subcutaneous adipose tissue. (Cheryl laughs). [Greg had recently lost fifty pounds.]

It seems important to many couples that the bed is made with common covers, so their unity is symbolized visually when they first come to bed. I think no matter what goes on during the night regarding covers, the unified start is a symbol for many people that they are a couple and are intimate. Some couples, like the two quoted immediately above, Vic and Maria, Cheryl and Greg, sleep under separate covers. But it is no coincidence that both couples have a routine time in the morning for snuggling in bed under a common cover. It is challenging for couples to use covers in a way that works for both partners in terms of comfort, temperature, and perhaps personal modesty or security. But it seems that most couples at times use common covers as a symbol of their being a couple and being intimate.

THE COUPLE SYSTEM

To maintain a relationship, people have to find ways to mute, tolerate, reduce, insulate themselves from, or otherwise deal with their differences. Temperature differences are real, and they are also paradigmatic of all the other differences a couple might confront. Temperature differences can be matters in which what one partner needs costs the other physical discomfort and can block the other from sleeping. One can also speculate, with temperature as the paradigm for partner differences, that part of the attraction of the differences that bring a couple together could be that one partner can help to satisfy vital needs of the other—for example, a person who is often uncomfortably cold at bedtime may be powerfully drawn to a partner who is always warm and who radiates heat.

SEVEN

Talking and Touching

TALKING AND TOUCHING are central to couple relationships. It is with their words that partners work out their lives together, support and argue with one another, make the big and little decisions that are necessary for a shared life, are themselves with each other, work out what is true and real for them, and even entertain each other. For many couples, the bed is an important place to talk. As I indicated in chapter 1, this is especially so for couples whose lives are crammed with work, commuting, household responsibilities, parenting and other family commitments, religious activities, and various individual pursuits. For them, the bed is often the primary place, perhaps the only place on many days, to talk. A few couples said that they talked with each other when they awakened in the morning, but far more couples said that they often talked at night when they first came to bed. Similarly, the bed is often the place where couples get most of their snuggling, holding, and touching with each other. For many, that physical contact seems vitally important, meeting essential individual and relationship needs.

TALKING

ROUTINE BEDTIME CONVERSATION

There seemed to be a routinization to the bedtime conversation of many couples in that of all the possible things they might communicate about they focused on a relatively narrow range of topics. Perhaps those topics were key to building and maintaining their relationship, what counted in their values and concerns, what was safe to talk about given their differences and shared history, and what they each felt they needed to know and to have the other know. Bedtime conversation might involve many different matters, but it often included each partner summarizing the day's activities for the other and discussing individual or couple plans for the day or days ahead.

Some people said that there were occasions when they wanted, even needed, to talk about a specific heavy issue—a serious illness in the family, for example—before going to sleep. If they did not talk about the issue, they were unlikely to fall asleep soon, and if they did fall asleep they were likely to awaken during the night obsessing about the issue. In some couples it was clear that the heavy things had to be talked about before the partners fell asleep.

> SANDRA: Our son was diagnosed with a language disorder. . . . Once he was labeled with this, trying to figure out what his future would be, how his future would be different from what I had expected his future to be. Or would it be different? Or how would we get him to where he would want to be? . . . I don't think I lose a lot of sleep over that. (KEN: Unun) I think it's because we, I talk. My husband's a very good listener most of the time (Ken chuckles), and so I talk, we talk it over before I go to sleep, so that I can relax to go to sleep.

WE DON'T TALK ABOUT THAT WHEN THE CHILDREN ARE AROUND

Bedtime talk did not only go on because the two partners happened to be together then. There were special properties of the bedtime routine that made it more likely that bedtime would be when the couple would converse. The process of getting ready to go to sleep removed distractions. For example, they left household chores behind, gained distance from children and others who lived with them, turned off the lights in other parts of the house, stopped talking on the phone, turned off the cell phone, and turned off the television set in the family room. If they had a bedroom television set, they might both be awake after they turned it off. As they prepared to sleep they might be in a mood to plan for tomorrow, and that might require couple interaction. They might see going to bed as a last chance to catch up on each other's news of the day. The bed and bedroom might have romantic tones, and the intimacy of being alone together, with many daily distractions and masks stripped away, might mean that bedtime was when it was easiest to express feelings for each other and to connect emotionally. Also, some parents waited until bedtime, when their children were asleep or otherwise unable to overhear, to talk about private matters.

SANDRA: There's been a will dispute in my families, and it's been a major stressor. There are legal issues and depositions and all that kind of stuff. . . . We don't typically talk about that when the children are around, and so the only time that they're not around is (KEN: bedtime) bedtime, and so we go to bed and talk about it.

She Talks; I Listen

Consistent with what others have observed (e.g., DeFrancisco, 1991), in the heterosexual couples I interviewed, if the two partners differed in who initiated talk and how much they talked once they were in bed, it was typically the woman who initiated talk and talked more. In some cases, it seemed that one reason a woman talked more was that she worried more and so had more to air.

SANDRA: We talk the most about stressors; something's bothering me. . . . We'll either talk about it like last thing at night, or this morning I woke up first and so I was thinking about, oh, we're gonna do shades and stuff. We're . . . trying to figure out what's the best deal. And so that was on my mind, and so as soon as he woke up then we laid in bed and talked about it. So it's kind of either in the morning or the evening. Don't you think? (KEN: Umhm) That's probably where we have the most intimate, most important conversations . . .

ME: Would you say one of you is the person who's more likely to bring up issues?

SANDRA: I think I am. Don't you? (KEN: Umhm) . . . You're more laid back. . . . Things don't bother you as much.

That women in heterosexual couples seemed to worry about more things than men did can be interpreted in several ways. If women carry a heavier load, not only because so many are employed outside the home but also because they carry a heavier load of maintaining family harmony and meeting family member emotional needs (Strazdins & Broom, 2004), household responsibilities (Bianchi, Milkie, Sayer, & Robinson, 2000), responsibilities for children (Yeung, Sandberg, Davis-Kean, & Hofferth, 2001), and responsibilities for communicating with family members (Leach & Braithwaite, 1996; Lye, 1996; Rosenthal, 1985), they would have more about which to worry. And with lives so full, they may have few opportunities other than at bedtime to process things with their partner. Also, if there are power differences in heterosexual couples that give men more autonomy to deal with various matters and women less (Tichenor, 1999), the woman's worry would be an expression of needing to consult more often than a man needs to.

SOMETIMES HE GOES TO SLEEP WHILE I'M TALKING

As might be expected with women more inclined to talk at bedtime than men, there were heterosexual couples in which she wanted to talk at bedtime and he wanted to sleep. That could be frustrating and challenging for either partner.

> DAN: Going to sleep, she talks. When I go to bed, it's usually to sleep. . . . Usually she's talking about what she needs to do tomorrow, what I need to do . . . things that happened during the day. She just goes on about stuff like that, when she's actually very tired and I'm very tired. (KRISTEN: Yeah) She'll just have this stuff running through her head that she has to get on the line before she goes to sleep. (KRISTEN: Umhm)
>
> ME: And you listen to her.
>
> DAN: I'm laying right there. I don't have any choice (he and she laugh).
>
> ME: You could fall asleep while she's talking.
>
> DAN: I do. I do sometimes.
>
> KRISTEN: Sometimes he does, but when he falls asleep it's not out of boredom or out of (DAN: No, it's just 'cause I'm tired). Yeah. He works really hard, so if he falls asleep while I'm rambling on, then it's sincere exhaustion.

If bedtime conversation was made difficult or impossible because one of the partners fell quickly asleep, one way partners who wanted to talk accomplished that was to try to talk about important matters well before bedtime.

> ME: Is that okay with you that he falls asleep so quickly? Or do you ever want to talk to him?
>
> JULIA: We've been married so long (chuckling), I learned to do it beforehand. . . . Once his head goes like this, I might as well forget it, because he's very out of it. Very deep sleep. So I just know that if I, if we want to talk, we do that before we decide to go to sleep.

Some women had learned to be tolerant of a man's falling asleep so quickly.

> SUSAN: (Laughs) He can fall asleep standing up.

ME: Does that ever annoy you that he can fall asleep so easily?

SUSAN: . . . If he's falling asleep when I'm trying to talk to him (chuckles) about something really important, and I want his attention, but after all these years I've kind of accepted that that's just him. . . . I read articles about it, and it seems to be easier for men to fall asleep. When they're tired they just go to sleep.

I do not want to overstate the gender difference. Women, too, might fall asleep very quickly. Related to that, in two of the three lesbian couples I interviewed, there was a difference between partners, with one inclined to talk at bedtime and the other inclined to fall asleep almost as soon as they lay down.

LATE NIGHT EMERGENCY TALK

As much as everyone valued sleep, and as much as some people seemed impossible to stop from sleeping, in an emergency, people could force themselves to stay awake, alert, and actively involved in conversation.

NANCY: We were . . . in bed. And we got a call from my brother, who had that very day . . . been diagnosed with leukemia, and I was the first person he called, and I remember being on the phone with him, and he was telling me about what he just been diagnosed, and I kind of whispered to Pam what was going on, and she immediately got up and went on the computer to start looking up some information, just to find out more about it, and I just remember that night was just horrible. And we talked, and I do remember crying most of that night.

TOUCHING

There is a gap in the psychological and medical literature concerning physical contact needs and practices of adults. There is a large literature on the needs of infants and young children to be touched. There are literatures on sexual relationships, inappropriate touching, therapeutic touching, touching in nursing practice, the contact needs of the elderly, and touching at the end of life. But other than generalized statements on the adult need for touch (e.g., Fanslow, 1990) and my own work on couple touching when in public (Rosenblatt, 1974; Rosenblatt & Cleaves, 1981) I have found nothing on adult needs to be touched or on the frequency, forms, and situations for adult-adult touching. I would like to frame what the couples I interviewed had to say about touching at bedtime and in bed in terms of a literature about adult needs and patterns regarding touch. But there is not a literature that I can find.

What did people have to say about touching? Many couples are so busy and spend so much of each day physically distant from each other that they have little or no time to touch. So for many, the physical contact they have in bed is extremely important. Most couples said that they snuggled, spooned, kissed, or otherwise touched once they were in bed.

Touching in bed could be about meeting physical, emotional, and psychological needs that might not be met elsewhere. Touch is also a symbol. When a couple snuggles, spoons, or kisses, their actions say that they have a special relationship. Perhaps nobody else in the world ever touches either partner in those ways. So touch at bedtime is about symbolizing the intimate nature of the couple relationship.

Another way to look at the snuggling, holding, and touching of couples who share a bed is that there may often be a sexual element or questioning involved. One or both partners may experience the physical contact as sexual and may enjoy or perhaps not enjoy the contact in part because it implies, feels like, or symbolizes for them the sexuality in their relationship. The physical contact may also at times be a question about sexual intercourse, with the partner's response either moving the interaction into intercourse or not. And some of the physical contact a couple has is postcoital, with a sense for one or both of them of sexual satisfaction, intimacy, release, and shared pleasure.

When Partners Do Not Go to Bed at the Same Time

Achieving adequate physical contact at bedtime is a challenge for any couple in which one partner stays up after the other goes to bed. How does a couple make physical contact in bed if they do not go to bed together? One solution is that many couples who go to bed at different times have physical contact when the first of the two partners heads for bed, even if it's just a kiss goodnight.

Another solution for some couples is that after the second partner to go to bed arrives in bed they touch.

> JOE: Usually I . . . wake up when she comes to bed. . . . If I'm awake I will welcome her.
>
> REBECCA: Yeah, yeah, he does. . . . I'll come right over to him, and I'll put my hand on him. . . . We usually sleep facing outward, but when I come to bed he'll turn toward me. He usually kisses me and

snuggles me and pulls the covers up over me. . . . Sometimes he wakes up, sometimes he doesn't. I always tell him I love him. Sometimes he replies. Sometimes it's just a grunt.

In some couples who go to sleep at different times the cuddling routine may begin with one partner asleep.

SUSAN: Even when he's sleeping I still snuggle up to him. . . . I start out spooning . . .

ME: If you're asleep and she comes to bed and spoons, do you know that?

ADAM: Yeah, I wake up briefly.

SUSAN: Yeah, usually sometimes you mumble something indiscernible like, abababa. Then you go back to sleep.

As is said in the preceding chapter, cold feet, cold hands, and cold bodies may limit contact when a partner first comes to bed. But even with that limit, and even if one partner is asleep when the other arrives in bed, many couples still touch in bed in ways that communicate love, affection, and intimacy.

OKAY, THAT'S ENOUGH; I GOTTA SLEEP NOW

As important, rewarding, pleasurable, meaningful, and reassuring as physical contact may be after first arriving in bed, many people said that they needed to disengage in order to sleep or after they had slept for a while. Some couples who routinely moved apart after their initial bedtime cuddling seemed to have a mutually understood signal that it was time to move apart. It might be a verbal signal or one partner turning away. Sometimes it was a push. One woman talked about wiggling in order to get her partner to move away. In some couples, one partner waited until the other fell asleep and then pulled away.

ROBERT: It's a conscious thing for me to make sure that we're together. And then as soon as she's asleep, I'll pull my hand out and move around so I can get comfortable.

If one partner generally wanted prolonged contact and the other did not, how did they resolve the difference? One way was to have a shared understanding that made the difference seem appropriate and natural. For example, some people who wanted less contact would say that because of their family background or their culture of origin it was necessary that they have a degree of distance. It was a way of saying, "Don't blame me; it's my genes or my culture."

VIC: My family [is] German-Irish. I don't remember my mom giving me a hug. In my entire life growing up, I don't remember my dad doing that. And I don't know if that's cultural or just dysfunctional, but (laughs) I think it's a little bit of both. And so when I met her and she's this, you know, lovey-touchy, at one hand it was refreshing, but at night it was irritating, because I wanted to go to sleep, and I don't think it's really, I mean even now I feel good holding you and touching before sleep, but not during. I gotta have my space.

ALMOST ALWAYS WE LAY TOUCHING

Some couples remained in physical contact all night. For them, one challenge was how to maintain contact while doing a normal amount of rolling, tossing, and turning during the night. Couples who stayed in contact had ways of coordinating their movements in bed. One couple, for example, had two spooning positions and announced when wanting to switch from one position to the other.

DIANA: We spoon. He always keeps me warm.

ME: Is he behind you or are you behind him?

DIANA: Well we have a position we call A, where I'm behind him, and then B is the other way.

ME: Which is the more common one?

DIANA: We always start out in A, and then we later turn to B. And then I think we spend more time in A.

ME: How does it get signalled that it's time to turn to B?

DIANA: We just announce it. (AARON: umhm). A . . .

ME: Do you fall asleep in contact then? (AARON: Umhm). (DIANA: Umhm).

NOT TONIGHT, HONEY; I'M TIRED

Although physical contact was a high priority for the majority of couples, situations arose that overrode the desire or "should" to be in contact. For example, in some couples, the cuddling routine was skipped if either partner was very tired. Sometimes a person had "a bad day" and wanted to go to sleep without physical contact. Respecting a partner's desire not to make contact was often not a problem. But if the lack of contact went on night after night, difficulties might arise.

Perhaps to head off difficulties, some people would force themselves to snuggle even if not in the mood. One could say that, in a sense, they were not respecting their own needs, but sometimes they could find that the snuggling put them in the mood for snuggling.

> SUSAN: Sometimes I'm not in the mood for cuddling, and if he tries to snuggle I'm like, "Eh, leave me alone. . . ." And vice versa. Sometimes he just doesn't feel like snuggling, and so I respect that, 'cause I know how it feels. . . . Other times when I can tell he really wants to snuggle and I'm not in the mood, I just try not to make an issue out of it, and then eventually whatever it is that's bugging me that makes me not want to snuggle kind of fades away.

Snuggle with Me This Way, Not That Way

The ways a couple has contact in bed are shaped by their learning what works and does not work for them. Some examples of contact that couples had tried that had not worked are mentioned in chapter 2. Another situation of learning to limit physical contact occurred in some heterosexual couples in which the man was very muscular—from physically demanding work or weight lifting. Some women could not stand having a heavy, muscular arm resting across their body.

> MATT: Sometimes I put my arm around her.
>
> MARY: He used to put, yeah (MATT: Yeah). It was just like a heavy weight. (MATT: [laughing] Weight) (laughing) "Get away from me!"
>
> ME: Okay, so that didn't last long.
>
> MARY: No. (MATT: Yeah, no.) God, it was like a one hundred pound weight on you where you couldn't move.

Some men with muscular arms said it was frustrating not to have someone to put an arm around.

> ME: If you put your arm around her, it's your left arm that's around her?
>
> TIM: Yep.
>
> CYNTHIA: Yeah, yeah.
>
> TIM: That usually doesn't happen. "It's too heavy!"
>
> CYNTHIA: (Laughs) "Get off" (Tim laughs). . . . His arms are too heavy. . . . It's like . . . something's got me pinned down. . . . "Too heavy." Yeah (chuckles) so, no. We've always been very separate. (TIM: Yeah).

Similar to the problem of heavy arms, some people experienced a partner's leg as too heavy to allow it to lie across them.

> STEVE: There's been times when she's thrown her leg across me and it's kind of too hot and too heavy, and "Move your leg," (chuckles) "Let me have some room here."

A related problem was when a partner sweated excessively. Some people could not stand to snuggle if the partner was very sweaty.

For some couples there was also the challenge of sexual arousal. If a woman in a heterosexual couple wanted to snuggle and not be sexual there might have to be limits on how they snuggled. Snuggling one way might be gently connecting and only that. Snuggling another way might be sexually arousing to the man and then there was the question of where to go with that.

> CHERYL: I like sleeping together. I like the closeness. I like to cuddle. We both like to cuddle. If we don't cuddle before we go to sleep, it's not right, and the same in the morning. I think that's real important. One funny thing, when we cuddle together when we go to sleep, I throw my arm over him and I'm all up next to him, but I can't do it the other way. I can't have him cuddling up to me. I have to cuddle up to him.
>
> ME: Do you know why?
>
> CHERYL: Yes. You want me to tell? Because he will become aroused, and then I cannot sleep (laughs) being poked. So when we snuggle for sleep, it has to be with me snuggled up to him, instead of him up to me.

We Used to Sleep Real Close, But Now We Need More Space

Some couples said that over the years they had moved to less physical contact in bed. It often seemed to be partly because one or both partners had come to want more space and because they had left behind the romantic and sexual rush from physical contact that was common in the first months or years of bed sharing. For some couples the movement toward less contact at bedtime and toward more personal space was founded on a sense that they could move into contact whenever it suited them and that their relationship was fundamentally secure and emotionally connected.

> ME: Do you remember when you first started sharing a bed?
>
> CHRISTINE: Yeah, when we first did we were stuck together like glue . . .

GEORGE: Yep, it was really nice at the time. And we enjoyed each other a lot.

CHRISTINE: And then it got to the point where we were claiming our own space, but at least one part of our bodies was always touching (GEORGE: Oh, yeah). You have an arm over (GEORGE: Uh huh) the other one (GEORGE: leg or), legs crossed, but now it's not really like that anymore. (GEORGE: unun) But we don't care, 'cause . . .

GEORGE: Oh, yeah, we know that we can just go and cuddle. . . . And the other person will say, "Cool." . . . That also helps with being able to say, "You know what? I want my space right now, and I know you understand that."

It may not be easy at first to change a pattern of physical contact. Laura remembered how alarmed she felt the first time Zack pulled away from her.

ME: On the nights when you get in bed together, do you touch at the beginning of the night?

LAURA: Usually, yeah. . . . When I'm tired and going to bed, I'm tired (chuckles), and I fall asleep. But I remember the first time when we *didn't* snuggle when we went to bed. And I thought, "Well, he's really mad tonight." (Zack laughs).

ME: When was that?

LAURA: Oh, it's years ago. We've been in this house for thirty-four years. And it was before that.

I Would Have Liked to Have a Snuggler

Because two people in a close relationship differ in many ways, it is not surprising that there were couples who differed in how much physical contact they wanted at bedtime or while sleeping. In some couples, one partner persisted in wanting contact while the other persisted in blocking it. When people differed in desired contact, it seemed that almost always the one who generally wanted more contact initiated it.

ME: When you're both in bed, do you snuggle?

SHARON: If we do I'm the one that makes the snuggling attempt. He's not really a snuggly person.

ME: So he tolerates it.

PETE: I don't really tolerate it. (SHARON: Pretty much). It's fine if she comes over and wants to snuggle. I'm just not one that kinda goes over to another person and starts hugging and stuff. Never been that way.

As with other couple differences, it was not necessarily easy to come to terms with a difference in how much physical contact was desired, but many couples had. Several people talked about wishing they had a partner who liked physical contact more, but also about learning to accept a life without much contact.

GRACE: He isn't a snuggler. I suppose I would have liked to have a snuggler, but he's not a snuggler, so you get used to not having a snuggler.

When Dad Had His Heart Attack I Needed More Holding

Sorrow and worry had come to bed with some of the couples I interviewed, and sometimes a partner who felt sad or worried wanted to be cuddled, held, or hugged.

DONNA: After my dad had his heart attack, I think I required a lot more affection before we went to sleep.

ME: So you would snuggle up more?

JEFF: Yeah (DONNA: Yeah).

ME: You would hold her more?

JEFF: Yep.

DONNA: . . . I needed the reassurance.

Perhaps Jeff and Donna had enough history together for Jeff to know what Donna needed in difficult times, or perhaps he had sufficient empathy to sense what she needed. But there could be problems when one partner wanted to be held and comforted and the other partner did not know what to do. Here is an example from an interview I did in bereavement research with a couple who had experienced the death of a child.

IRIS: I'd lay in bed and cry at night, and he'd lay over near me and be embarrassed and not know what to do (laughing).

TODD: Yeah, I didn't know exactly how to handle it when she'd be crying, didn't know what I could do to make her feel better. Not that I didn't want to. But I guess I was just at a loss on what to do.

IRIS: I think we were very frustrating to each other, because I would speak of all my emotional reactions to things people said, and I'm missing Jeff. And then he'd get upset with me, because he sees it from more of a cerebral point of view (Rosenblatt, 2000, p. 47).

Perhaps Iris had not been in a good place to ask Todd for what she needed, so both were frustrated, and he might have been confused. But clearly some couples I interviewed either had sufficient empathy or had learned how to deal with situations of sorrow or worry.

KAREN: When mom died that was very, very, very hard. . . . I don't think I slept very good.

RICHARD: No, you didn't. . . . A lot of times . . . like anniversary of her death . . . she'd start crying, with no explanation at all, and then it'd take me a while to figure out.

KAREN: And just snuggle. Just cuddle, just hold, just snuggle.

ME: So he put his arm around you.

KAREN: Oh, yeah. Yeah. I (laughing) burrow . . .

RICHARD: She just needs to be held at that particular time. And just not say anything. (KAREN: Yeah). She doesn't need to be talked to.

Not providing a partner with the holding and other support the partner needed in a difficult time was not necessarily a failure of empathy or learning. Sometimes a partner who felt needy did not receive the help she or he wanted because of not wanting to awaken the other to ask for the help.

ME: With the problems you had with your brother, then the suicide, you were having a tough time sleeping (LINDA: Umhm). Did you and your husband have different kinds of contact in bed when that was going on?

LINDA: Well, yeah, because I cried a lot and my husband was very supportive. . . . I guess there was probably some nights where I wanted him to be there a little bit more than he was, but I didn't wanna wake him up.

GENDER AND NEEDING PHYSICAL CONTACT IN BED

In heterosexual couples I interviewed, more women than men spoke of wanting touching, snuggling, and to be held in times of sorrow or worry. There might be many reasons for the gender difference. Some women might have felt more free than their male partners to express emotions of sorrow and worry. More women than men might have been willing to admit that they wanted to be comforted. Then too there may be basic gender differences in sleep patterns that underlie the gender differences in times of sorrow or worry. As was said earlier in this chapter, more men than women can fall asleep quickly and sleep deeply, even in tough times.

> ME: When the dog died, were you upset that Eric just went to sleep?
>
> ANGELA: Yeah, I was. I was mad. Because I'm like, "What are you doing? You're going back to sleep?" I was grieving. I was upset. . . . But learning how he is and his personality, yeah, he'll just go right to sleep. . . . It's not because he didn't love the dog, or love me, but that's just how he deals with things. He just, when he's ready, goes to sleep.

I do not want to overstate the gender pattern. Some women said they fell asleep easily when sad or worried and some men said that they did not. And some men sought or accepted holding and comforting in difficult times.

Then We'd Talk

In tough times some people needed to talk. Some couples said that they would have long bedtime conversations about what was upsetting them. Some people, like Sandra, might even awaken their partner in the middle of the night to talk about what was sad or worrisome.

> SANDRA: I would wake up and I couldn't go back to sleep, 'cause I was thinking about my father, and so I'd wake my husband up (chuckles), and then we'd talk, and then I'd go back to sleep. He'd use like guided imagery to help me relax and try to take me to a place that was a happy place.
>
> ME: You wanted him to do that?
>
> SANDRA: Umhm. Yeah, I asked him to do that. . . . I didn't get up and try to go someplace else because I thought I got most comfort from being close to him.

Clinical Depression

When a person is clinically depressed, all of the person's thinking, actions, feelings, and interactions can be affected. So, of course, clinical depression will show up in bed. Some of the ways it can show up are covered in chapter 9, but here I want to address the part of depression that has to do with going to bed sad or worried. With clinical depression, a partner's support, conversation, and physical contact in bed are no cure, but they can still be very much appreciated by the person who is depressed.

ME: When you hit the bottom with depression, did you want to cuddle or talk more or less?

SHANNON: Talking more. It's talking about the, "I hate me," and those types of conversations, and a lot of crying, and he'd end up trying to comfort me. . . . Before treatment I was suicidal a lot at night, and the nights were really bad, really difficult . . .

STEVE: Frequently we would talk, and cuddle, try to encourage her, but when you're dealing with somebody with depression there's really not much you can do (chuckles).

ME: Could you sleep as soundly when she was feeling that way?

STEVE: Yeah, yeah. After we dropped off there wasn't like an issue. The conversation we'd have before we went to sleep would obviously focus more around her feelings of inadequacy, her feelings of depression and sadness, but there was more cuddling involved, where she wanted to be held.

ME: Do you think that the cuddling was helpful or soothing in some way (SHANNON: Yeah), communicated something to you?

SHANNON: Yeah, it was *very* comforting. (little laugh) It just felt good to be held.

One challenge for a depressed person can be to limit talking about matters that could deepen the depression. Pam said that she had learned to limit what she and her partner Nancy talked about in bed. For Nancy, limiting conversation in that way was frustrating because it meant that certain problems could not be solved and certain issues could not be aired. Limiting conversation limited the relationship in ways that made her feel distant and distanced. But still, the limits helped Pam to cope with her depression.

PAM: There were periods of time where she would want to discuss or bring something up at night that was tense for me. It was like, "I don't want to talk about this stuff." And for me a lot of it was just learning to say, "No, I don't want to talk about it, and that's it." Because I think typically in the past I always gave in. . . . Who wants to talk about something that stresses you out right when you go to bed? 'Cause then you lay there half the night and you can't sleep . . .

NANCY: There was definitely a distance. . . . Laying in bed knowing that there were problems, but not having her willingness to talk about it. . . . Going to bed and knowing that the person right next to me, the closest person to me, couldn't share with me, or wouldn't share with me was hurtful. I felt very distanced from her. . . . There would be . . . these inexplicable episodes of crying, where she was really sad. And I remember holding you . . . while you cried.

THE COUPLE SYSTEM

In many ways the glue of the couple system is their talking and touching. The heart of the relationship and the core of what they value lies in the ways that needs are met by their talking and touching. And yet, as this chapter shows, it is not a simple matter to accomplish talking and touching. At bedtime, talking and touching compete with sleepiness; they may be blocked by the presence of children; they may be made more difficult by differences in when people want to go to sleep and differences in needs and what can be tolerated. And yet, in an emergency, many couples found a way. The tired partner stayed awake or was willing to be awakened in the middle of the night. Couple systems are imperfect; there are always rough edges; there are always new matters to deal with. There are often unresolved and unresolvable struggles. And yet most couples seemed to feel good about where they had come to with regard to talking and touching.

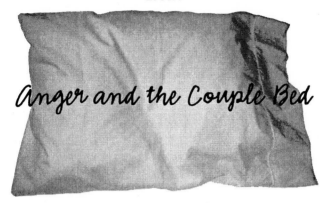

EIGHT

Anger and the Couple Bed

ANGER AND CONFLICT had at times come to bed with most, perhaps all, of the couples I interviewed. Most couples experienced anger and conflict with each other recurrently, sometimes at levels that were very intense. Most couples said they had experienced anger and conflict that they could not turn off just because it was time to go to sleep. It was hard for some people to share a bed with their partner when either of them was furious with the other or when conflict was unresolved. What did couples do in such circumstances?

THE WALLS ARE UP WHEN WE'RE ANGRY

When a couple did not resolve a conflict before their usual time to sleep or when they were locked into confrontation or angry feelings, one or both partners might have trouble sleeping. Often there was physical and emotional distance between them. Sometimes the physical distance was a matter of being separated by a few more inches. A few inches could mean a great deal.

> KRISTEN: When we go to sleep and I'm angry, I will physically roll away from you. The constant touching that we have when we sleep, legs over legs and arms and everything, there's none of that. So the walls are up.

With the physical distance went a psychological distance, a sense of not being so much friends, not having a partner one could fully rely on, not sharing so much. For some couples, the physical and psychological distance was not a matter of inches but of one going to another room to sleep.

ANGELA: Most of the time, if I am very angry, I'll go sleep in the other bedroom. . . . I just need time by myself to process things. . . . I don't like to go to bed angry, and I know you don't either. It's not the most comfortable thing to do, and so we try to work things out before we do go to bed. But I personally don't let things go right away. I'll stay mad, and . . . I have that focus or that feeling of still being upset, and it takes me longer to get over. . . . So sometimes I will go sleep in the other bedroom.

For Angela and others, sleeping elsewhere might allow time to cool off and to think things over. Thomas, who is quoted immediately below, said something that perhaps many people who went elsewhere to sleep when angry might have felt, that sleeping together when very upset with the partner seemed unauthentic, fake, not real, symbolizing a closeness and a belonging together that did not fit the angry feelings.

ME: Do you ever go to bed angry with each other.

THOMAS: Umhm. (MOLLY: Yeah). Yeah.

ME: How does that affect your sleeping together?

MOLLY: We don't sleep well.

THOMAS: . . . I'll go downstairs and sleep. . . . Typically I don't want to be in bed if I'm really angry. I don't want to be part of it.

ME: Part of?

THOMAS: Something that's not real, more fake, or not authentic. Just, that's something that I don't want to be part of . . . just coming to bed and lying on it. My view is that it's fake. It's not authentic. It's not intimacy. And I don't want to be part of it.

ANGER KEEPS ME AWAKE

Some people said that when they went to bed angry they had trouble sleeping. They obsessed about the issues, what was said and done, what they should have said, what might happen if the issues were not resolved, and what the issues meant for their future as a couple.

ROBERT: It's really hard for me to sleep when something like that's on my mind. . . . It definitely affected me laying there for a good hour and a half before I could even think about going to sleep.

In heterosexual couples, it was more often a woman than a man who was unable to sleep, who would remain awake and obsessing about a conflict.

ME: If you can remember back to times when you have gone to bed angry, how does it affect your sleeping?

MARTHA: I don't sleep.

AL: Doesn't affect mine at all (Martha laughs).

MARTHA: I don't sleep, because I hash it around, and I can think of more things to say (chuckling), and I want to wake him up (chuckling).

AL: My idea is fall asleep and wake up in the morning and it'll be all better.

THE WHOLE THING IS LEARNING

Sooner or later almost all couples were faced with the challenge of learning how to deal with bedtime anger. One of the common things they said they learned was that anger, upsetness, and distance are not disasters. They can and will come through to a better place. Many couples eventually learned how to understand and respect their different ways of dealing with anger and to feel more confident that a difficulty would be resolved.

ANGELA: The whole thing is learning each other and how each person reacts to each situation and learning when to quit. I need to process things; I need time to think about things, and he will more just want to sit and talk . . . until it's resolved. And we're still learning to respect . . . what each other needs . . . or if it's something that we're fighting about or upset about, to give each other that respect and the time that you need to process that information in order to have an honest response. . . . I need time to think. . . . I do remember saying that a couple of times, "Let's just talk about it in the morning. . . ." It's gotten better I'd say the last six months. . . . We're finally understanding what each other needs.

Some people learned that something they did when upset with their partner "just wasn't worth it." What was not worth it varied from person to person, but often what people seemed to learn was that it "just wasn't worth it" to stay awake fuming.

KAREN: If I'm really irritated and I know that he's tired and doing his falling asleep thing, I'll sit up and read a book. It depends on how worked up I am. If I just say, "Okay, forget it," it might take me longer to fall asleep, but I don't think I've ever stayed up all night and fumed. I guess I've learned . . . that it's just not worth it.

In some couples the learning involved one partner realizing that her or his preferred way of dealing with conflict and anger would not work with the partner.

JANET: It was much more frustrating when we first (CAROL: Yeah) were getting to know each other. . . . She wanted to talk at ten o'clock at night, and I was done.

CAROL: . . . If we were having some sort of disagreement, then it's hard for me to let it go and go to sleep, (JANET: Yes) 'cause I can't sleep anyways if there's something that isn't resolved. But I learned. . . . If there's a difficulty I go to sleep upset and deal with it another time, because after a certain point it's kind of diminishing returns as far as (chuckling) whether or not we're gonna solve it tonight anyway. If she's tired.

JANET: . . . We've learned to do the processing during the day (CAROL: Yeah). We really schedule a lot of time together. We're the typical lesbian couple in those areas. We spend, I know it could be more, but we really do (CAROL: Umhm) devote a lot of time to each other.

Some couples found more constructive ways of dealing with anger at bed-time than storming off to sleep in a different room.

MARIA: Do you think we go to bed angry at each other a lot?

VIC: I don't think we do as much as we used to. . . . The early times in our marriage, sometimes I'd get really upset and go off to the other room and go to bed. . . . Or you would grab your blanket and take out and go in the guest room. (MARIA: . . . but now we don't do it at all.) We don't do that. . . . I've recognized that . . . you know how to push my buttons and I know how to push yours. And it's a matter of rec-ognizing what you're doing. . . . It's like, "Okay, she's worried about something, and so she's getting into her control mode. . . . I gotta just . . . deal with what she's worried about instead of the control thing. . . . (MARIA: I can be quite controlling) . . .

MARIA: I just think it's interesting that you're thinking about how it's all my thing. You're not talking about the times when whatever it is that we're arguing about is maybe your thing, but anyway I do agree that when I get real controlling you've been a lot better at not engaging . . . which helps.

Most couples said that they had worked out agreements about how to deal with anger at bedtime. Susan and Adam, for example, had agreed that even if angry they would always say something connecting and loving when going to bed, even if they could not resolve the problem then.

SUSAN: Another rule is that even if we're in an argument, or we're not in agreement . . . that it doesn't mean that we have to solve the fight before we go to sleep, but we don't go to sleep in an angry status. We have to say something like, "I love you" or "good night" or "we'll talk about it in the morning," give each other a kiss, even if it's just a little peck because we're really mad, but we established that rule in the beginning of our relationship, because both of us had gone to bed angry in our first marriages a lot, and then the first few times we got in an argument, we did that and it was awful. And I couldn't fall asleep, and I would cry, and he couldn't fall asleep. And we finally said, "This is crazy; let's learn a lesson from the (chuckling) first time around, and let's not do this. . . ."

ME: Can you both sleep when you've had an angry argument?

ADAM: Yeah, I can.

SUSAN: Yeah, I can now. I didn't used to be able to. I used to have this need to just fix it right now or, "Oh, my God, this means everything's over; we're gonna get divorced. . . ." Then I realized that that was just a completely ludicrous way to look at it. And then I also had to realize that if I've tried (chuckling) to make him stay awake and . . . resolve it with me that it was like picking at a scab and never letting it heal. And he would just get more tired and more frustrated, and it wouldn't solve anything.

Another way of looking at the rule couples like Susan and Adam had developed, of saying something positive and connecting even though they were still feeling angry and upset, is that the rule helped them with the paradox of being upset but loving. It seemed that many people felt that being upset was inconsistent with being loving, and the inconsistency could be uncomfortable, even threatening. By emphasizing the loving part of the relationship they were, in a sense, saying that it was the loving part of the relationship that would endure and that they wanted to endure. It was a way of saying the positive part of the relationship was not going to go away and could be counted on to continue after the current anger and conflict had dissipated.

There were other rules that a substantial number of couples said they followed in dealing with anger and conflict at bedtime. The rules did not guarantee happiness and did not prevent feelings of anger. But they seemed to have made anger and conflict situations less nasty, scary, or overwhelming by giving couples routine things to do when angry at bedtime and giving them the reassurance that their relationship would survive.

We Try to Never Go to Sleep Angry

Some couples agreed to follow the rule about never going to sleep angry because at least one of the partners decided that going to sleep angry was a mistake.

> MIKE: I used to hold a grudge. And I won't. To me that's not a good thing to do. I try to avoid it. And she always avoids . . . going to bed that way. Always. Settle things, get things out in the open, get things taken care of before you go to bed.

Some couples said that the idea of resolving a conflict before going to sleep came from a parent or parent-in-law.

> ME: Do you ever go to bed angry with each other?
>
> CHARLES: Very rarely.
>
> LINDA: We try to get out of that before we go to sleep.
>
> CHARLES: Yeah.
>
> LINDA: . . . That's one thing my Dad told me when we were first engaged, ". . . Never go to bed without resolving something. If you go to bed angry, it's gonna fester, and by morning it's probably gonna be worse."

Some people said that their motivation to resolve problems before falling asleep was that they did not want to wake up in the morning with the problem and the anger unresolved.

> BEN: Usually we work it out before going to sleep. (CAROLINE: I think so). . . . I don't like going to bed on a bad note, 'cause then I think you wake up with the problem hanging over your head, and that's no fun. So I'd rather just stay up and work it out. (CAROLINE: Yeah).

Some couples who had the rule of not going to sleep angry reflected on times when they did go to sleep angry and how awful that had been. Peacemaking before going to sleep seemed to either resolve the issue or to set up a framework for resolving the issue later.

ME: Do you ever go to bed angry with each other?

NATALIE: . . . On rare occasions that happens, and when it does, it's awful. (JOHN: Umhm). He cannot sleep. That will cause him to grind his teeth.

JOHN: I like to get that worked out before we go to sleep. (NATALIE: Umhm). We always come to some sort of resolution, even if it isn't always the most satisfactory. We always work on a solution before we go to sleep . . .

NATALIE: It's usually the kind of thing where we remind ourselves it's not that we don't respect each other. . . . Then we're able to sort of suspend the argument until the next day or until we can be more productive with it.

WE JUST PUT IT OFF TO ANOTHER TIME

Some couples had the rule that they would put off dealing with their anger until the next day or a more distant time. There was a sense of playing for time and that in that time they might become calmer or issues that were so inflaming would become much less so, or even disappear entirely.

Some couples also talked about the importance of the timing of making up. One had to be sensitive to the other person and the conditions. For example, Mitch and Kathy learned that it was pointless to try to make up in the morning because Kathy did not like to talk then. She was busy getting ready to go to work or church and was irritable if Mitch talked to her.

Some men in heterosexual couples seemed to hope that issues would go away if ignored, but their partners did not necessarily agree. A woman might feel that the two of them would have to address the issue sooner or later but that one advantage of putting off dealing with it at night was that they might not have the energy to deal with it then because they were tired.

KRISTEN: "Out of sight out of mind" is his claim, that if we don't talk about it, it will just eventually go away. And mine is (chuckling), "If we don't talk about it now, you're gonna hear about it, because it's not resolved until it's resolved." So it's just a matter of we know it's gonna be brought up and it's gonna be resolved, but we just sometimes don't do it that night. Don't have the energy.

DAN: Don't have the answers.

KRISTEN: Yeah. Take a night and think about it.

Some people also said that with the passage of time, a person might think the issues over and come to a different view of them.

STEVE: I don't think that arguments necessarily have to be solved before you go to bed. Sometimes they make more sense the next day anyway. Things have more perspective.

Eric and Angela said that, for them, waiting until another time was often about waiting for the effects of alcohol to wear off.

ERIC: Most of those times when there is a strong disagreement, they've been flared up due to drinking. . . . If you have a couple of beers and whatever the thing that is bugging you comes out. . . . We've been working on just, "That's it; we'll talk about it later." (ANGELA: Yeah) . . . Sometimes when we're irritated with each other, then we'll just go to different rooms.

ANGELA: . . . Yeah, it does seem like if we do have a disagreement, we've . . . had a few beers. . . . We decided after the couple disagreements that we did have, "Okay, if we're upset about something, we'll talk about it in the morning, 'cause it's gonna be there in the morning and probably have a clearer head."

I think another reason why things were easier the next day for some couples was that they pulled away from the closed loop in which one or both partners kept making more or less the same arguments, arguments that the other might understand but not be swayed by.

ME: Do you ever go to bed angry with each other?

RICHARD: Oh, yeah.

KAREN: Oh, absolutely. I think that's just part of life (laughs).

ME: How do you sleep together then?

RICHARD: I sleep fine. (Karen laughs) I really don't have a problem going to sleep. It may keep me up a little bit longer. . . . But I found between us the best thing is just keep my mouth shut. (Karen laughs) Go to sleep.

KAREN: Deal with it later.

RICHARD: . . . Most of the time by morning or by afternoon it's washed over. . . . I can't really say that it keeps me awake, unless she keeps me awake by continuing on and on and on (Karen laughs) about something. No, I'm the type of the person that if you explain it to me once I usually understand. She likes to go over it many times, just to make sure I get it right.

I do not mean to imply that couples always resolved their disagreements or that playing for time meant that they could think and talk their way out of any problem. Some issues could not be resolved, in which case what a couple might gain by putting off dealing with the issue might only be an acceptance that it was not a matter that could be resolved.

AND THEN WE MAKE UP

Many couples said that they eventually resolved an angry encounter by making up. As they talked about it, "making up" seemed almost always to require words.

DONNA: Most of the time we do talk it out in bed at night (JEFF: Umhm). If something's happened during the day we talk it out that night, in bed or whatever.

Couples were diverse in how they begin to resolve anger or conflict. William and Julia talked about often beginning the making up process by turning their anger into something safely playful.

WILLIAM: We try to make up (JULIA: Yeah) before we hit the sack. (JULIA: Right).

ME: How do you do it?

JULIA: . . . I just say (chuckling) (WILLIAM: Are you still a jerk?) Yeah. We just have a silly thing. (William chuckling) We just say, "Are you still a jerk?" And then that usually just gets us talking about it.

Nick said that pestering his wife Sarah would start a peacemaking process, though Sarah said his pestering only made her more angry.

ME: Do you ever go to bed angry with each other?

NICK: Not really me. But she has gone to bed (chuckles) mad before.

ME: What's that like?

NICK: . . . If she goes to bed mad, then I kind of pester her, and try to get her to laugh or bug her until she gets over it.

ME: Is that how you'd describe it too?

SARAH: Yeah, and I get more mad because he's trying to bug me.

Rebecca and Joe said that they might go to sleep angry, but then Rebecca would wake Joe up and apologize. For her, and perhaps for some others who were interviewed, what was intolerable seemed to be not that she was upset but that she and her husband both were upset. That, for her, seemed a real threat to the relationship and meant that she would want to apologize and quite possibly be sexually intimate.

ME: Do you ever go to bed angry with each other?

REBECCA: I've tried (small laugh).

JOE: (chuckles?) I guess it's happened, yeah . . .

REBECCA: I'm volatile. But it doesn't last very long. I will get upset about something, and so, yes, I will chew him out and I will nag. But if he gets upset while I'm upset, then it bothers me and I can't stay mad at him. If I know that I'm pushing at him, it does bother me, and I've tried to stay angry at him before. You know how they say, "Never let the sun go down on your anger?" I cannot do that. I will wake him up and apologize . . .

ME: Are you glad she does it?

JOE: Yeah. Sometimes I'm still angry up to the point that she apologizes . . .

ME: And then does it become a romantic moment?

JOE: Sometimes.

Lovemaking after (or even during) a bedtime conflict or bout of anger can be understood in various ways. Sexual intercourse can emphasize that, despite the conflict and anger that could be taken as a disaffirmation of the couple relationship, the relationship continues to be intimate. Another way of understanding it is that it might be difficult to engage in without forgiveness, so the process of getting to lovemaking is in part the process of getting to forgiveness.

Among the thirty-nine heterosexual couples I interviewed, there were six cases where the woman generally apologized or reached out when both were angry and only one where the man generally apologized or reached out. It's not an enormous difference, but perhaps it suggests that women are more likely to be peacemakers, more skillful at rearranging personal feelings and putting peacemaking inclinations to words, or carry more of the load of keeping the relationship on an even keel. Women may, on the average, also be more emotionally reactive to couple conflict (Almeida et al., 2003) and more threatened by continuing emotional distance. So more women than men might feel strongly compelled to make peace.

Some women who said they were often the person who started the peacemaking process blamed themselves relatively often for the conflict. Perhaps there is validity to their perceptions, but perhaps because they had the role of the peacemaker they might have felt greater responsibility for conflicts.

> REBECCA: One of the reasons why I can't stay angry at him is because I need to be with him. And that's not all there is. That's a very negative way to put it, that I'm losing my security if I'm angry at him, but I thought about that before. I'm not saying I'm sorry because I'm trying to just get something. (JOE: Right, yeah). I'm saying I'm sorry because usually I am the witch. . . . I can get very sarcastic. And I can needle a lot, and so usually it is my fault, and I do feel very sorry for that, but there is that other sense that if I don't apologize I can't be close to him.

That women may more often be peacemakers than men does not mean that women more easily let go of anger. There were plenty of men in heterosexual couples who shrugged off or ignored disagreements or loudly said their angry piece and then were finished feeling upset (see Rubin, 1976, pp. 146–148). But the woman in the couple might still feel upset because the issue was not resolved or because of what she or her partner said. She might also be upset because the man seemed to be shrugging the issue off.

> SHARON: I kinda hang on to stuff long after he doesn't even know what the hell it was all about. He forgets it like that (snaps her fingers) . . .
>
> PETE: I've never been a person to hold on to something that way. I just learned a long time ago that that's gonna make even more unhealthy, holdin' on to stuff and letting it fume and burn and just fester. . . . It's like having a big old pimple that just doesn't go away. It's just like, pop it and get rid of it and move on. I don't see any sense in hanging on to stuff. Life's too short . . .
>
> ME: Does it make you angry when he's like that?

SHARON: Sometimes, because I think that the problem isn't even resolved. And he's already forgotten about it, so to me it feels like it's not important to him. So if it doesn't bother him at all, then I feel like he doesn't care. And if he doesn't care, then he doesn't care about me.

THE COUPLE SYSTEM

The dance of the couple system does not stop even when partners are angry. There are still patterns of interaction to what they do when they are angry. The relationship of anger to couple sleeping illuminates the ways that couple sleeping is central to the couple relationship. The bed is often the place where interaction happens. It is frequently where the couple relationship is symbolized and where it can be measured. No wonder that so many people had so much to say about going to bed and to sleep angry, about the challenges of being angry at bedtime, the difficulty of sleeping when angry, and about making up processes that were connected to the bed and to shared sleeping.

NINE

Illness and Injury

IF EITHER PARTNER is ill or injured, that may disrupt the sleep of the injured person (e.g., Ewan, Lowy, & Reid, 1991) and also of the person's sleeping partner. Physicians treat individuals, but health problems show up in the couple sleeping relationship, sometimes in profound ways.

AN OBSERVING PARTNER AS DIAGNOSTICIAN

Chapter 1 indicated that a substantial part of what people could say to me about sleep came from one partner being awake during the night and observing the other. Sometimes a partner observed something about the other's sleeping that had the potential to help with a health problem that had not been diagnosed by a physician. For example, Joe's observations about Rebecca's sleeping helped to solve Rebecca's headache problem.

> JOE: We went out and bought a big, fluffy pillow, and Rebecca took [it], and I had one that was (REBECCA: It didn't say "big fluffy pillow." It said "medium"), yeah, well (laughs), and I had had one that was not quite as high, and Rebecca was complaining a lot about headaches. And she didn't know why she was getting these headaches, and I noticed that when I'd see her in the middle of the night, when she'd be asleep, she was not usually laying on this pillow (chuckles). She'd have her head just on the bed itself. . . . And I finally said to her, ". . . When you're asleep, you're never laying on your pillow. I wonder if the pillow is bothering you. Maybe it's too high." So we traded pillows, and she hasn't had headaches since then.

105

Sometimes one partner's observations of the other's sleep had the potential to save the partner from what could be a life threatening health problem. For example, as is indicated in the chapter 13 discussion of sleep apnea, sometimes a partner who was awake recognized that the other recurrently stopped breathing. Observing the sleep apnea was a step toward the partner with apnea receiving medical treatment that could reduce or eliminate this potentially life-threatening problem. However, that did not mean that everyone with sleep apnea responded to a partner's observations by seeking medical care.

> ME: Do either of you have what they call sleep apnea, where you skip breaths?
>
> MARTHA: I'd like to have him tested for that . . .
>
> AL: I think that is her imagination. (MARTHA: No) I have no idea whether I do or not.
>
> MARTHA: No, because you'll take a deep breath and it'll go for a while, and then you kinda (repeated snoring-type noise:) "cha-cha-cha" when you start up again. That's a real good sign.

ILLNESS THAT DISRUPTS SLEEP

Almost any illness can affect couple sleeping. What follows is a discussion of the six illnesses that the couples most often mentioned when talking about how illness could interfere with couple sleeping.

MIGRAINES

Migraine headaches may make it difficult for a person to fall asleep or may awaken a person during the night. Once awake, a person with a migraine might act in ways that awaken the partner. Kristen's nighttime migraines would often force her out of bed to take a bath to try to relax. The sounds of the bath would awaken her husband, Dan. And sometimes she was in such distress that she would need him to rush her to urgent care or a hospital emergency room.

> KRISTEN: A lot of times I'm up in the middle of the night, sitting in the bathtub, 'cause that kind of helps me relax [when I have a migraine]. Or if they're the kind that makes me sick to my stomach I [camp] in the bathroom. Or he brings me in for a shot. When I've got a migraine, sometimes it hurts to sit upright, because my head throbs, and then to lay back it hurts to have the pressure on the back of my head. Even a fluffy down pillow is uncomfortable, and so . . . I just can't sleep . . .

DAN: I don't bother her when she has migraines. I let her be. Just keep asking if she wants me to take her to the urgent care or the hospital. . . . [I might] rub her face or . . . her shoulders. I leave her alone unless she asks for something.

Heart Disease

The partner of someone with heart disease could conceivably sleep with tense alertness to the possibility of a medical emergency. Cindy was so concerned about Ed's heart disease that his staying downstairs late at night to watch television could send her into a panic about the possibility that he had just had a heart attack.

CINDY: If I wake up and it's like three, four o'clock in the morning, and . . . he hasn't gone up [to bed] yet, I get scared. I think, "Oh, my God. He had his heart attack." (laughs)

ED: There's occasional days when I . . . get caught up watching something.

CINDY: So I always rush down [and] say, "What's going on?"

Diabetes

Sleeping with a partner with diabetes, one may be alert to the possibility of the partner going into diabetic shock.

BARBARA: He's diabetic. . . . We've had episodes where we've been woken up in the middle of the night where his blood sugar plummets . . .

ME: Are there times when you feel like you're on guard or some part of your mind is on guard . . . ?

BARBARA: Yeah. Oh, yeah. 'Cause I know after that one episode happened, I think that was more (HANK: Yeah), like wanting to make sure. I would wake up, I'd always wake myself up just to . . . make sure he was breathing.

Several people talked about being prepared to respond immediately to a partner's diabetic shock by providing the partner with a drink of fruit juice or telephoning 9-1-1.

PETE: Every once in a while I would go into insulin shock (SHARON: Oh, the insulin shock, yeah), sometimes at night. You're sleeping and blood sugar's so low that I'd go into shock. . . . You start to shake and quiver and you swallow your tongue . . . and she notices that right away, and so she . . . grabs a glass of orange juice or whatever, and then she's fightin' with me tryin' to get me to . . . drink it . . .

SHARON: He went through a spell where he was doin' that (PETE: a lot) a lot, and I'd have to be in tune to that, so that I would . . . wake up to catch it and take care of it.

Depression

With clinical depression there can be quite an array of sleep problems (see chapter 7 for a discussion of one aspect of depression). The most dramatic challenge to the sleep of a person whose partner has clinical depression is that the depressed partner might attempt suicide. In one couple, the repeated attempts of the wife to commit suicide led the husband, with her cooperation, to tie her wrist to his at bedtime each night. Some nights he would sleep fitfully, with the possibility of her trying to kill herself always on his mind. Some nights he would stay awake guarding against her killing herself.

> PETE: She would try to kill herself . . . so I would tie my wrist to her in bed, with a cloth. . . . Our hands were together. So if I fell asleep, and she tried to untie it or get up, I could feel her. . . . Sometimes I would sit up at night and just watch her, so that she wouldn't get up and try something . . .
>
> SHARON: It affected my sleep. It affected his sleep . . .
>
> PETE: I would actually stay up. I'd actually have the TV goin' at night, and watch TV so I could watch her.

Postsurgery Pain and Sensitivity to Jostling

When a couple sleeps together while one of them is recovering from surgery, a challenge for the partner who is well is not to jostle the recovering partner.

> MICHELLE: When I went through the surgery that was kind of a tough time. . . . I didn't want him to jostle; I didn't want to be moved. I ended up with a lumpectomy, which is just taking the tumor, but drainage in here, and so I had for about what? four or five weeks (TONY: Yeah) the drainage tube. And it was cumbersome, and I just really wanted him to leave me alone. Which he was pretty good about.

ME: So he didn't snuggle up to you then.

MICHELLE: Not usually (small laugh). I think you pretty much stayed on your side of the bed (chuckling) for a few weeks. (TONY: Yeah). . . . It was pretty much just, "Leave me alone and let me get through this."

For anyone trying not to jostle a partner recovering from surgery it might be a challenge to get a good night's sleep. Anything that changes the usual ways one lies in bed and moves can interfere with sleeping. Also, when people were trying not to be in contact or to jostle each other, they would have little of their normal snuggling, cuddling, or sexual contact. The decline in touching and sexuality could make sleeping difficult.

COLDS AND THE FLU

Many couples said that they continued to share a bed when one of them was sick with a possibly contagious cold or the flu.

ME: If either of you is sick with a bad cold or the flu, do you still sleep together?

WILLIAM: Yeah. We just don't kiss then. (JULIA: Yeah)

ME: So you stay entangled like you usually do?

JULIA: We usually . . . do. 'Cause we're so used to sleeping (WILLIAM: Umhm) close together. I know, we shouldn't. We probably pass it on (chuckling) to each other.

STEVE: We don't sleep separate . . . when we're sick. We figure we probably infect each other anyway just daily living.

When two people shared a bed and one of them was sick with a cold or the flu, the other might not be able to sleep well. The partner's wakefulness, the sounds of the illness, and the tossing and turning that might go along with it, could disrupt the other's sleeping.

INJURY

Injuries make it more difficult to get a good night's sleep (Janson et al., 2001). Many people I interviewed had the experience of coming to bed with painful injuries—particularly to the back, knees, ankles, and shoulders. A few of the injuries were from ordinary household activities or had occurred during recreational activities, but many were work related. In fact, the majority of people I interviewed who had blue collar jobs had stories of serious work injuries that affected individual and hence couple sleeping. It is a comment on workplace safety that the couple relationship carries part of the cost of unsafe working situations for working class couples. Business cost accounting does not report how much sleep workers lose because of injuries on the job, let alone how much sleep the people who share beds with workers lose. But it is clear from a number of interviews that workers in blue collar jobs not only exchange their time for the pay they receive, they also exchange their health, their sleep, and the sleep of their partner.

One way an injury affected couple sleeping was that when one partner was injured, the other might go to great effort not to move in bed in a way that jarred the injured partner. That might make it harder for the uninjured partner to get a good night's sleep. Also, while lying in bed, an injured person might move in difficult-to-control ways and might have to shift positions relatively often, which might mean that the uninjured partner was awakened often.

> KAREN: [While working,] I . . . went down a flight of steps. I . . . ended up damaging my back and my ankle. And it took me two years to get back to a job. So I did lots of physical therapy and a lot of rehab. . . . So that was an adjustment for both of us . . . the therapy and the comfort and different things . . .
>
> ME: Do you still have discomfort some of the time?
>
> KAREN: Oh yes.
>
> RICHARD: She has a permanent disability. (KAREN: Yes, yeah). . . . She would wake me up with these, what would you call 'em? Violent . . .
>
> KAREN: Oh, the leg jerks?
>
> RICHARD: The leg jerks, yeah. 'Cause she'd get like nerves shots up her leg.

Injuries that took any time at all to heal typically deprived a couple of their usual snuggling and cuddling and their usual sexual relationship. Sometimes physical contact disappeared. Some couples, like Karen and Richard, found new ways to be in contact.

> KAREN: I'm the creeper; I'm the snuggler, so I'm constantly moving over (laughs). . . . He's got a bad shoulder right now, so it's hard for him to turn for spooning.

RICHARD: So I'll usually put my arm out here, and then she'll (KAREN: yeah) snuggle with me for a while, and then she'll turn over and I'll turn over, and we'll go to sleep. . . .

ME: Sometimes does he roll over to you to hug you?

KAREN: Very seldom, because of his shoulder now. Before he would. Before, [he would] spoon with the arm around me.

Dan had a blue collar job that periodically caused him to come home with severe back pain. Although he and Kristen continued to sleep together when he was in great pain, the pain he felt when he moved at night would awaken Kristen.

In some instances, an injured person needed the whole bed, which relegated the partner to sleeping elsewhere.

GEORGE: I've had two instances since I've been with her that I've had back spasms. And those few times I claim the whole bed to myself. . . . I can't be cramped up in one corner. . . . I slept on my side, with a pillow in between my legs, and a heating pad on, and that helped a lot.

ME: When he's like that, where do you sleep?

CHRISTINE: I would sleep out here [on the couch].

It was striking that when blue collar workers who had been injured talked about their injuries, if they complained about something or somebody they would typically talk about the problems their sleeping partner created for them. I would have thought they would talk instead about how the work situation was at the root of their problems. Richard, whose wife Karen is quoted earlier in this section of this chapter about severe injuries she had received in a blue collar job, had chronic and apparently incurable problems with his shoulder as a result of his own blue collar job.

RICHARD: Because of my shoulder now sometimes it's more comfortable for me to lay on my back and put [my arm] out like this. Well, she doesn't give me that much room. . . . It would be nice if I had the room for that, but normally when she rolled over and has gone to sleep . . . her feet may be touching or whatever, but there's room for me to put my arm. Well, there's other times that she's closer than that, so I can't do that, so I end up putting it up here, and because I have, I don't know if it's tendons or whatever is pulled here. When I wake up in the morning if it's been this way all night, I literally have to take the arm and (grunting) pull it over. It hurts quite a lot.

Perhaps statements like the one from Richard only seem to focus blame on the spouse because the interview focused on the couple relationship. But the focus on the spouse could mean something ominous about how workers in the United States think about what causes problems with the body. Perhaps Richard accepted that work would cause pain. He was still working at the job that caused so much harm to his shoulder. Perhaps the damage on the job was, for him, a given, with no responsibility for his injury attributed to his employer who hired people to do work that damaged shoulders. If so, that left the potential for a great deal of pain and frustration to be focused on Karen, who was the person Richard thought of as capable of making choices that caused him more pain and discomfort or less.

THE COUPLE SYSTEM

Although it can seem as though shared sleeping is a burden when one of the partners is ill or injured, the case can be made that shared sleeping at that time can be enormously useful and important. In fact, from an evolutionary perspective, sleeping with someone else can be partly about staying alive. It is not simply that the other is a guard or protector against outside dangers. Nor is it only that the other is helpful in keeping one warm on cold nights or is a partner in reproducing. It is also that the other may be able to react in life saving ways to health conditions that arise and may help to make healing processes easier, more speedy, and more likely to come to a good completion.

Shared sleeping also means that the external environment intrudes into the couple bed sharing relationship in that any illness or injury one partner brings from the outside has the potential to affect the other partner's sleeping and the couple relationship. Whether it's a cold virus brought in from the outside or back spasms acquired on a physically demanding job, the difficulty comes into the bedroom and has the potential to affect the sleeping of both partners and the touching, talking, sexuality, and so on that are such an important part of couple bed sharing.

TEN

How Can You Sleep So Soundly When I'm So Wide Awake?

SLEEPLESSNESS IS ONE of the most common complaints people present to physicians (Neubauer, 2003, p. 1). Perhaps one-third to one-half of adults in the United States at least occasionally have insomnia (Aldrich, 1999, p. 129; Ancoli-Israel & Roth, 1999). Many people I interviewed had times when they lay in bed wide awake long after lights out and long after they hoped to be asleep. Many had times when they awoke in the middle of the night and could not go back to sleep.

Sleeplessness is not necessarily bad. It can be a time for creativity, insight, and discovery. However, most of the people I interviewed who talked about sleeplessness spoke of it only as a problem. Sleep deprivation makes one more irritable, less able to remember, and somewhat depressed (Ware & Morin, 1997). Sleep deprivation can make one accident prone and inefficient. It can make one fall asleep while driving (Gander, Marshall, Harris, & Reid, 2005; Ohayon & Zulley, 2001) or at work (Nakata, et al., 2005). In this chapter I focus on sleeplessness as it shows up in the couple relationship.

GENDER AND SLEEPLESSNESS

Women do not have a monopoly on nighttime wakefulness, but in the heterosexual couples I interviewed women were roughly twice as likely as men to say they had long periods of wakefulness after lights out or in the middle of the night. This fits the literature on the gendering of wakefulness. Women are more likely than men to have difficulty sleeping (Akerstedt, Fredlund, Gillberg, & Jansson, 2002; Aldrich, 1999, p. 129; Frisoni et al., 1993; Hislop & Arber, 2003a, 2003b; Li, Wing, Ho, & Fong, 2002; Middelkoop et al., 1996; Ohayon & Zulley,

2001). And the gender difference seems to become greater beginning with menopause (Baker, Simpson, & Dawson, 1997; Neubauer, 2003, p. 11). One way to understand the gender difference is that women are more likely than men to lose sleep because of stressful life events (Gottlieb & Green, 1984).

> SHARON: Sometimes I'll have a really bad night where I must be worrying about my kids or everything just too much. I just worry too much. It's stupid. And then I just can't fall asleep.

Hislop and Arber (2003a) made a strong case for the idea that women are wakeful so much of the time because women carry such a heavy load with regard to housework, emotional care of the family, child care, elder care, and maintenance of family contacts with others. Their analysis might apply to the women in the heterosexual couples I interviewed, but almost no woman I interviewed talked about the basis of their wakefulness that way. Almost every woman who experienced a great deal of sleeplessness seemed to experience it, like the woman quoted above in this chapter and the women quoted immediately below, as due to something inherent in themselves or due to a specific issue at work or at home.

> ANGELA: My mind . . . continues on with the day I think. And I think I tend to dwell on things.

> AMY: When we were first married, probably our first three years . . . were real volatile (KARL: Umhm), real awful. And that was probably part of the staying awake was between my job and the tension here, some crud that was going on with his ex-wife. It was just like there wasn't much in life very stable. That's a lot of what used to keep me awake at night. . . . I can have really intense complete battles in my mind sometimes. . . . I'd repeat the arguments, three or four different ways, so by then you're so obsessed on it then sleep is just not even an option.

Making it an issue about something in themselves or in their home or work situation might make matters seem less out of their control. That is, it might be empowering to think of oneself or one's relationships as the source of sleep problems, because then there is a possibility that one can solve the sleep problem on one's own. But still, like women in the Hislop and Arber (2003a) focus groups, many women I interviewed who were often sleepless felt things were out of their control in the sense that they had tried all the solutions to sleeplessness that they could imagine and none had worked well enough or consistently enough.

IF MY PARTNER CAN'T SLEEP I CAN'T EITHER

There were couples in which the wakefulness of one did not seem to disturb the sleep of the other, or only disturbed it briefly now and then. But there were also couples in which the wakefulness of one interfered quite a bit with the sleep of the other. So a person who was awake because of worry about work, a relationship, or a money problem became a challenge to the partner's sleeping. What awakened the partner or kept the partner awake? It could be movements of the bed as the wakeful partner tossed and turned. It could be heavy sighs. It might be something subtle, like the wakeful partner's breathing not being like the breathing of someone who is sound asleep.

> MOLLY: Often if one of us has trouble going to sleep it disturbs the other person, even if you're being totally quiet. It's just kind of odd. There's been times when I've had something on my mind and can't go to sleep, and you wind up staying awake. (THOMAS: Umhm. Or vice versa.)
>
> ME: . . . How do you think the other one picks it up?
>
> MOLLY: You can feel that they aren't asleep, and hear it in their breathing. I can hear it in his breathing when he's not sleeping.

Often for people who were wakeful, the choice of what to do when they could not sleep was as much about not bothering their partner as about getting themselves to sleep. Some said that they left the bedroom in order to allow their partner to sleep well.

> CHRISTINE: He has so much to do, and he gets up much earlier than I do. I want him to get his sleep. I don't want to be disturbing him, so usually when I can't sleep, I'll just come out here, maybe watch TV or . . . read, until I feel more able to go back to bed.

When Sandra had trouble sleeping, she sometimes had to awaken her husband in order to talk things through.

> SANDRA: Oftentimes what I'll try to do is resolve whatever it is that I'm thinking about or that's bothering me, but if it's something that I just can't get off my mind or is something that I really have to . . . discuss with him, then I'll wake him up.

If a person who could not sleep wandered away from the bedroom, the partner might awaken and go looking for the missing person, concerned that something was wrong and wanting to offer help.

AMY: He'll see the light down here if I'm reading . . . or if I'm in the computer room with the door shut and he sees that, then he'll stand there half awake and goes, "Are you okay?" 'Cause he knows sometimes I'm not okay, and that's why I'm up. . . . If I was really upset about something, then sometimes . . . he'd maybe throw on sweats and come down and sit with me for a while, or ask if I need to talk.

In some couples, the partner who found it easy to sleep might be able to help the wakeful partner get to sleep.

BEN: The only times I've had trouble sleeping . . . was if we dealt with [something really horrible at work]. Then I'd lay down and be like, all I could see was this [really horrible scene], but then having somebody there I just don't really think about it.

ME: So sleeping with her has helped you sleep.

BEN: Oh, I think so, yeah . . .

CAROLINE: I just let him vent about it, and usually once he talks about it and gets it off his chest, he's like, "Okay." He can calm down, and then I'll just rub his leg or give him a kiss or something, and say [something] comforting.

LIGHT SLEEPERS AND HEAVY SLEEPERS

Some people are usually or always light sleepers. They awaken easily. A faint sound, a slight movement of the bed, or a change in the light coming into the bedroom may awaken them. Some people are usually or always heavy sleepers. Almost nothing awakens them, not even the blasting sound from a clock radio turned to high volume. When one partner is a light sleeper and the other a heavy sleeper, problems may arise. A light sleeper can be awakened easily and often by things a partner does and can find that very irritating. A heavy sleeper can sleep through anything, and that can irritate or even alarm the light sleeper when she or he wants the heavy sleeper to wake up. How do couples in which one is a light sleeper and the other a heavy sleeper deal with their difference?

WAKE UP!

Among the couples I interviewed, a common pattern in the relationship of lighter sleeper and heavier sleeper was that the lighter sleeper would awaken to something—perhaps a suspicious noise—and then awaken the heavier sleeper so that the heavier sleeper could be an ally in investigating and perhaps confronting whatever awakened the lighter sleeper.

WILLIAM: If there's a noise, you wake up first. (JULIA: Yeah, I do).

JULIA: . . . I am the lighter sleeper . . . and I'll say, "William," if I hear something.

WILLIAM: You say (imitating a frightened questioning:), ". . . What's that noise?" (she laughs) And then I'm going, "What noise?" And then I go out . . . and I'm going around. I don't know what noise you're talking about.

Some partners resented how deeply a heavy sleeper slept. Sometimes the resentment was subtle. For example, a light sleeper's seemingly humorous story about a partner who is a heavy sleeper not awakening when something that could awaken almost anyone else occurred could also be about the concern and anxious annoyance the lighter sleeper felt that terrible things could happen and the heavy sleeper would be no help.

KARL: Nothing wakes me up (laughs). I can sleep through just about anything . . .

ME: Do you feel like one of you is more likely to wake up if there's a strange sound outside or in the house or if it starts raining? (KARL: Not me [chuckles]) . . .

AMY: We had a car crash . . . about one hundred feet from our bedroom window. . . . So we had cop cars back there and an ambulance, and I was out on the deck talking to my neighbor across the backyard, and went back and I never woke Karl but went back to sleep, so I didn't bother him. So when he got home the next day I said, "Boy, that was really somethin'." He goes, "What?"

KARL: I didn't even hear the ambulance or . . .

AMY: Nothing, nothing. I heard the slam when it hit the post, and all of sudden it's flashing lights and everything. Yeah, I'm probably a light sleeper.

Living with a heavy sleeper could be frightening if one had reason to believe that in case of danger the heavy sleeper would be impossible to awaken.

SHANNON: Pretty much once I'm asleep, I'm asleep. I guess I've been told I can sleep through anything. There was a fire in the other building a few weeks ago. I never even heard the sirens. I was oblivious.

STEVE: A couple times the fire alarm's gone off in this building and, either the smoke alarm or the big fire alarm out in the hallway, and she slept right through it; I could not wake her up to get her out. If we really had a fire in this building . . . she'd burn up. There'd be no way I'd get her up.

The heavy sleeper could resent being awakened, perhaps partly because for a heavy sleeper waking up is quite an effort.

ME: Does his waking up easily when there are sounds help you to feel safe?

MARY: No (chuckles, both laugh). It's not safety at all. . . . It's like when your kids are little and you got to get up all night long with them.

Mary's way of characterizing her resentment, that "It's like when the kids are little," can be understood to mean that she did not like being awakened, but she could accept it. Couples in which one partner was a light sleeper and one a heavy sleeper seemed to get along despite the difference partly because the heavier sleeper recognized that they differed. Then there was nothing personal or malicious about the lighter sleeper reacting to something during the night in a way that awakened the heavier sleeper.

Don't You Know That Doing That Wakes Me Up?

A lighter sleeper can easily be awakened by actions of the heavier sleeper. This book is filled with evidence of that. For example, difficulties with a partner's snoring or tossing and turning are sometimes about a light sleeper being awakened by things that others would sleep through. Similarly, touchiness about having the windows open or not, the thermostat set at a temperature that is too low or too high, or the partner going to bed at a different time could be about concerns a person who sleeps lightly has that if things are not right she or he will be awakened. Light sleepers may be able to do things to make it easier to sleep—for example, sleeping with ear plugs or with pillows covering their ears. But they also need the cooperation of their sleeping partner in order to get a good night's sleep.

ALCOHOL, CAFFEINE, AND MEDICATIONS

Some people talked about alcohol, caffeine, and certain medications affecting sleep, both of the person using them and of the person's partner.

Alcohol

In the medical literature, alcohol consumption is a predictor of complaints of insomnia (Haermae et al., 1998; Janson et al., 2001; Li, Wing, Ho, & Fong, 2002), but only one couple I interviewed said that alcohol consumption was connected to sleeping problems. In that one couple, the partners seemed to feel there was a current and very serious problem with alcohol. They seldom went to bed together and often slept apart because the person who used alcohol heavily had trouble getting to bed or could not go to bed until thoroughly drunk. Her sleeplessness as she worked on becoming sufficiently drunk, or her drunkenness, coupled with her partner's discomfort with the drunkenness, often led to them spending the night apart.

Caffeine

Echoing what research on caffeine usage shows (e.g., Dekker, Paley, Popkin, & Tepas, 1993; Riedel, 2000; Smith, Maben, & Brockman, 1993), quite a few people said that taking caffeine, taking too much of it, or taking it too late in the day created sleep problems. The caffeine made it difficult to fall asleep, made for restless sleep, made for lower quality sleep, and made it more likely that the user would awaken during the night.

If a person had trouble falling asleep or slept restlessly because of caffeine, that could be a problem for the partner. Amy insisted that her husband Karl cut back on caffeine because of his kicking in his sleep whenever he consumed a considerable amount of caffeine. After he cut back, the kicking subsided.

> AMY: You indiscriminately inhale caffeine (KARL: Yes). You don't watch your caffeine intake. (KARL: No I don't). Although at one point when he was first starting to kick, I asked him to please not after supper drink any more of the high test Coke, and that did help.

I interviewed people who consumed awesome amounts of caffeine each day—for example, twelve cups of coffee or eight cups of coffee plus two liters of caffeinated cola—but who reported falling asleep easily and sleeping without difficulty. So at the level of how people experience their own sleeping, high intakes of caffeine might not be a problem for some people. But many people said caffeine was, at times, a problem for them or their sleeping partner.

Sleep Medications

Quite a few people had tried at least one medication to help them to sleep. Some sleep medications were prescribed by a physician, while others were bought over the counter. Different sleep medications supposedly deal with different underlying causes of sleep difficulty. For example, one medication might help with depression, another with relaxing at bedtime, and another with physical pain.

> MICHELLE: I have some arthritis in my knees and back, and if they're bothering me at bedtime, I will take some Tylenol PM, which has an antihistamine in it, which makes you drowsy. It works. But not as a rule do I need to take something to sleep with. It's that my back hurts or my knees hurt.

> DAN: When I worked third shift, if I couldn't sleep and as a last resort, I would take a couple of shots of Nyquil. And that would put me out. But that was like a last resort, where I'd been up all night, and it was like one, two in the afternoon, and I knew I had to go to bed, [because] I had to go back to work (chuckles) that evening.

Consistent with what is reported in the literature on sleep medication (Roehrs, Hollebeek, Drake, & Roth, 2002; Sproule et al., 1999), more people I interviewed who said that they took medications to help them sleep had used over-the-counter medication than used prescription medication. And, like Michelle and Dan, the people who took over-the-counter medications typically took them only occasionally.

Only a few people I interviewed had been on a prescription medication for a long time and seemed to feel that they needed the medication in order to sleep adequately.

> BRENDA: For a total of thirteen years I was trying everything I could think of to battle insomnia, short of sleeping pills. Because I just thought that I'd try all the alternatives, and I never did find anything that had a lasting effect. And so I started taking sleeping pills in '94, and I've been taking different combinations and dosages ever since. . . . Now that I'm medicated, I sleep through more than I would like to, 'cause I used to be a very light sleeper, and the slightest noise would wake me up, and so I think that if there was no medication in the picture I'd still be a very light sleeper.

When medications work without serious side effects they can be a boon to the person who is having trouble sleeping, which probably means they are also a boon to the person's partner.

In some couples, the person who took sleep medications was not the person who had the serious sleep problem but the partner of one. In particular, a few people with a partner who snored loudly took medications that helped them to sleep despite the loud snoring.

> CYNTHIA: I would say maybe forty percent of the time I'll take, usually I take either a Tylenol PM or Tylenol makes an over-the-counter called Simply Sleep, and I'll take a couple of those.
>
> ME: It must really knock you out.
>
> CYNTHIA: Yeah it does, yeah. And I'll do that also if his allergies are bad and I know the snoring is going to be an issue. I'll just take something to knock me out for the night. And that usually helps.

THE COUPLE SYSTEM

In a couple system, people are connected. So it should be no surprise that some people had trouble sleeping only because their partner had trouble sleeping. And it should be no surprise that some people who had trouble sleeping benefitted from their partner's efforts to help them. One doesn't have to think of this perspective as a critique of a medical model that sees sleep problems as only individual ones. More than one model can legitimately fit the phenomena. However, it seems important to emphasize that a medical model focused on individuals does not invalidate a systems view of couple sleeping or of couples in general.

Almost every chapter in this book talks about ways that the sleep of couples is shaped, limited, helped, undermined, or infused with the effects of modern technology. That technology includes contemporary bed manufacturing, central heating, air conditioning, television, sleep apnea devices, ear plugs, bedding, alarm clocks, reading lamps, housing that separates the sleep area of an adult couple from the sleeping area of their children, doors and locks, rice bags heated in microwave ovens, indoor bathrooms, and sleepwear. This chapter adds to the list by making clear that the technology of manufacturing alcoholic drinks, caffeine products, and sleep medications has an impact on the sleep of many couples. The couple sleep system is embedded in a larger system of modern technology.

ELEVEN

ALL THAT IS EXTERNAL to the couple can affect couple sleeping, through impacts on one or both partners. This chapter explores the two systems external to the couples interviewed that most often had a major impact on couple sleeping: the workplace and coresident children.

THE INTRUSION OF WORK INTO COUPLE SLEEPING

SHIFT WORK

Shift work can be hard on the sleep of the person doing the shift work (Akerstedt, Fredlund, Gillberg, & Jansson, 2002; Akerstedt, Knutsson, et al. 2002; Haermae et al., 1998; Lee, 1992; Melbin, 1987, ch. 7; Regestein & Monk, 1991), hard on the partner's sleeping, and hard on the couple relationship (Smith & Folkard, 1993). When two people work shifts that do not coincide, their shared sleep may be limited. For many people, the ideal of couple sleeping is for partners to go to sleep and wake up together at or close to the same time. But the sleep of couples whose work shifts do not coincide is often out of synchrony. That can take a toll on the couple relationship.

> TIM: Out of all the years we've been together that's been the tough pattern, four years of third shift, a year of second, back to third, then back to second for two years. There was all those years I worked second. That's when she'd already be in bed when I got home. Third shift, the one year when our daughter was first born . . . I got home at eight in the morning, slept for two hours, then she went to work. And then

when our daughter needed to take her nap I'd sleep for another hour
and a half. She'd be home from work, we'd eat supper, and I'd sleep
for three hours and . . . go to work. . . . As far as like a normal family
sleeping it hasn't been us over the years.

For couples who work different shifts, it might only be weekends, holidays,
and vacations that they sleep together.

PETE: We didn't sleep together very much, because I worked nights, and
she worked . . . days. . . . The only time we'd get to sleep together was
when I had two nights. And that went on for twelve years . . . while we
were raising our kids that we basically only had two nights a week
together. . . . We spent twelve years basically hardly ever in a bed together.

Sarah worked different shifts on different days. It seemed that no matter
which shift she worked she and Nick could interfere with one another's sleeping and miss the connection and joy of going to sleep and waking up together.

NICK: She works three to twelve and I work generally strictly during
the days. . . . Sometimes on the weekend she'll do twelve-hour days.

SARAH: I get up at like 5:15, so sometimes I get up earlier than him,
so I interrupt him sleeping by resetting the alarm. . . . Most of the time
I work evenings, so then he gets up before me. . . . When I work
evenings, I get home about twelve, and he's already sleeping. [But]
then he wakes up when I come home sometimes.

NICK: For another hour or so . . . until she winds down.

Cindy said she was always angry when her husband worked the late shift,
angry that he was not there and angry that he did not want to go to sleep as
soon as he came home.

CINDY: I was really angry that he wasn't there, or I'd wait and wait
for him to get home, and then when he was there he'd say, "I gotta
calm down before I go to sleep, so I can't come to bed."

A major challenge of shift work is that someone who wants the comfort
and security of sleeping with her or his partner can be blocked from that by the
sleep patterns required by shift work. One way some couples handled that was
for the partner who did not want to sleep alone to sleep with a child or grandchild. For example, Cynthia did not like sleeping alone, so when Tim worked
the night shift she brought their seven-year-old daughter to be with her.

Shift work can deprive a couple of communication time, emotional intimacy, and physical contact. Sometimes, to deal with that, the person who was not on shift work would alter her or his sleep schedule to match as closely as possible the sleep schedule of the shift worker. Susan would put off going to bed until Adam came home from working the late shift. For her, not only were communication, emotional intimacy, and physical contact with him important, she also felt better if he was the last person she saw before she went to sleep.

> ADAM: I'm working four in the afternoon till one o'clock in the morning, so normally I get home at about 1:30. . . . Then she's up watching a movie or on the couch sleeping.
>
> SUSAN: Yeah I kind of wait up for him. . . . Some of it is just wanting to see him at the end of his day, even if it ends in the middle of the night. Just to connect with him for a few minutes and see how his day was and have him be the last person I see before I go to sleep.

If shift work kept them from sleeping together, couples developed ways to make sleep as comfortable as possible for both of them. For example, they might agree to set the thermostat so that both of them slept at a preferred temperature. There was also the question of whether or how to make the bed when it was in use the majority of hours in the day. Sandra wanted Ken to make the bed as soon as he got out of it, although, with her shift schedule, she was going to get into the bed almost as soon as he made it.

I'M ON CALL

Being on call so that one might be paged or phoned from work has been shown to reduce sleep for the person on call, make for greater tiredness on waking up, and lead to a more disturbed family life (Imbernon et al., 1993). How does being on call affect couple sleep? Three people who I interviewed carried pagers so if there was a problem at work they could be "beeped" and either have to call into work to address the problem or go into work to fix it. On the nights when the pager sounded, both partners lost sleep and part of their shared time in bed.

BRINGING WORK TENSION, CONCERN, AND INVOLVEMENT TO BED

Many people I interviewed had a job that could not be left at work. They might bring home actual work to do. But much more commonly they might come home thinking about what went on at work that day or what they had to do at work the next day. They might be concerned about work quality, the problems someone at work was having, a mistake they made at work, or the possibility of layoffs. Often they brought these work issues to bed. People who continue to obsess about work are more likely to have disturbed sleep (Akerstedt, Knutsson, et al., 2002).

> BRAD: As a teacher you have things that would weigh on you, so then you'd wake up and you'd say, "Oh, Jeez, I gotta go do that." Then you'd get up and you'd write it down, and then when you're laying there you're thinking, and you're thinking.

> GREG: Sometimes . . . I wind up with my mind racing as details of the stuff I'm working on refuse to absent themselves, so sometimes I will either have trouble going to sleep, or I'll wake up at four in the morning, pretty much have no choice except to do some work, simply because it's not possible to sleep.

Sometimes when one person in a couple lay awake thinking about issues at work, it awoke the other person.

> ME: If you have stresses at work that you bring home, do they show up in your sleeping?
>
> AARON: Yeah.
>
> ME: What happens?
>
> AARON: Lay there and think.
>
> ME: Do you know when he's doing that?
>
> DIANA: Sometimes. Sometimes he wakes me up by just fidgeting.

Sometimes a partner who was upset about work issues awoke the other partner in order to talk about what was upsetting.

> VIC: I used to be able to fall asleep just like that. But in the last year, since all of the stuff that went on [with my job] . . . it's been more difficult . . .
>
> MARIA: That was hard on me. . . . It was just a really hard time for Vic and so he wasn't sleeping and then he wanted to talk, and so I would wake up to be with him and to talk with him, and then I had to get up and go to work. . . . It was really hard.

Sometimes a partner's solutions to the stresses of work interfered with the sleep of the other. For example, Barbara's decision to leave a job that was making it difficult for her to sleep made it harder for Hank to sleep because then he had sole responsibility for bringing in the family income.

Some couples tried to deal with job tensions by making it part of their bedtime conversation. A sympathetic conversation might help to relieve the tension and could be a wonderful couple connection. Also, some couples found that their ordinary unwinding routines helped them deal with job tension.

CHILDREN AND COUPLE SLEEPING

BABIES

Baby feeding, comforting, changing, and burping during the night will certainly disrupt parent sleep. In heterosexual couples, it was much more likely that the woman would be the person to lose sleep doing nighttime infant care.

> BRENDA: I had a spare bed in [the baby's] room, so I didn't spend too much time in the marriage bed when she was a baby. It was impossible. As soon as I'd go back to bed, she'd cry. I would try sleeping in a different room, pillows over my head and ear plugs, and he'd try getting up with her, and I'd express some milk. And we just tried everything. And . . . it was that Mommy thing. She could be next door, and if she woke up I'd know it. Even if she hadn't cried yet. We were so connected. So I never slept. And she slept through the night for the first time when she was three and a half. (laughs) Yeah. So I was pretty wasted.

A premature baby could complicate parent sleeping even more. At first, there were the recurrent visits to the hospital and ongoing anxieties about the baby. When the infant finally came home, she or he was small and needed to be fed often during the night. And the parents might feel that they had to watch the child's breathing closely, even during the night.

> LINDA: Both of us became extreme light sleepers, because one thing with preemies is they . . . have a habit of forgetting to breathe. . . . She slept in a crib in our room . . . [and we] constantly were going over there to make sure that she was still breathing. But she was at the hospital for three months, so for three months basically he and I really didn't sleep that much. I guess . . . for fear that the phone is gonna ring, which on many times it did. . . . Neither one of us would be able to sleep that much, and the hospital had a twenty-four hour visiting thing so we'd just get up and maybe go see her because we weren't that far. It was tough.

All of 'Em Liked to Sleep on Our Floor

A child who was old enough to walk and who was having trouble sleeping might come to the parents for reassurance or a warm and snug place to fall asleep.

> ME: Do any of the kids ever show up in your bed?
>
> SANDRA: Unfortunately (chuckles), yes. Mostly the youngest one. . . . She always comes to my side first, and then I may tell her, "go to Dad's side, just crawl in bed with him . . ."
>
> ME: When a kid shows up on her side, does that wake you?
>
> KEN: Typically it doesn't. Only if she makes the kid get in (laugh) on my side. . . . I could be sleeping and then all of a sudden I'll wake up and I'll feel like I'm sandwiched.

Monica and Don's children liked to sleep on the floor of their parents' bedroom. It might be easier for the parents to sleep with a child on the floor than with a child in bed, but having a child asleep on the floor could be hazardous.

> MONICA: All of 'em at a younger age liked to sleep on our floor. So then you gotta be careful you don't step on 'em if you get up at night or if I come to bed later.

Older children went to bed later than before, and it might be difficult to get them to bed. That might mean that parents then had later bedtimes than they wanted, and it might give the parents less time to be alone together before going to sleep. Children out late in the evening could also undermine parent sleeping.

> AL: They have a twelve o'clock curfew on weekends, but we stay awake for them. (MARTHA: In bed) Or she would.
>
> MARTHA: Yeah, yeah. So I would read until whenever they came home, and they could come in the driveway, and then I'd turn off the light right away. Then I'd be fine. They add worries. I'm sure we slept a little bit more difficult then.

Child Nightmares

The nightmares of a child could interfere with parent sleeping. It might be just the sounds of the alarmed child intruding into parent sleep, or it might be the child's need to be reassured that drew at least one parent to the child's bedside. One couple had a son whose nightmares would send him running, while still not awake, out of his bedroom and into danger.

> DEBRA: That was a *real* disruption from sleep. I tell you.
>
> HENRY: Oh, oh. That really was. We really worried about that, because see he slept upstairs, and that's the danger, those stairs. And he'd come bursting out. You feel he could fly right down there, fall down them stairs. (DEBRA: We were afraid).

GRANDCHILDREN CAN BE EVEN MORE CHALLENGING

Three couples had grandchildren living with them either part of the week or on a full time basis. With grandchildren, the usual issues of child intrusion on adult sleeping were present (crying at night, nightmares, a younger child showing up in the adult bed, an older child out late). But grandchildren brought additional challenges. At first, the grandparents might not know the grandchild's sleep habits well enough to relax with the grandchild asleep.

> SHARON: If he gets up, you're gonna know it. . . . "Grandma!" He sleeps up here, and we're clear down on the other end of the hall downstairs, and he knows where we are. I leave the light on. I'm like, "You know where I am if you need me." When he first came with us, he did have a few nights. Remember? But now he's fine. He sleeps through the night, and he's fine. He's usually in bed when we get up, still sleeping. I used to worry about him. I'd get up and make sure he was still there, 'cause I . . . thought he'd go out the door and be wandering in the woods. . . . I didn't know what kind of sleeper he was or where I'd find him.

One couple had to accommodate to a granddaughter's preferred way of falling asleep by lying with her until she fell asleep.

> CINDY: We usually . . . have her fall asleep in our bed, then carry her to her bed. Or another thing we've done is she is so used to sleeping with somebody when she goes to sleep, she's never had her own bed, except at our house. I go in her room, lay down on a single bed with her, wait for her to fall asleep, and then I go back to our bed. One of the things we've run into too is she is very used to, when you go to sleep, everybody goes to sleep at the same time. So then I'll go up there with her, and I tell her she and I are goin' to sleep. She will not

go to sleep till [my husband] finally comes up there. And then it's okay with her if he's in our bed and I'm in her bed, but she has to have somebody with her till she falls asleep.

A lesbian couple with grandchildren who frequently visited (but did not sleep at the house of their grandmothers) changed their pattern of sleeping together in part so one of the partners could get to work earlier and home earlier so she could have more contact with the grandchildren.

THE COUPLE SYSTEM

The couple system is in contact with and embedded in many other systems. The influence of these systems is not kept out of the bedroom, even by a locked bedroom door. Work and children were the two external systems that had the greatest influence on couple bed sharing and sleeping. There were other external influences that were very significant in the lives of specific couples. For example, a lesbian couple was enormously influenced by terrorist acts and threats from a homophobic neighbor. Another couple was strongly affected by the health care system. But by far the most common among the strong influences on couple bed sharing and sleeping were the workplace and coresident children.

In trying to characterize what is "normal" in couple sleeping, it seems crucial that the external systemic forces that limit, intrude into, or alter what goes on in the bedroom be accounted for. To understand a couple who struggles with their shared sleeping, we must examine the relationship of work, children, and other external factors to their struggle.

TWELVE

Bathroom Trips, Tossing and Turning, Resless Legs, Sleep Talking, Grinding Teeth, and Nightmares

THERE ARE A NUMBER of individual activities that can occur during the night that can disrupt a partner's sleep. Each of the issues discussed in this chapter is such an activity. And, in the case of nightmares, sometimes the partner of a person with a problem can be of great help in dealing with what could be quite upsetting.

NIGHTTIME TRIPS TO THE BATHROOM

Many people I interviewed paid nighttime visits to the bathroom. Did those trips affect a partner's sleeping? Not necessarily.

> JULIA: I go to the bathroom more during the night than you do, much more, so does it wake you up at night? (He shakes his head 'no') No, nothing wakes you up (they both laugh).

But typically the choice of a person with whom to spend one's nights is, among many things, a choice of who will wake up when one goes to the bathroom during the night. Sometimes, among the people I interviewed, it was only a matter of the partner noticing for a moment and then going back to sleep.

> ROBERT: I rarely remember watching her go to the bathroom and come back. I remember her sitting down and laying there and saying that she just went or she's really got to go. . . . Then she'll get up and go, but I never remember watching her walk to the bathroom.

If the partner getting up to go to the bathroom had serious health problems, there might be an element of concern connected to the partner leaving the bed during the night.

KAREN: I have woken up and he's not there. And it's like, "Oh, oh. Where'd he go?" If I hear him in the bathroom that's fine. If I don't hear him, it's like, "Where is he?" And I think I'm even more so that way since he's had his heart problems.

On a trip to the bathroom, some people made efforts not to disrupt the sleep of the other—for example, not flushing and not stepping on squeaky floor boards.

HENRY: When you get older you have to get up and go to the bathroom more often . . .

ME: Do you hear when he goes to the bathroom?

DEBRA: Sometimes. Probably most of the time I don't. . . . He knows where all the squeaks are . . .

HENRY: I try and step along the side board there where (chuckles) people have less walked, and grab a hold of the door thing, 'cause if I step out in the middle, I might squeak somethin'. I'm always tryin' to tiptoe over to the bathroom, and tryin' to shut the door without makin' any noise.

Although for some who were awakened, it was a matter of noticing and going almost instantly back to sleep, a few had trouble going back to sleep. Consistent with what is in the literature on women living with men whose prostate problems lead to frequent nighttime trips to the bathroom (Shvartzman et al., 2001), some people experienced substantial sleep loss as a result of partner nighttime bathroom trips.

ME: Do either of you get up during the night to go to the bathroom. (LISA: I do). (WALT: Yeah, pretty frequently). Both of you? (LISA: Umhm). When one gets up does that wake up the other?

LISA: Sometimes, not always.

WALT: Yeah, I'd say, ten percent, twenty-five percent of the time . . .

ME: When she gets up and that wakes you, can you go back to sleep?

WALT: Sometimes, sometimes.

ME: But sometimes you lie there for a while. What are you doing?

WALT: Trying to fall asleep, getting frustrated, so I'll sometimes do the "Ninety-Nine Bottles of Beer on the Wall," and sometimes that helps. But it's aggravating, 'cause I know I'll lie awake for two hours and then the alarm will go off.

If She Goes Then I Go

Just as snuggling, chatting, and pulling covers back and forth from one another are part of the dance of sharing a bed, so, for some couples, are the trips to the bathroom at close to the same time. In at least nine of the couples I interviewed, if one went to the bathroom the other often would go immediately afterwards. Perhaps it was a matter of the first trip to the bathroom waking the other, and the other then deciding, "I'm up. Why not go to the bathroom now, rather than waking up later to go?" Perhaps it was the thought, "My partner is up. If I go now, I won't wake her/him later by getting up." Perhaps in some cases it was a matter of one partner's going to the bathroom stimulating the other to think about her or his body, which led to the thought, "I really need to go to the bathroom!"

TOSSING AND TURNING

Tossing and turning can arise from many different sources. Among the most common mentioned were trying to find a comfortable position, trying to relieve aches and pains, rearranging blankets, not being able to fall asleep, the distress of a dream, and stress from work or school. As many people said, one partner's tossing and turning could disturb the other's sleep.

DONNA: He was writing a huge paper [for school]. . . . That's probably the worst sleep we have ever had, because . . . I swear he was like fighting demons in his sleep, because he was so restless, and he turned and rolled and kicked and punched. He just didn't sleep well. . . . He'd roll over with much more gusto than normal; he'd wake me up.

ME: When he's rolling does that wake you up?

LIZ: A lot.

ANDY: I flip, constantly. I don't know why. I just do. I roll over and over and over.

With tossing and turning, it might be the bouncing of the bed that blocks a partner from sleeping. Sometimes the problem was that the tossing and turning pulled blankets away from the partner (see chapter 6 for more on blanket wars). Sometimes the problem was that the person who was tossing and turning made physical contact with the partner, which awakened the partner. At an extreme reached in several couples, one partner's tossing and turning might physically harm the other.

> CINDY: I don't know if you've heard this one, but for a while he was rollin' on me, and I'd get actual bruises on my breasts.

. There might also be more subtle effects on one partner's sleep of the other's tossing and turning. A partner's tossing and turning might move one to a less deep sleep (Wellman, Bohannon, & Vogel, 1999), so even though it did not awaken one it might make it more likely that one's sleep was not restorative or that something else would awaken one.

We Had to Do Something about It

It can be challenging to learn to sleep through a partner's tossing and turning. The following came from a newlywed couple.

> ROBERT: We got married on Friday and went up north, and by the time we got there we were both just dead tired. So we both slept fairly well through that night. . . . We had two nights there at that hotel, and the next night we both slept really good again. We came back here, and the very first night back here . . . was horrible. It was more because of [my] waking up every time she woke up to turn. . . . When the other one moves so the other one wakes up because you moved.

In more established couples, a person who tossed and turned typically had learned how to reduce the difficulty the tossing and turning created for the partner. For example, Hank talked about how he learned to roll over in ways that did not pull the blankets off Barbara.

Research by Wellman, Bohannon, and Vogel (1999) suggests that tossing and turning problems are more challenging for a partner when the couple sleeps on a mattress that allows for greater motion transfer. So it makes sense that one couple dealt with the difficulties created by the man's tossing and turning by purchasing a mattress that was two separate units. Then the man's "flopping" did not bounce the woman so much.

> SHARON: It used to be like sleepin' with a flopping whale. . . . He'd flop around to the other side of the bed, and every time he'd send me flying . . . off the bed.

PETE: Yeah, when I'd turn. . . . So we got a . . . Comfo-rest bed, so you have two separate sides and can adjust the softness and hardness, and now if I do that, she doesn't feel me. SHARON: It helps a lot. It was that or get separate beds (PETE: Right), because he would flop so much . . .

ME: And . . . it would wake you up?

SHARON: Oh, yeah. Every time. So I . . . decided I couldn't sleep with him like that, so we thought we'd try . . . separated mattresses. . . . So when he's floppin' around he's not throwin' me off. . . . That Comfo-rest thing . . . helped a lot.

Occasionally when one partner's tossing and turning became too disruptive, the other partner might decide to sleep elsewhere for the night or might evict the tossing and turning partner from the bed.

AMY: It's my idea of what it would be like to be in bed with a two hundred pound marlin fish that's flopping. . . . If . . . it begins to bother me, and I begin to feel like I'm going to get knots in my stomach, which means then I'll be awake the rest of the night, then I just wake him up . . . and tell him to go downstairs, and he shifts beds. And then we both sleep.

People who had experienced injury from a partner's tossing and turning adapted ways to protect themselves. For example, Cindy, who was quoted earlier in this chapter as having been bruised when her husband tossed and turned, learned to protect herself by shielding her body from his blows.

CINDY: I started sleepin' with a stuffed animal just to have a stuffed animal between us . . . as protection from him (laughs).

Cindy was not alone in laughing at the problems created by a partner's tossing and turning. As was mentioned in the chapter 6 discussion of blanket wars and could be mentioned with regard to almost every other problem discussed in this book, some couples laughed as they talked about their difficulties with tossing and turning. I think the laughter did not solve the problems but made the problems less threatening to the couple relationship.

SUSAN: One night I was tossing and turning. . . . I was trying not to move, but I just couldn't get comfortable, and finally he woke up and he goes, "Will you stop moving?" And I said, "If you don't like it, get a sleeping bag and go on the couch. I can't help it; go sleep on the couch." He goes (chuckles), "Why should I? I've got a sleeping bag right next to me." And I (laughing) laughed so hard. It was a good comeback at three o'clock in the morning (laughs). (ADAM: It was a one liner. Yeah). So our kids the next day go, "Why were you guys laughing so loud at three o'clock in the morning? You woke us up." I can appreciate his humor (laughing).

RESTLESS LEGS

According to the National Center on Sleep Disorder Research (2000), roughly two percent to fifteen percent of adults in the United States have restless legs syndrome. The syndrome involves involuntary twitching of the legs (and occasionally the arms) that occurs irregularly, particularly when a person is resting or sleeping, and creeping or crawling sensations in the legs (Aldrich, 1999, p. 175). A related syndrome called "periodic limb movement disorder" is similar but does not involve the creepy/crawling feelings (Aldrich, 1999, p. 181). A person with restless legs or periodic limb movements may not usually have a good night's sleep because of trouble falling asleep and because of being awakened by the movements and feelings. The person may even have to get out of bed during the night in order to deal with the problem.

Sleeping with someone whose legs frequently move can be difficult; however, as Donna indicated, some people can adapt to a partner's limb movements.

ME: When his leg is moving back and forth like that, does it make it hard for you to sleep?

DONNA: In the beginning it did. It took me a while, 'cause it felt like the bed was just like vibrating.

Some people felt there were things that could be done to reduce the leg movement problems. Amy said that Karl's leg movement problem could be temporarily reduced by exercise and perhaps by lowering his stress level.

AMY: I really think it's more that he doesn't get any physical exercise, and it seems to be when it's stress. . . . You just had a week's vacation with exercise and fresh air, so (she chuckles) I'm sure within about ten days he'll be back kicking, but, no, he's been good this last week. That's why I think it's emotional and exercise.

Lisa said that alcohol intensified her leg movements, so avoiding alcohol gave her and perhaps her partner a better night's sleep.

LISA: Certain things will trigger it. If I have too much wine I notice my legs will twitch more and cramp in the night.

Amy is quoted in chapter 3 as saying that sleeping with Karl was easier after they bought a king size bed. With a larger bed the chances of being kicked by Karl's twitching legs were minimized, and with a more massive mattress perhaps his leg movements bounced the bed less.

Donna was quoted earlier in this chapter as saying how hard it was to share a bed with Jeff when they were first together. She and Jeff talked about the learning she had done in order to sleep through his leg movements.

DONNA: It took me a while to get used to him doing that and to not wake me up . . .

JEFF: I know she's had to learn to . . . put it out of her mind or just get used to having that happen.

SLEEP TALKING

Fifteen percent of the people I interviewed said that they or their partner sleep talked.

ROBERT: Probably a good two or three nights, half the time, I have noticed that she'll say something in the night.

TERESA: Our very first year we were married, he was learning to do (BRAD: Oh, ho, Morse code), Morse code, and that he talked in this dotty-dot-dit, did-da-da.

BRAD: Umhm. Da-did-did-da-da. That was fun (laughs). Di-da-dit-dit (laughs), B's Bravo.

TERESA: . . . I got that all night long. . . . I almost learned 'em because he'd (laughing) say them so much.

A partner's talking or calling out, even a partner saying what sounds like a single word, might awaken a person. Being awakened can be a hassle, especially for a person who has trouble going back to sleep.

Some people learned to sleep through a partner's sleep talking. Partly it was a matter of learning that the other was sleep talking, so one did not have to come fully awake to try to understand what was not addressed to one and was probably not coherent. Partly it was a matter of learning that a sleep talking episode did not usually go on very long (Aldrich, 1999, p. 269), so the few words that one heard were probably the end of what was going to be said. For some people, another part of dealing with a partner's sleep talk was not to become upset by it. They learned not to take it personally and even found humor in it.

> JOHN: Her idea of talking in her sleep is to sound completely awake when you know that (laughs) she's not. And it's generally things like, "Nope," "Nope," "Nope." It's not like, "No, no," panicky. It's just like matter of fact, "no," that kind of sound, and it's very funny. It's really hilarious.

Making sleep talk a source of amusement can make it seem safe and easy to live with, rather than something about which to feel annoyed and angry.

DANGEROUS SLEEP TALK

A few people talked about occasional sleep talk that could be entangled in something dangerous. Eric sometimes hurt Angela as he talked in his sleep, because his sleep talk was angry and aggressive and might be accompanied by aggressive lashing out with his arms.

> ME: You hear him talking sometimes.
>
> ANGELA: Yeah. . . . Just a few words . . .
>
> ME: But those words wake you up?
>
> ANGELA: Umhm, because usually when he's talking, it's [part of an] aggressive dream . . . and it's very loud words, like he's in a fight. And so yeah I wake up immediately because he's moving and talking at the same time (Eric and Angela laugh).
>
> ME: So that gives you some warning.
>
> ANGELA: Yes, oh, I've gotten it a few times, from the arm coming down, but just can't move away quick enough (chuckles). But yeah, there is some warning, definitely, because I hear that, and now I know what to expect.

Angela dealt with the possibility of violence accompanying Eric's sleep talk by moving to the edge of the bed as soon as she heard him sleep talk.

Sometimes sleep talking accompanied sleep walking, and sometimes sleep walking involved danger to the sleep walker and perhaps even to the entire household. Susan recalled a frightening episode when Adam's sleep talking was accompanied by his walking to the kitchen and turning on the gas stove burners. She was sure that the episode was a result of his working long hours, and so her approach to making herself, Adam, and everyone else in the house safer was to push Adam to cut back his work hours.

> SUSAN: He worked about seventy hours a week, and it was really getting to him. . . . He wasn't sleeping well. . . . He got up one night and walked out to the stove, and turned on all the knobs and yelling about something, and I was like, "What are you doing?" And then he started talking to me like I was one of the guys [where he worked], thought he was talking about adjusting a [machine], and I said, "This is the stove. You're gonna burn the house down (chuckles). You need to go to bed." And of course when you're talking to someone who's talking in their sleep, they're just looking at you with this glazed over look in their eye, and that's when I realized, "This man has got to quit one of the jobs."

Adam did quit one of his jobs, and his dangerous sleep walking and talking had not recurred.

GRINDING OR CLENCHING TEETH

Some people had at times awakened with a sore jaw, been told by a dentist that their teeth were worn down from nighttime grinding (sometimes called "bruxism" or "bruxing"), or been treated for tooth or jaw problems stemming from nighttime tooth grinding or clenching. During episodes of bruxism, it is not uncommon for a sleeping partner to be awakened by the sounds of teeth grinding against teeth (Broughton, 1994). There were five couples among those I studied where one partner said that she or he lost sleep because of the other's grinding or clenching teeth.

All of the people who were bothered by a partner's tooth grinding or clenching had ways to stop it. David said that calling out, "Cut it out," would temporarily stop Heather from grinding her teeth in her sleep. After she developed painful temporal mandibular joint disease, she had six months of therapy to learn how to stop the grinding. It worked. She stopped grinding her teeth, and David slept more easily.

George nudged Christine to stop her nighttime tooth grinding, but she usually resumed grinding so quickly that it might take him many tries at stopping her before he could fall asleep.

> GEORGE: It's never woken me up, but trying to get to sleep is sometimes a problem (CHRISTINE: . . . It's a very annoying noise). . . . I

don't know how anybody can grind their teeth like that (she laughs).
Just putting pressure on your jaws and grinding back and forth, but
anyways . . . I usually . . . nudge her or push her a little, and then she
stops. . . . But then a couple minutes later she might start . . . again.

In some cases it seemed that the way to minimize tooth grinding was for
the person who did the tooth grinding to avoid intensely stressful situations.
For example, Sharon's problems with grinding her teeth started when her adult
son moved back home, bringing his new wife and their baby along.

ME: Do either of you grind your teeth at night?

SHARON: I did for a while. Remember when our daughter-in-law
was living here?

PETE: Oh, that's right. . . . I think the dentist even talked to you about
putting a mouth guard . . .

SHARON: Yeah, he said, "I can get ya a mouth guard." And, "No, I'm
just gonna get rid of the problem," so we went on a vacation and we
told them all to be gone when we came home. We kicked them all
out. Yeah, we, I kicked them all out. . . . And that was the end of that.
But they would be fightin' right above us. . . . It was so awful with the
baby and her and him . . . I would take my pillow and stuff and I'd . . .
go sleep on the trampoline . . . in the backyard.

Once the son, his wife, and the baby were gone, Sharon's jaw problem
cleared up.

In a few couples where tooth grinding was not currently a problem, one
partner had in the past developed chronic pain or even serious damage to the
teeth or jaw as a result of tooth grinding, and so the person had sought treatment. The treatment might include wearing a bite guard at night, learning
relaxation techniques, or even going through surgery. Having a solution to the
pain and other problems stemming from tooth grinding protected the person's
partner from losing sleep over the tooth grinding.

NIGHTMARES

Perhaps forty percent to fifty percent of adults admit to having at least occasional nightmares (Broughton, 1994). It might be partly because of nightmares
that there is so much focus on individual sleep in U.S. society and so little on
couple sleeping. In nightmares a person can seem dreadfully alone, with no help
from anyone else. On the other hand, although a nightmare is always the expe-

rience of an individual and although it occurs in the depths of the individual mind, it can be very much a couple matter.

Some people talked about occasions where one partner would do things that entered into the other's nightmare. For example, a partner's snoring could become the sound of the frightening animal in a person's nightmare.

> REBECCA: I can pretty much predict when I'm going to have a nightmare. . . . He snores. . . . And that's where the dream has changed, because now, instead of having another human being attacking me that I'm trying to run from . . . it's . . . a huge, giant gorilla who's about to kill me or it's a wolf or some kind of demonic entity that's about to kill me.

More often, among the couples I interviewed, nightmares were a couple problem because a person having a nightmare did things that interfered with a partner's sleep. In roughly a third of the couples I interviewed, one person had nightmares that at some time (perhaps once, perhaps often) led to the other being awakened.

She Flew across the Bed, Right over the Top of Me

Some people, while still having a nightmare, acted on what was happening in the nightmare in a way that awakened the partner.

> RICHARD: She had a dream one night about the storm and that was when our son was little. Right?
>
> KAREN: (Laughing) Oh, that one.
>
> RICHARD: She went flying across the bed, right over the top of me, just ninety miles an hour.
>
> KAREN: (Laughing) I got to the baby though, didn't I?
>
> RICHARD: "The baby, the baby." She had had a dream that the storm . . . was blowing the baby out the window. . . . The shortest path there was across me.

Consistent with research reports of frequent, intense nightmares for many Vietnam veterans (Chiaramonte, 1992; Neylan et al., 1998; Wilmer, 1996), a Vietnam veteran's night terrors of being in battle led to dramatic action as he attempted to reach safety while still asleep. His wife was repeatedly awakened by his terrified flight to safety.

MIKE: I'm a Vietnam veteran, and I used to suffer from terrible night-mares and would go flying through the, you know, run into a wall or something. . . . I was running for shelter. And I'd run into windows. I've run into walls; I've run into the dresser, and it would just drive her crazy.

Look Out!

Some people called out during a nightmare. When Josh would call out, Margaret was instantly awake. Her asking him what was going on awakened him, but he went back to sleep quickly. She did not.

MARGARET: Josh will blurt out something that is very scary, like, "Look out!" And of course . . . I am, whoa, wide awake. . . . "What happened?" And he'll say, "It was just a bad, bad dream" (snoring sound). And he goes back to sleep.

Can You Go Outside and See if There's a War?

In some couples, the person having a nightmare might wake up unsure of what was dream and what was reality. So the person might awaken the part-ner on the assumption that the nightmare events were or might be real. For example, Rebecca recalled a nightmare she had about being in the midst of a war.

REBECCA: I thought there was a war outside. I was going to send him outside to look and make sure. . . . I remember waking up and being extremely scared, because I thought we were in Kosovo, and it was a war.

JOE: She woke me up and said, "Can you go outside and see if there's a war?"

Sometimes the lost sleep of someone whose partner had a nightmare occurred because the partner would awaken seeking reassurance or wanting to talk about the nightmare.

ROBERT: She'll wake up terrified. There's nights where she wakes up, and she'll wake me up, 'cause she just feels so horrible.

BARBARA: If I'm very shaken I'll wake him up . . .

HANK: She makes a comment to me a lot of times afterwards, "We were getting to a point in the dream where I had to wake myself up." . . . We'll talk for a few minutes, and then if she's done . . . I just fall back asleep.

DONNA: If I've had a bad dream . . . I normally roll over and scoot over next to him, just to kind of, I don't know, just because I want to know he's there.

Helping a Partner Escape a Nightmare and Calm Down

A person who was awakened by the heavy breathing, twitching legs, and moans of a partner having a nightmare might try to save the partner from further distress by awakening the partner.

KRISTEN: I have a recurring nightmare. . . . He'll wake me up in the middle of it, so that it doesn't go any further and kind of tell me, "Everything's all right. It's all right. It's all right."

ME: How do you know she's having a nightmare?

DAN: 'Cause she starts breathing heavy and twitching.

ME: Do either of you have nightmares that wake you up and maybe you then wake your partner up?

MARIA: Once in a while. (VIC: You have; you get 'em).

VIC: . . . I can tell when she's having one. She'll start moaning (Maria laughs). You do (chuckles). You do. You make sounds like, your breathing picks up.

MARIA: Yeah, that's right. You do sometimes wake me up. And I'm relieved that you do. . . . If it's really bad, we'll wake the other person up and just ask to be held.

In one couple, there was a fear that unless a nightmare was stopped it might lead to a heart attack.

ZACK: I'd be on the verge of the bull chasing me, and me gettin' cornered or something.

LAURA: That's when I wake him up . . .

ME: Are you afraid something will happen to him if you don't wake him up?

LAURA: . . . He was not healthy. . . . His mother died at forty-eight from a heart attack. And maybe that was in the back of my mind.

ZACK: Yeah, there was a time when we had heart problems that way.

LAURA: And when the kids were little I wasn't working, and there was a feeling of, "Oh, what would happen" if something did happen to him, because we didn't have insurance.

Some people who were awakened from nightmares by calming and reassuring words from their partner were glad of it. For example, when I asked the Vietnam veteran what his wife would do when he had one of his nightmares, he said she would:

MIKE: Just try to calm me down. And after ten, fifteen minutes you realize your not back there again. You are here. You are safe. . . . If there's thunder, she may have to peel me off the ceiling.

Janet and Carol talked about Carol's nightmares and Janet's efforts to calm and reassure her.

CAROL: A lot of times I would end up trying to yell and run . . . and you know how you can't move, and you can't really make a lot of noise. . . . Then she'd wake me up (JANET: I did), which was really nice.

JANET: Yeah, I did that if I can tell . . . something bad's happening.

CAROL: Yeah, and then I could get past it and get back to sleep. . . . (JANET: It stops the story). Then I could get away (chuckles). (JANET: Then we'd cuddle again. And she'd go back to sleep). There've been a few times . . . where I've really had to get up, and she'd get up with me, and talk or have (JANET: tea) a cup of hot chocolate or something because I couldn't . . . (JANET: She'd go back and dream the same dreams), yeah. I couldn't get out of it.

Sometimes the calming involved *not* talking about the nightmare, because the person who had the nightmare was trying not to think about the nightmare realities. Sometimes the calming involved words but not touching, because the touching could become part of a nightmare that had not quite been left behind. In an extreme case, a woman whose nightmares were connected to her having been sexually assaulted could not be touched by her husband until she had a great deal of psychological distance from a nightmare.

KRISTEN: Sometimes I actually wake myself, because I realize I'm sitting up in bed. And then I must have said something or yelled. . . . He can't reach over and hold me, because that's part of what the nightmare is about. . . . He's learned that just really terrifies me. So he from a distance reassures me that everything is fine. . . . I was attacked in college. And it's a nightmare of that experience. . . . It took a while to explain what was going on to him, but now he knows, because of the nature of the dream, for him to reach over and hold me is completely counterproductive. So he knows exactly what to do to kind of bring me down and make everything okay.

WE'VE GOTTA GET SOME SLEEP

Fear of nightmares can make a person reluctant to go to sleep, which can reduce how much sleep the partners have each night. In those cases, one challenge for the person's partner might be to find ways to get the person to sleep.

CINDY: I was afraid to go to sleep a lot of nights. I didn't know what I was gonna dream about or what I was gonna remember.

ME: So in that situation what would your husband do?

CINDY: Most of the time just hold me or get my mind off and tell me, "Whether you like it or not, you do have to sleep" (chuckles).

When person A's nightmare would disrupt the sleep of person B, what did couples do? Sometimes what made a difference was just continuing to sleep together. For many of the people I interviewed who had nightmares at some time, nightmares decreased in frequency and terror the longer the couple shared a bed. Perhaps being in the couple relationship reduced feelings of aloneness or of being vulnerably on one's own that were the foundation of some nightmares.

SUSAN: I used to have nightmares almost every night. . . . In my dream I knew I was crying out. . . . But he would wake me up. He saved me from my nightmare monsters many times. (ADAM: Umhm) And gradually over the . . . years . . . I stopped having them so regularly. And now it's a rare thing. . . . I was [always] at that one point when you're having a bad dream and you know it's a dream but you can't get out of it. Maybe that's at the point where people become more vocal, and then he would wake me up, and I was so relieved because you're kind of trapped in that realm. And I think that it was a combination of that and my life with him has been emotionally much more secure than my life ever was.

Some couples worked at eliminating whatever might set off nightmares— for example, being careful about what was watched on television, what was read, what was eaten or drunk at night, or the movies and plays they attended. Sometimes imposing something neutral between an experience that might set off nightmares and the time one went to bed helped to head off nightmares.

JOE: One of the reasons in the last couple of weeks that Rebecca's been staying up and listening to music is . . . if you don't, well, (REBECCA: I have nightmares) she was reading a book about Tre-blinka, and she's said that if she doesn't listen to music or do something relaxed before she goes to bed, she'll have nightmares about it. So she, the last couple of weeks, has been doing that just about every night. (REBECCA: Right).

THE COUPLE SYSTEM

Most of what is written in the medical, psychological, and sociological litera-ture on the issues discussed in this chapter is about individual experience. One sees a physician as an individual if one's sleep is frequently disrupted by bath-room trips. One sees a dentist if one is grinding one's teeth. Disturbing night-mares might send one to a physician for medications or to a therapist to work on the issues underlying the nightmares. But, as this chapter shows, each of these problems can be a couple concern. I do not want to overstate the extent to which they become couple issues. Some people sleep through a partner's nighttime trips to the bathroom or tooth grinding or sleep talking. And some couples have found ways to ameliorate the problems discussed in this chapter or the effects of the problems on the partner's sleeping. Still, when two people share a bed, there are a number of different ways in which what goes on with one partner during the night can become a couple experience. In the labyrinth of the mind and the privacy of body functioning, we are alone with our need to go to the bathroom, our feelings of restlessness, the sensations that drive rest-less legs, the dream activity that becomes words spoken in our sleep, the grind-ing of our teeth, and our nightmares. But if we share a bed, all these private matters can become matters for a partner to deal with as well.

THIRTEEN

Snoring and Sleep Apnea

SNORING

THE FILM IMAGE of smiling newlyweds joyously beginning their sweet and loving future leaves out that it is likely that if the couple stays together long enough one of them will have years of sleep difficulty because the other snores. According to the people I interviewed, snoring is one of the most common sources of frustration in couple sleeping. A partner's snoring can make it impossible to go to sleep and can wake one repeatedly each night. Some snorers can achieve loudness levels that exceed pollution control agency standards for maximum acceptable outdoor nighttime noise (Wilson et al., 1999).

Some people I interviewed said that they were bothered by a partner's snoring for a few weeks and then they were not. It may be that they accommodated to the snoring the way many people accommodate to recurrent noises from the household heating system, passing traffic, or airplanes overhead. But consistent with a clinical literature (Armstrong, Wallace, & Marais, 1999; Ulfberg, Carter, Talback, & Edling, 2000) some people whose partner snored said that they could not get used to it and could not tune it out. They talked about waking each morning feeling tired, going through the day sleepy, inefficient, error and accident prone, and unable to think very clearly because their partner's snoring so disturbed their sleep.

> BARBARA: I remember thinking when we were first married, "Am I ever gonna be able to sleep?"

As was mentioned in chapter 1, many people only knew they snored because their partner had told them they did. Snoring can be thought of as a "disease of listeners" in that the reports of bedmates and others drive the presentation of snoring as a medical problem to be treated (Schmaling & Afari, 2000). In my interviews, some people who were told they snored found it hard to believe. They might even deny that they did it. A snorer's doubt and denial could add to the frustration of the partner whose sleep was disrupted by the snoring.

> MADELINE: What's funny to me is I'll point it out. Like I'll wake him up sometimes . . . and I'll say, "You're snoring," and he'll deny it. . . . "I just went to sleep. . . . You've been snoring the last two minutes." . . . That's what's frustrating is that you deny it.

So for a few couples it was one of the challenges of dealing with snoring that one partner did not know he snored (and it is more often a "he" who snores—Lugaresi, Cirignotta, & Montagna, 1989; National Sleep Foundation, 2002) and even doubted the other's accounts of the snoring. It is difficult for a snorer to make changes when he thinks there is nothing to change. What is a partner to do if the snorer denies snoring? Some people had threatened to use a tape recorder to provide concrete evidence of a partner's snoring. But only one had actually done so.

> KAREN: I even went so far as to put on a tape recorder one night, and recorded him snoring. . . . The next afternoon I said, "I got something I want you to listen to." And he just could not believe that was him. . . . (RICHARD: I don't know who slept with her that night, but it wasn't me) (Karen laughs). He insisted it wasn't him. Total denial.

A few snorers came to accept that they snored when on a camping or fishing trip with friends because they were then told by their friends what they had been told by their partner—that they snored loudly.

Whether a snorer accepts that he or she snores, a partner whose sleep is disturbed by the snoring will try to cope. Coping is easier if the snorer accepts that he or she snores because then there are more possibilities for dealing with the snoring. In any case, what did the people who I interviewed say about how they tried to cope with the snoring? What follows is a list of approaches to snoring that at least a few snorers or partners of snorers said they found helpful.

IF THE SNORER LOSES WEIGHT

As people put on weight they are more likely to snore and to snore loudly (Lugaresi, Cirignotta, & Montagna, 1989; Wilson et al., 1999). Some interviewees said that if the snorer gained weight the snoring became worse, and if the snorer lost weight that reduced or eliminated the snoring.

MONICA: I'm sure his snoring has gotten worse because he's gained weight.

ME: Do either of you snore?

CHERYL: He used to, and he lost sixty pounds when he became diabetic, and he doesn't really snore anymore.

Although Cheryl's husband no longer snored after losing sixty pounds, some snorers said that, for them, stopping snoring was a matter of losing only a few pounds. When Natalie would tell John that his snoring had become worse, it was usually that his weight had gone above 220 pounds. He did not find it terribly difficult to drop the few extra pounds.

IF THE SNORER REDUCES ALCOHOL INTAKE

Consistent with the clinical literature (Lugaresi, Cirignotta, & Montagna, 1989), some people said that they snored more when they drank alcohol, or more alcohol than usual.

SARAH: If we have gone out for a couple of drinks, he snores.

To deal with alcohol related snoring, the obvious approach to reducing or eliminating the snoring would be for the snorer to give up alcohol. One man periodically gave up alcohol, and each time he did, his snoring abated.

MONICA: He snores really bad, and it's gotten worse the older we get, and last night was a horrendous night.... He had a union meeting, and I figure they had beer at it, 'cause I could kind of smell it when he came home, and he snored so bad last night I couldn't fall asleep. And then when I finally did I kept getting woken up by his loud snoring.... When he's given up beer the few times he has, he snores a lot less.

TREAT COLD, SINUS, AND ALLERGY SYMPTOMS

Some people said that they only snored when they had colds, sinus infections, or allergy problems, or when they had those problems they snored most loudly. So some snorers took a decongestant or antihistamine to try to clear breathing passages.

PAM: I had chronic sinus infection, and had the operation to have my septum cleared out . . . but it didn't help.

NANCY: She still snored a lot after that, but I think you're on some kind of nasal medication now.

PAM: Yeah, I started taking a nasal medication now, so it's not as bad.

NANCY: I haven't been interrupted in weeks.

Getting to Sleep First

Some people said that they could sleep through a partner's snoring provided they fell asleep before the partner's snoring began.

SUSAN: If I fall asleep before he starts snoring, it's okay. I won't wake up. But if he starts snoring and I haven't fallen asleep yet, you might as well be hittin' a piece of metal with a ball peen hammer right behind my head. I just can't fall asleep then.

Some people tried to get to sleep first when they knew their partner's snoring was likely to be more intense. For example, Susan tried to get to sleep first when Adam had consumed alcohol.

SUSAN: If he has a few beers forget about it, he's gonna be snoring all night. . . . He'll go a couple weeks without snoring, and then if he has a couple glasses of wine with dinner and a couple of beers later on then that night I know he's gonna snore. So I try to (laughing) go to sleep before him.

Nudging or Rolling the Snorer Over

Waking a snorer might stop the snoring long enough for the partner to get to sleep or might cause the snorer to shift position in a way that stops the snoring for a while.

DONNA: I normally just kind of wake him up enough that he stops.

ME: You push him with your hand?

DONNA: Yeah. I'm gentle about it. I just kind of gently, or I'll just touch him, and he wakes up enough he stops. I roll over and try to quickly fall asleep . . .

ME: Do you wake up when she gives you a push?

JEFF: Half the time I don't know that she's doing it, unless she wakes me up and she's talking to me. . . . Then there's times that she snores. A lot of times it'll just be a . . . little nudge. And that gets me to stop. Well, it doesn't get her to stop (chuckles), and I have to give her a good jab sometimes.

Get Off Your Back

Consistent with the clinical literature (Lugaresi, Cirignotta, & Montagna, 1989), some people said that snoring was more likely to go on and be intense when the snorer was sleeping on his or her back. So if a partner could get the snorer to roll onto his or her side, that stopped or reduced the snoring.

ME: What do you do when he snores?

SARAH: I nudge him, so he turns over. I tell him to turn over.

ME: He mostly snores when he's on his back?

SARAH: Yep.

ME: So you get him on his side.

SARAH: Yeah.

Interfering with the Snorer's Breathing

Maybe it was as much an expression of exasperation and anger as an attempt to control partner snoring, but some people said that interfering with the partner's breathing would temporarily stop the snoring.

LIZ: Every once in a while I'll pinch his nose (laughing) and cover his mouth when he's bugging me with that snoring.

Talking to the Snorer

Angela said that sometimes a few words to Eric, even if they did not awaken him, could be enough to stop his snoring.

ANGELA: All I can focus on is that noise, and it annoys me; it really frustrates me. What I'll do is, "Eric, you're making," because . . . he knows he does it, 'cause he's woken up from that noise. And he'll ask me, "Did I just do that?" "Yup," and so basically I just will try . . . to . . . have him roll over on his side. . . . So he'll try to do that for just a few minutes, and then he'll end up rolling back on his back. And then it'll start again. . . . I would say maybe five out of the seven nights of the week, I can sleep with him. If he's super, super, super tired, those are the nights that I can't. That's when he doesn't respond to my, "Eric, you're making the noise" . . .

ME: What do you do when she says that?

ERIC: . . . I just kind of do like (chuckling) the comedians say, "Note to self (Angela and I laugh); I'm breathing heavy." . . . Then I just try to concentrate on . . . breathing where I'm not making the noise.

Breathe Right Strips

Some couples had tried Breathe Right Strips on the snorer's nose. Although some research shows that nasal strips do not alleviate snoring (Michaelson & Mair, 2004), Breathe Right (2005), which manufactures nasal strips, claims that the strips help in some instances to control snoring. Consistent with the Breathe Right claim, the couples I interviewed reported mixed results, with some feeling that the strips helped.

CYNTHIA: He will use [the Breathe Right Strips] once in a while, and they do help somewhat but not a huge difference.

SUSAN: Those strips work for him. . . . So if I can wake him up enough . . . he'll put one on, grumble about it the whole time, but he'll do it (laughs).

Ear Plugs

Some people said that ear plugs helped them sleep through a partner's snoring.

SUSAN: I have a series of things that I do now including keeping my military ear plugs next to the bed 'cause if it gets really bad and I lay there and I think I'm gonna suffocate him if he doesn't stop (chuckles), I put the ear plugs in.

Ear plugs did not necessarily eliminate all problems with a partner's snoring, but especially if combined with other things, ear plugs helped some people.

NATALIE: The hard thing for me was he sometimes snores (JOHN: I snore. That's right). . . . And I sleep with ear plugs. . . .

ME: Do you hear him through the ear plugs?

NATALIE: Yes. . . . Usually I'll put a pillow over my ears.

Going to Another Room to Sleep

A few couples said that the partner of the snorer might leave to sleep on the living room couch, a guest room bed, or a bed that was a child's until the child grew up and moved out, what Hislop and Arber (2003a) call a "contingency relocation." Among the couples I interviewed, a temporary move to another bed was reserved for nights when the snoring was especially annoying, when the snorer had a cold, sinus trouble, or allergy attack that was likely to bring on or intensify the snoring, or when the partner of the snorer was especially in need of a good night's sleep.

> SHARON: If I feel like I'm losin' that much sleep, I'll sleep alone for a night or two and catch up. But we married each other for better or worse, and that's just part of the "worse" is the snoring, I guess.

> PETE: I'll usually wake up if she leaves the bedroom, and I'll know she's gone. . . . In the morning, I'll ask her, "You left the bed last night again." And she'll say, "You're snorin' so darn loud you're shakin' the windows." "Okay, okay. That's fine." It doesn't hurt my feelings.

Surgery

Snoring problems may be reduced or eliminated surgically (Armstrong, Wallace, & Marais, 1999), and a few couples I interviewed had investigated such surgery. But nobody I interviewed had actually had surgery. Sarah knew about the surgery and thought Nick should have it to control or eliminate his snoring. He did not disagree, though at the time of the interview he had not had the surgery. Martha, who talked about her struggles to deal with Al's snoring (hitting him, stuffing Kleenex in her ears), was exasperated that he had not gone for surgery for his snoring. My impression is that surgery is a step that snorers are very reluctant to take.

SLEEP APNEA

Sleep apnea is a temporary cessation of breathing during sleep. It might involve skipping only a single breath, but often it is a suspension of breathing for many seconds, perhaps even more than a minute. In extreme cases, there might be dozens of apnea episodes during each hour of sleep. Almost all the apnea that people I interviewed described involved a time of not breathing that ended with an unusually loud snoring, choking, explosive, or sucking-in sound. According to the National Sleep Foundation (2005), sleep apnea affects roughly five percent of the adults in North America. It is potentially life threatening. And it may make it almost impossible for a partner to get a good night's sleep.

Consistent with the clinical literature (Victor, 1999), some people I interviewed who had sleep apnea were unaware of it until their partner told them about it. In fact, a clinician may have to question the bedmate of someone with sleep apnea in order to learn about the presence and severity of it (Bonekat & Krumpe, 1990). In my interviews, people said that sleep apnea seemed almost always to go on during snoring. Consistent with the sleep medicine literature (Aldrich, 1999, ch. 13; Dancey et al., 2003; Victor, 1999; Ware, McBrayer, & Scott, 2000), the people I interviewed who said they had sleep apnea were likely to be overweight, older, male, and back sleepers.

Some interviewees said that they could sleep through a partner's episodes of sleep apnea. But others had their sleep disrupted by their partner's apnea (Ashtyani & Hutter, 2003; Beninati, Harris, Herold, & Shepard, 1999). They might have trouble falling asleep because of the apnea, or might not be able to sleep through some of the episodes. Their sleep might be undermined by the loud noises at the end of each episode of sleep apnea or by the loud snoring that is common with apnea (Aldrich, 1999, p. 204). Also, they might not be able to sleep because they were alert to the possibility that the partner would not resume breathing.

> MICHELLE: I listen to him sometimes. And sometimes he doesn't inhale (laughing), and I, "Oh, come on! Take a deep breath!" (laughing) I don't know if it's sleep apnea or what, or he just has irregular breathing, but sometimes I think, "Is he gonna take another breath? Come on!" Then he goes (loud snorting sound), and I "Okay." (laughs)

It is easy to understand why a partner's cessation of breathing might keep one awake, or awaken one, and be alarming. "Will he ever start breathing again? Should I call 9-1-1 or start CPR? If he goes too long without oxygen will there be brain damage? Will he have a heart attack?" If the partner of someone with sleep apnea knows the facts about sleep apnea he or she knows that it taxes the cardiovascular system so much that it can lead to heart attack or stroke (Aldrich, 1999, pp. 220–221).

The end of an apnea episode typically involves the person having the episode waking up enough to start breathing. The repeated awakening, perhaps dozens of times per hour, means that the person is sleep deprived even if in bed for a normal amount of time. The person will awaken in the morning feeling very tired and might go through the day feeling irritable and depressed. Sleep apnea makes one more accident prone (Aldrich, 1999, p. 220; Barbe et al., 1998; Engleman, Hirst, & Douglas, 1997) and may mean that one will feel drowsy at work. It means that one may have difficulty concentrating, learning new tasks, or performing monotonous tasks at work (Ulfberg, Carter, Talback, & Edling, 1996). It also means that one may fall asleep at inopportune times—for example, while driving (Horstmann et al., 2000; Shiomi et al., 2002), while talking to someone face to face, while at work, or while talking on the phone.

GETTING THE PARTNER BREATHING AGAIN

Some people whose partner had sleep apnea said that they would lie awake tensely during an apnea episode waiting for the partner to resume breathing. They might count the seconds, with a plan that if more than some specific amount of time passed, they would awaken the partner. Some people said that they elbowed, poked, or nudged a partner during a sleep apnea episode to get the partner breathing again. A person who is not aware that he has apnea or who does not regard apnea as a problem might not be grateful to be elbowed.

> KRISTEN: He . . . has sleep apnea. So I will elbow him to get him to breathe again . . .
>
> ME: So you'll be asleep and you'll wake up because you know he's missed a breath?
>
> KRISTEN: Yeah. Yep.
>
> ME: Do you know when she elbows you that she thinks you've stopped breathing?
>
> DAN: Not if I'm sleeping. But I do when I'm awake. I just don't breathe. (KRISTEN: Yeah). And (laughing) obviously I have enough air. . . . Why do I need to breathe constantly if I have enough? But I don't notice it. We'll be laying in bed, and I won't be asleep yet, and she'll nudge me and say, "Breathe." (Kristen chuckles) And I'll take a breath. . . . Or I'll be watching TV and she'll be rubbing my back, and she'll have to tell me to exhale. It's not like I'm going to forget to exhale. I just haven't done it yet. I hold my breath all the time. . . . I don't see the problem.
>
> KRISTEN: It's just uncomfortable for me to know that you're laying there not breathing. It's a concern. . . . I do wake up when he's not breathing. . . . Many times a night.

According to the people I interviewed, elbowing, poking, nudging, or other efforts to restart a partner's breathing seemed generally to help for the moment.

> ME: When you wake up and have a sense he hasn't breathed, what do you do?
>
> KAREN: . . . Elbow, nudge, roll over (laughs).
>
> RICHARD: So far that's worked. I keep coming back.
>
> ME: Do you know when she does it?
>
> RICHARD: I may know that she does it, but I guess that I've always thought it was because I was snoring. . . . But she's mentioned to me that that's why she would shake me, 'cause I'd stop breathing and she'd get scared.

TREATMENT FOR SLEEP APNEA

Some people with a partner who had sleep apnea were so concerned about the partner's health and sleep deprivation (and perhaps their own sleep deprivation) that they urged the partner to seek medical evaluation. Motivating a partner with sleep apnea to seek treatment is not simple, because just as with snoring, people with sleep apnea may deny or minimize their problem (Engleman, Hirst, & Douglas, 1997). But sometimes a partner's urging or the problems the sleep apnea was creating moved a person with sleep apnea to seek medical help. In a time of managed care, when health maintenance organizations and insurers are under pressure to limit medical expenditures, a physician might take a wait-and-see attitude if the person with apnea seemed to get a reasonable amount of sleep most nights.

> JIM: Whenever I've talked to a doctor it's always been: When it just starts disrupting your work and your actual day-to-day life, then you should come see me. If it's an occasional thing where you feel drowsy maybe once a week, then he said it wasn't that big of a deal.

A physician who thought the sleep apnea was serious would typically refer the person to a sleep clinic. The problem would be deemed serious if the person was obviously sleep deprived most days or if the person had a health problem that, in conjunction with sleep apnea, could be life threatening. For example, a person with heart disease who also had sleep apnea would typically earn an immediate referral to a sleep clinic.

KAREN: What brought it to a head was after his heart surgery. You know, the stopping and the starting and everything, so at one of his checkups I said, "This is really a problem, and isn't this creating more stress for his heart?" "Oh, yeah." And it was a real short time they had him in the sleep study, real, real short time. I hear of people having two, three, six months waits. Unun. No. He was in like . . . maybe within four days.

There are several thousand clinics in the United States that specialize in diagnosing and treating sleep disorders (Shariq, 2005). Sleep clinics address a wide range of sleep problems, including snoring, insomnia, restless legs, sleepwalking, and sleep that is not restorative. But here I focus on sleep clinics as places for treating sleep apnea because sleep apnea is almost the only problem that interviewees talked about with regard to seeking sleep clinic help.

Jack, who had gone through a sleep clinic evaluation, had tried out several different approaches to his sleep apnea problems suggested by the clinic staff, including sleeping with a C-PAP (Continuous Positive Airway Pressure) machine and mask.

JACK: I went to a sleep clinic, and I tried a C-PAP machine and a Bi-PAP [Bi-Level Positive Airway Pressure] machine, then a dental appliance. I was working with my pulmonologist.

Sometimes a clinic evaluation led to the conclusion that a person's sleep apnea problems were real for the person and the person's partner but not so severe as to call for radical intervention.

WALT: I went through an all night study . . . and they did an evaluation and put all the sensors on and then told you to go to sleep. . . . They evaluate the REM rates. . . . They said that, "Yeah, it's not normal." It's not critical or anything but.

Two people who had gone to a sleep clinic had radically changed their sleep routines in accordance with clinic recommendations. That did not mean they necessarily felt good about the clinic. Both of them had strong reservations about the adequacy of a clinic sleep study done in very artificial circumstances. Richard had reservations, but still he complied with the clinic recommendation to sleep with a C-PAP machine and mask.

RICHARD: I snore very loudly. . . . They claimed that I was interrupting my sleep sixty times an hour. . . . It doesn't seem like that, but when they do those type of studies you're not in your own bed. . . .

You tend to be uncomfortable in a strange environment, so under normal circumstances in my own bed, if I'd been tested there, it probably would have been less. But even so they've determined that I wasn't getting good sleep.

ME: After that study did they treat you in any way?

RICHARD: I have a mask that I wear. (KAREN: A C-PAP machine). A C-PAP machine.

ME: Does that help?

RICHARD: Yeah.

Ed and Cindy, in contrast to Richard, were enthusiastic about Ed's clinic experience. Ed started sleeping with a C-PAP machine after a sleep clinic evaluation. Consistent with research reports that C-PAP machines can be helpful (Montserrat et al., 2001; Sin, Mayers, Man, & Pawluk, 2002), the machine helped him, as it did Richard, to sleep better and more safely. And also, consistent with the findings of research by Parish and Lyng (2003), Ed's use of a C-PAP machine improved Cindy's sleep.

ED: Four years ago I . . . went in because I was constantly snoring, and that was really driving her up a creek. So I'm on a C-PAP machine, and so that took care of the snoring . . .

CINDY: Snoring wasn't the only thing keeping me awake, 'cause what he would do is snore and then he'd have the periods where he didn't breathe, the sleep apnea attack . . . and I'd be going (plaintively:), "Breathe, please." . . . I said over and over again, "You have to go to the doctor and tell him that your breathing is stopping." So he finally went, and they recorded how many times he quit breathing, because they kept him overnight . . . how many times he moved around and kicked his legs and got rid of his blankets, and the whole bit. And now if he tries to sleep without that thing, I miss the kind of white noise even, because I'm just so used to it.

It seems rather a paradox that for some couples, moving through what seemed a very unnatural clinical evaluation in a sleep lab to adopting wearing a very unnatural mask markedly improved the very natural process of sleeping. But another way to think about it is that the sleep clinics fight very unnatural fire (sedentary living, rich diets, and so on) with very unnatural fire (the evaluations and masks) in order to counteract the unnatural conditions that undermine sleeping.

A few people with sleep apnea were advised to have surgery to alter their breathing passage. Nobody I interviewed had gone through the surgery, but in every case where someone was using C-PAP or similar equipment, the interviewee said that the equipment helped both partners to sleep better. It is consistent with the literature on C-PAP treatment that for patients who continue to use C-PAP equipment, sleeping generally improves (McFadyen et al., 2001). The literature further suggests that use of C-PAP equipment improves the marital relationship of the user (McFadyen et al., 2001) and the sleeping of the user's partner (McArdle et al., 2001; Parish & Lyng, 2003). Sleeping with a C-PAP mask also tends to improve the driving of people with sleep apnea (Horstmann et al., 2000).

THE COUPLE SYSTEM

For many couples, snoring became an important part of the couple system in that it affected the partner's sleep. It may influence when the two partners go to sleep, what they do during sleep, how they interact during sleep, how well they sleep, and how they function when awake. Some partners of snorers had learned a lot about dealing with snoring—how to tune it out, when and how to touch or poke the partner, and so on. But snoring was relatively intractable in that despite considerable time, learning, and effort, there were still quite a few couples who experienced snoring as a problem.

With sleep apnea, it is also clear how interdependent people who share a bed are. Their systemic connection means that one's sleeping problem can easily become the other's, and that by sharing a bed, a person with a life threatening sleep problem may receive genuine help in fighting the problem. People may have started out sharing a bed because of sexual attraction, the desire to have somebody to touch and cuddle, the desire for safety from the dangers of the world, and many other reasons that have nothing to do with facing physical health problems. But the reality is that by starting out on the journey of sharing a bed for the reasons they did, they reached a point where the bed sharing addressed and might help with serious health problems that they had not anticipated. Katz (1999, pp. 71–89) has written about "riders," things that go along with decisions but that were not at all anticipated when the decisions were made. I think the experience of sleep apnea and the couple efforts to deal with it were "riders" to the couple decision to start sharing a bed. The sleep apnea was an unfortunate "rider," but the fact that the partner of the person with sleep apnea could be a force for identifying the problem and getting the person help was a very fortunate rider.

FOURTEEN

Safety, Intimacy, and Why Couples Sleep Together

FOR SOME PEOPLE, sharing a bed was partly about safety. For example, some said that when their partner was away they felt more vulnerable. The creaking sound in the hallway and the strange scraping noise in the backyard were more worrisome when there was nobody in bed to turn to for help.

> MICHELLE: [When I'm home alone] I just hear more things. If I'm spooked, I'll actually keep my glasses on.
>
> TONY: Yeah, I come home quite often [after she's fallen asleep] and take her glasses off.
>
> MICHELLE: Yeah. Because if I'm spooked in the house, then I want to be able to open my eyes and see what's going on, and so I won't take my glasses off. So if he comes home and my glasses are on, then that's a signal that I was spooked when I went to bed. That and every light in the house being on.

> MONICA: Because we're next to the woods, it'd be really easy for somebody to come in our house. And alls they gotta do is break the window in the back door down there. Yeah, when he's gone, I always am a little bit on edge.

Nightmares were less terrifying, less overwhelming, or could be distanced more easily when one could awaken to find the partner there.

> EMMA: I remember times when I'd wake up by myself and have a bad dream. . . . [I'd be like] a little kid scared of what's under my bed or

what's in the closet. But I do feel a lot safer and a lot more comfortable when he's here when I do wake up with bad dreams.

When the partner was away, some women were so apprehensive about being home alone that they had friends or relatives come to sleep with them or they stayed the night with friends or relatives.

REBECCA: I told him after [his stint] with the National Guard, "I'm not doing this again." . . . When he goes on his two weeks, I try to spend as much of the time as I possibly can at my parents. I don't like it when he's gone.

LINDA: I don't like to be by myself, especially at night. . . . When we were first married . . . I would force myself to stay awake so late if he was gone, and I would have every light on, and when you would go on your fishing trips . . . I'd have to make sure that no one was anywhere in the house. And I'd walk the house, and look under every bed and look into every closet. . . . Many times I'd have a friend sleep over. . . . On occasion I would go over to my parents, and stay over there.

Although one man also said he felt more vulnerable when his wife was away, he did not seem to feel as vulnerable as she did when he was away. It seemed typical that, in heterosexual couples, if someone felt vulnerable or more vulnerable sleeping alone, it was the woman.

ME: How is it different when you're sleeping by yourself?

MARIA: Oh, I don't like it at all. It's really hard. Some of it is just fear of someone breaking in. And so I never really sleep very well when he's gone. I always have a phone by my side. . . .

ME: So you feel safer when he's around.

MARIA: Yeah. It's amazing. I take it for granted when he's there. I just feel safe, and it's just wonderful. When he's not there it's just very different. . . . What's it like for you?

VIC: . . . I . . . get kind of lonely at night. But . . . I don't feel too threatened, when I'm alone, by external things. It's more a worry that I'm gonna have worries and not be able to sleep. But not so much external stuff, like somebody breaking into the house.

JUST THE PROXIMITY THAT HE'S RIGHT THERE IS VERY COMFORTING

When people talked about the companionship or the positives of sharing a bed, security and safety were often mentioned, more by women than men.

> ME: Do you feel safer with him in bed with you?
>
> MADELINE: Umhm. Umhm. Yeah (chuckling), even though he might not be responsive. . . . We have a cottage up [north]. And a lot of times I'll go up there myself. And my comfort level is higher when you're there. . . .
>
> ME: Do you feel safer with her in bed?
>
> JIM: I never really thought about it (chuckles). I feel safe, probably by myself as much as with her.

Why do more women than men speak of feeling safe when the partner is in bed with them? In most couples, the man was bigger and more muscular than the woman. The only people who spoke of themselves as fighters were men. In a world where some men attack women, quite a few women said that they felt vulnerable. One woman who had once been sexually assaulted talked about feeling safer at home with her husband present.

> MICHELLE: I don't think I would feel as safe if I were in a different room or a different bed. Just the proximity that he's right there is very comforting. . . . I don't think men in general have this chronic sense of being at risk, or having this vulnerability about them. But I've got this experience in my past, so I'm acutely aware of that's probably what this stems from, but I don't know if other women who have not had this experience feel this way, but I was alone when this happened, and I know how inadequately prepared I was to deal with it. So just to have another person on my behalf is incredibly protective. It makes me feel *so* much more comfortable, and so much more capable of dealing with this if this were to happen again. . . . There is that . . . vulnerability that he's able to set aside for me, that he's able to make go away. So that when I climb in bed with him, I feel completely . . . surrounded, completely protected, that nothing's going to happen. It's a good feeling.

Quite a few heterosexual couples had stories of the woman feeling concerned by a sound in the night, waking the man, and the man going to investigate.

CHARLES: Noises that are out of the ordinary ... will wake me up. . . .

ME: If you hear a sound that worries you do you wake him?

LINDA: Yeah, (CHARLES: Yeah) yeah, yeah.

ME: Can you get him to do something about the noise?

LINDA: Sometimes. I have to really push him.

CHARLES: Well, yeah, but it's not because I'm too tired. It's because there's nobody in the house.

LINDA: But I want to know.

CHARLES: We have a security system in our house, and she thinks she hears somebody in the house.

LINDA: It's for peace of mind, 'cause then all I do is I lay there and then all of a sudden wheels start turning, and ... that little noise all of a sudden becomes bigger and bigger, and then I can't go back to sleep.

I FEEL BETTER KNOWING THAT SHE FEELS BETTER THAT I AM HERE

Some men felt good about being relied on for safety. They felt it was part of their role as a man, or it made them feel more confident and competent to have a partner turn to them for safety.

ME: How do you feel about being relied on?

JOE: . . . I like the fact that she does think that way about me, and I guess in a way that's kind of the way I am. . . . I'd want to make sure that she doesn't get hurt. It's fine with me, and actually I guess I kind of like somebody looking up to me and knowing that I do have the capability of providing that security.

ROBERT: It gives me a better feeling knowing that if something did happen and somebody did need to go look in the closet to make sure there was no monster in there just waiting to come out and kill us (Emma giggles), you know what I mean? That I feel better knowing that she feels better that I can be here.

In accepting the role as protector, some men were clear that they would be dangerous to anyone who broke into the house.

ME: Do you feel kind of protective of her?

BEN: Yeah, in the sense that I'd hate for somebody to break into our house, 'cause they'd get my whole wrath (Caroline laughs).

But William said that he was not competent to deal with a real threat. For him, being relied on for safety was absurd.

> WILLIAM: The thing that gets me is, in the middle of the night, when you wake up and you say, you hear, (sounding frightened:) "What's that noise?" (normal voice:) . . . I don't know, and I don't care, because I'm too tired and if it's bad enough, they're gonna come and kill us anyway, so what the heck. What am I supposed to do?

WHEN WE ARE APART, WE STILL TALK

Sometimes a couple sleeps apart because of the demands of a job, obligations to family-of-origin, a stay in the hospital, or something else. When that happens, couples act in ways that illuminate their usual pattern of sharing a bed.

When one of the partners was out of town, many couples said that they talked to each other over the phone. In fact, the talk often occurred around the time the couple would usually talk as part of their bedtime routine. So the bedtime talking routine was maintained.

> MARIA: If we are apart, I think we almost always talk, like late at night, right before we fall asleep, so that helps some.
>
> ME: How does that help?
>
> MARIA: Mm, it's comforting just to know that the other person's thinking about you.
>
> ME: Do you feel like your interactions on the phone are pretty congruent with what they would be if you were together?
>
> VIC: Yeah, it's kind of a daily wrap up sort of thing. And wish her a good night's rest and just peace and that I'm thinkin' about her. That's the reason I call you before you go to bed, because I know you get worried (MARIA: If you're camping or something. Then I know you're safe), and I want to be there for you in that way.

I'll Sleep in Her Spot

With the partner out of town, some people slept in the spot in the bed that the person who was out of town usually slept. Why might that be? Some people found sleeping alone to be intensely lonely and used pillows or children to try to reduce the loneliness of occupying a bed alone.

ME: I gather you've had times when you've slept apart, because he had work (WILLIAM: Yeah) out of town or meetings or something (JULIA: Yeah). How does that affect your sleeping, when you're sleeping apart?

JULIA: I turn his pillow the long way, so it's like a body.... [When] we used to have the kids, I would have the kids sleep with me.... Our daughter has, probably until a couple of years ago, if Dad would be out of town, she would sleep with me, 'cause I don't like it. See my mom is like twenty years older than me ... and my dad died in 1997, and so I don't want to, she hates being a widow, and I don't want to, I don't even want to think about that. I don't like it. It's very lonely, and I see her, and I just, "Oh, I just don't like it." And I don't like to sleep [alone]. I don't like it.

Nancy called me the morning after my interview with her and Pam to tell me that she had forgotten to say that when Pam is out of town, she sleeps on Pam's side of the bed. She said she does so because then she can smell Pam's odor and because it is comforting to have Pam's spot in the bed. Also, Pam sleeps on an inside wall, and there's comfort and security for Nancy in sleeping on the inside wall when she is alone.

I Don't Seem to Sleep as Well as I Do When He's Home

Some people said that it was much more difficult to get to sleep when the partner was away, to stay asleep, or to get high quality sleep. The partner was so central to the routines of getting to sleep and staying asleep and to the feelings of connection and security that were foundational to falling asleep and sleeping well.

AL: It doesn't bother me sleeping alone when she is in the house, but when she is gone, then it definitely affects me sleeping. It takes me longer to fall asleep, and I am more restless.... Something isn't right. You're missing part of something.

MARTHA: It's comfort knowing that you're there though.

AL: Yeah. Yeah. It's a comfort.

MARTHA: It's like when he's up at the lake and I'm here.... I feel very uncomfortable when he's gone. More so when he's hunting, 'cause then I'm really worried. But, yeah, it's comfort, it's part of the partnership, it's part of the deal. Yeah. And thirty-four years is a long time.

ME: Do you sleep better or less well when he's out of town?

CYNTHIA: I don't think I get as good a quality of sleep. I don't seem to sleep as deep as I do when he's home.

DONNA: The few times that he's gone away for a night or a weekend or whatever, I sometimes have trouble falling asleep.

One sign that the ordinary bedtime routine is part of what is missed and that the ordinary bedtime routine gets people to bed is that, as some people expressed, with their partners away, the people I interviewed went to bed quite late. When the partner is home, in their ordinary routine are all the reminders and cues about taking the path to bed, including the partner's words about it being time to get to bed.

ME: Do you remember how it was sleeping with him out of the house and not in bed?

MICHELLE: I tended to stay up until about three in the morning. . . . I could sit and read, I could sit and watch cable TV, I could sit on the internet. There was no restrictions on my time, and he wasn't saying, "It's time to go to bed."

ANGELA: On those days when he's gone, it takes me longer to fall asleep because I miss him being there. I miss going to bed with him. . . .

ME: What do you miss? What isn't there?

ANGELA: That regular routine that we've gotten to know. That comfort level that, yep, he's here with me, he's safe, we're together, that type of thing. I miss him holding me.

When the partner was away, some people made accommodations to deal with what the partner ordinarily provided. One thing the partner provided was warmth, so in colder weather when the partner was away and it was difficult to get the bed warm enough, a person might wear warmer clothing to bed to provide the warmth the partner would ordinarily provide.

ME: You must have developed a sleep routine for the days he was absent.

DIANA: Yeah, I get cold, and so I have sweatpants. I sleep in sweatpants, where I just sleep in a t-shirt when he's home. But when he's gone I sleep in usually a sweatshirt and sweatpants. Socks in the winter. And that helps keep me warm. . . . It was hard for me to sleep with him out of town.

As was mentioned above in this chapter, some people were not comfortable sleeping alone when the partner was out of town and would bring a child or friend to bed with them.

ME: When he was [away] you had trouble falling asleep?

LINDA: Yeah. My daughter slept with me. . . . I feel more comfortable if I've got somebody in there with me.

ME: Some people I've interviewed find body pillows or . . .

LINDA: I tried that too . . . before [our daughter], on the nights when I would stay up. I would actually take a pillow kind of like to create like a person . . . right next to me. . . .

ME: Did it help at all to have the pillows there?

LINDA: A little, but still it was hard to go to sleep, and of course I'd hear every little noise.

Filling the void when the partner was gone could involve having controllable and distracting human sounds in the house and changing the rules for what the family dog was allowed to do. Sharon kept the television set on all night and sometimes brought the dog to bed to fill the void when Pete was in the hospital.

SHARON: He'd be in the hospital [and] I was lonely, so I would always have the t-, isn't that stupid? I would have the TV on all night. I wouldn't turn it off all night. I had to have it on all night. I don't know why. . . . The closet had to be shut. . . . And then the dog, sometimes, I'd even let the dog come in the bed.

WHY SLEEP TOGETHER?

With all the couple sleep problems discussed in this book it is not obvious why people choose to sleep together. Yes, many people value the cuddling, warmth, the security, the talk, and the sex. And, yes, many people find it difficult to sleep apart from their partner. But there are all those problems, and, consistent with the clinical literature (Akerstedt, Knutsson, et al., 2002), some people were clear that they would get more and better sleep if they slept alone. But almost everybody I interviewed continued to sleep with their partner. Why?

SLEEPING BETTER TOGETHER

Some people said they slept better when they were with their partner, even people who also complained that their partner disrupted their sleep by snoring, tossing and turning, stealing covers, and so on. Margaret was sometimes awakened abruptly by Josh yelling warnings in his sleep. Susan is quoted earlier in this book discussing Adam's snoring and other issues that had made it challenging for them to share a bed. But both Margaret and Susan insisted that they slept better when with their partner.

> MARGARET: I sleep better with him than without him. . . . I think I'm more secure knowing that he's there.
>
> ME: Secure from?
>
> MARGARET: If anything happens in the house, he'll get up (chuckles) and take care of it. If the dogs have to go out, Josh gets up. And when I'm by myself it's my awesome responsibility if something happens.
>
> SUSAN: I don't like that idea of sleeping in a hotel by myself. . . . It always takes me a really long time to fall asleep. . . . I'm up until three in the morning watching the television, trying to fall asleep, or staring at the ceiling, and it just makes me crazy. I don't like it. I can fall asleep in a hotel if we're together, but when I'm by myself, the older I get the less I like it.

Why would people sleep better with their partner if the partner's snoring, tossing and turning, and so on make it hard for them to sleep? Wouldn't they sleep better in a separate bed?

It's Unthinkable to Sleep Apart

Some people who had trouble sleeping with their partner found it hard to answer my questions about why they continued to sleep with their partner. For some, sharing a bed seemed so basic, so much about matters deep in the psyche, and so much taken for granted that they could hardly find words to explain why they shared a bed. It is as though they were asked why they kept on breathing. "Breathing? I don't think about it. I just do it." As Brad said when I asked about the possibility of not sharing a bed with his wife, "It would be just, it wouldn't be natural."

He, like quite a few others, seemed taken aback by my asking why he thought it was best for him and his partner to share a bed. He struggled to find words. Some people had to think for a few seconds before they could answer the question. It was a question for which often there was not a tip-of-the-tongue answer. But then when people did answer questions about why they continued to share a bed and what the advantages were to bed sharing, there was a core of what they had to say that I heard again and again.

It's the Ideal

Some people talked about sleeping with their partner as a personal and cultural ideal. For them, sleeping apart would be a failure, a falling away from the ideal, a denial of their couplehood, and a social embarrassment (see Hislop & Arber, 2003b, reporting similar statements from focus groups of women in England).

> AMY: When we were discussing what kind of beds to get ... I said we could get two twins. Then we could each have our own beds, and have what my mother calls "visiting privileges." (Karl chuckles) And I was actually okay with that. And Karl goes, "No, I want to be in the bed with you," so what I would say is probably in every couple, if not both, there's always one who likes the idea of physically being in bed with somebody. It's the old romantic snuggling. This is the way it's supposed to be if you have a partner. . . . It's like whoever you commit to as a partnership, there is this illusion that you should crawl into bed together at the end of the day, even if there's no sexual favors granted or given. It's a matter of that stripping everything from the day off, laying emotionally naked if not physically naked and vulnerable with the one person in the world that you should have the most trust with. And it's being able to do that at the end of the day, no matter what the world has treated you like. And I would call that sort of the romanticism of being in the same bed, the psychology that perhaps goes behind it for a lot of couples. And I think it's valid. I think it's a critical part of partnering.

Some people seemed to say that the ideal came from American culture, ethnic culture, or religious culture. Many people said things that made it seem that they had picked up the cultural ideal about sharing a bed from their parents.

> DONNA: My concept of people being married ... has a lot to do with it. People who are married sleep in the same bed. . . . My parents share a bed still. My grandparents shared a bed until they passed away.

The ideal might be reinforced by other family members' reactions when a couple did not share a bed.

> AL: Up at the cabin we have separate beds, and our kids think that that is just terrible.

INTIMACY

As is pointed out throughout this book, there are many practical reasons people sleep together—for example, for warmth on cold nights, for safety, for help in case of medical emergency, or for comfort when sad or worried. But what most people said when they explained why they continued to share a bed, even if at times it meant they slept less well, was that they wanted the intimacy of bed sharing. Intimacy involved a close, familiar, loving, personal relationship. It involved companionship, touching (including skin contact), talking that could be quite personal, sexuality, feeling one another's warmth, cuddling, and snuggling. With intimacy came feelings of security, closeness, reassurance, and perhaps romance. With intimacy a person would feel, not alone, but snug in the nest. There was a sense of familiarity, stability, sanctuary, and peace of mind. Intimacy affirmed and validated the relationship, and at times it was about truly being with the other. Most people who said they lost sleep because they shared a bed said, in various ways, that despite losing sleep they gained what they thought of as much more precious and essential to life than a good night's sleep, intimacy.

The couple intimacy that went with bed sharing was, for many, a closeness that was greater than what they had with any other human. It was a closeness in which they saw and touched each other in ways that nobody else saw and touched them. They felt each other's warmth, and the warmth could be comforting and nest making. They saw each other at the most vulnerable and when there was the least artifice. Some couples talked in bed about the most private and vulnerable of experiences and feelings. They touched, cuddled, and snuggled in a way that might satisfy the deepest of needs, physical and emotional needs that make being alone a tough, tough way to exist. They were sexual together and, yes, they could be sexual if they slept in separate beds, but in the same bed there was more possibility of spontaneous sexual pleasure. And there was ordinarily the sense that nobody else knew them so well or accepted them so comprehensively.

> MICHELLE: I like to feel him in bed next to me. I just like the feel of that warm body next to me. It's comforting. It's reassuring. It's nice (laughs).
>
> ME: I take it it's his warm body and not any warm body that would do it?
>
> MICHELLE: That's right! (guffaws) Thank you. I like to think so. . . .
>
> TONY: I think the same. I kind of like to know she's over there.

ME: What would it feel like if you were in separate beds? She said it feels secure.

TONY: Yeah, I think that's one word I'd use too. It's comforting to have her over there. . . .

MICHELLE: It is a wonderful, comforting experience. That's hokey, isn't it? (laughs) . . . It's wonderful to wake up in the morning and know he's there. It's nice to go to bed and know he's there.

KRISTEN: I love sleeping with him. I find it very comforting.

DAN: It's the same for me.

KRISTEN: Yeah. Just to wake up in the middle of the night and reach over and know that he's there. It's almost just a validation of the relationship, validation of love that we've got for each other. I think our relationship would be significantly lacking if we were in different beds. It just reaffirms the commitment that we have. Because sometimes you can say things and you're misinterpreted or you can do things, and they're unappreciated or they're misinterpreted. But when you're laying there side by side, and you reach over and touch someone, and they're there, and they respond and hold your hand, that's so affirming that you're there, you're together, and all is well.

DAN: All is well.

MIKE: It's the feeling of the companionship, the being able to know there's somebody else there beside you. I think it's just the . . . animal instinct of having a companion there. . . . This is kind of a stupid comparison. . . . Once you've had four wheel drive, you don't want to be without it. It's like once you've had companionship, you . . . want to have . . . a companion there. You want to have somebody. You want to have a sounding board if something goes wrong. You want to have somebody to hold. You want to have some physical contact. You want to have something there other than a dog. . . . You want to have somebody there who you can share things with. . . .

ME: Does sleeping in the same bed make it easier to share?

MIKE: Oh, yeah. I think so. Because a lot of time when you are snuggling in bed you'll talk a lot. I do. We do. You'll share different things that have happened or different thoughts, things that you want to do. When I've been between relationships, it made it harder to get to sleep, because you don't have that person there to rest your head on.

ME: If you were sleeping apart, what would you lose and what might you gain?

WALT: I think I'd lose a big part of the intimacy in our relationship, and just part of the joy of being married to her is being able to be with her in the morning. 'Cause when you're both working, that's kind of our ten minutes of quality time in a way, on weekdays. And it's nice in the winter. . . . . It's nice having another warm body in there. . . .

LISA: I feel that way too. I love physically being close. . . . That's really our time to be in our nest. . . . I much prefer sleeping with Walt than sleeping alone. It seems real safe and affirming to have that person there.

ME: What's the safety about?

LISA: The confidence that he's my person there. During the day I'm alone doing my thing. . . . At night when we go to bed, it's that real estate of the bed that is just totally apart from the world. There's no expectations there other than, "Thank God, here we are together." There's nothing that can really intrude on that space. I feel safe from a demand, someone asking me to do something, or having to be a certain way for anyone, having to look a certain way. . . .

WALT: Sanctuary.

LISA: Umhm. It's a wonderful way to end the day.

Actually We Do Sleep Apart Some of the Time

As has been said at various places in this book, for example in discussions of snoring and couple conflict, some couples slept apart some of the time. In some couples, sleeping apart some of the time made it possible for one or both partners to get a good night's sleep but also gave the couple some of the rewards of sharing a bed. So they had nights of what might be higher quality sleep and also nights of intimacy.

The shift to sleeping apart some of the time could be difficult at first because it could seem like pulling away from the ideal couple relationship and because of the loss of intimacy.

JANET: Until about three or four months ago we slept together every night, and then . . . she wanted to start staying up a little later. . . . So we decided, we have an option for her to be upstairs too, so then about four nights a week she'd sleep up there. . . . It was hard. We both came . . . into this relationship with a sense of very much wanting to sleep together and to share a bedroom and kind of the Betty Crocker stuff. . . . It was very symbolic to us of having a warmer, closer relationship. . . . So . . . when we decided to try this new thing, it was a little bit like, "O-oh (a worried sound). I know there's good reasons to do this, but. . . ." But it worked so well (chuckling), especially when she's been sick. . . .

CAROL: I felt a little like I was getting kicked out at first (Janet laughs), but . . . there's a part of me that kind of likes being able to do my own thing and not feel like I'm infringing on her sleep. . . . Now I don't have to feel guilty about keeping her awake. And I don't have to feel irked because I have to go to bed and I'm not sleepy and lay there and then have to come out here and the house is cold because we turned the heat down.

Proportionately more of the couples who slept apart some of the time were older. Some had snoring or health problems that intruded into the partner's sleeping. They were also more likely to have an extra place to sleep, because adult children had moved out, leaving extra beds vacant. Also, as was suggested in chapter 1, it might be less rocky to a marriage if a couple starts sleeping apart some of the time when they are older and have a long established relationship.

While sleeping apart, people are free to do what they could not or would not do with the partner in bed with them. It is a comment on the way that, for many couples, the ordinary couple routine restricts and controls what a person does that so many people deviated from the ordinary couple routine when they slept alone. As Carol said, in the quote immediately above, she liked her times of being free to do what she felt like doing. When people slept apart they could relish their freedom, for example, to use the whole bed, to sleep diagonally, or to read when they felt like it. Similarly, in their focus group study, Hislop and Arber (2003b) found that women who lived alone had more freedom than women who shared a bed with someone to engage in a wide range of strategies to deal with difficulties sleeping. Laura's comment about how things were different when her husband was away makes a similar point.

LAURA: If I sleep for five hours, then I'm awake. And sometimes if I just get up and go to the bathroom and go back to bed, then I can go back to sleep again. But five hours is about my max in sleeping. And when he's not there, then I might read or I might turn the TV on during that time. Or I might do puzzles. But I wouldn't do it if he were there.

THE COUPLE SYSTEM

Why do people share a bed, or share it as much as they do? The answers vary from couple to couple, but it seems that many people think that by sharing a bed they sleep better, they feel safer, they are warmer on cold nights, they are meeting important ideals, and they are more intimate. Many people seemed to say that sharing a bed is about intimacy, about doing what one is supposed to do, and about achieving an ideal. And yet, at another level, it is striking that, while saying that they sleep together, a number of couples do not always sleep together. Perhaps that is an important point about sleeping together, that it works for some couples in part because it does not go on all the time.

If one wanted to make a case about evolution and shared sleeping, it is clear that some people, particularly women, felt there was survival value in shared sleeping. What people had to say about safety can also be understood in the context of a gender ideology that has it roots centuries ago and that is a matter of contention today (Coltrane & Adams, 2003). The ideology includes the notions that women need the protection of men, it is the duty of men to protect women, and a woman without a man is a woman lacking in protection. I do not know whether anyone I interviewed would endorse that ideology, but what some people said could be understood as being influenced by or accepting of that ideology. From that perspective, what people were saying about safety could be understood to have a grounding in their sense of what it means to be a woman or a man. Then, too, they could be saying they were, by standards they held, proper women and men because of what they said about safety.

That so many people had difficulty sleeping apart from their partner means that sharing a bed is not simply a casual preference. It comes to be important and, in some ways, controlling in the lives of many people. The partner becomes central to the bedtime routine. The partner provides security, warmth, cuddling, companionship, and so on. Many people tried to make accommodations to substitute for what the partner usually provided, for example, talking on the phone to the partner, sleeping in the partner's place in the bed, wearing warmer sleepwear, or bringing one of their children into the bed. These might help, but their sleep might still be disrupted or start late or be of lower quality. The couple system makes its claims on people even when partners are apart.

FIFTEEN

Waking Up in the Morning

PEOPLE HAD MUCH more to say about getting to bed and to sleep and trying to sleep through the night than they did about waking up. Apparently, for most couples, the biggest challenges, the biggest rewards, the greatest intimacy, and the greatest frustration with one another happen before morning. Although there were couples for whom waking up was a time of great intimacy, for many couples waking up was primarily about getting ready for the day.

WE HARDLY SAY ANYTHING TO EACH OTHER IN THE MORNING

Because of work schedules, one partner might be out of the house before the other is awake. But even when both partners awakened at close to the same time in the morning, they might interact little or not at all. Perhaps one of them was not a morning person (see chapter 4). Perhaps they were apart in the morning because they took turns using the bathroom, or perhaps until morning caffeine kicked in, they lacked the energy to interact. Many listened to the radio or watched television as part of the morning routine, which could be a deterrent to interacting, though listening or watching together was experienced as togetherness by some couples. Many people said that they were absorbed in separately doing what it took to get out of the house and off to wherever they had to go in the morning. In fact, many people said that they tried to do their morning routine of getting ready to leave as efficiently as possible, which would leave little time for interacting.

> PETE: I make the coffee. . . . She usually goes back to the bedroom and gets dressed and into the bathroom. . . . We'll say something to each

other, but we're usually doing other things. . . . I'm usually . . . printing off bills for customers. . . . Or I'll be out in the living room going through my pills. And then she'll come out and probably say, "Good morning," and that's about it. . . . You get caught in these little routines.

In some couples, at least one partner felt there was value to the separateness that came when one of them was in bed and the other out of bed in the morning. For the partner out of bed, it was a needed time for quiet reflection, getting things done, and freedom from couple interaction.

TIM: I like to get a couple hours worth of stuff done before Cynthia decides to wake up. . . . I get my workout done, couple loads of laundry, empty the dishwasher from the day before, bathe [our daughter], get her dressed for school, feed her, if she got any little bit of homework to do (CYNTHIA: Yeah). We leave here by quarter to nine so I cram quite a bit in from five, five-thirty into that three, three and a half hour time frame.

SHARED WAKE UP ROUTINES

Many couples, even some who were separate quite a bit at wake up time, had morning wake up routines that put them in contact with each other at least briefly.

She's Usually My Alarm Clock

One part of some couples' morning routine was that one partner was the alarm clock for the other.

REBECCA: Alarms never wake me up. I rely on him to wake me up. . . .

JOE: I'll wake her up, and I make sure that she's awake. I know she'll say like, "Two more minutes," so I, "Okay, fine." (chuckling) . . . It's so routine that I generally come out of the shower and I don't comb my hair. I go and wake her up and then it's two minutes, so then I'll go back and comb my hair. . . . Then I'll wake her up again, and usually she wants another two minutes, and then after that it varies.

REBECCA: Or if I'm really tired, I say, "ten minutes."

JOE: Yeah, and then I give her two more minutes (chuckles). So I usually wake her up at least two or three times.

ADMINISTERING MEDICATION TO A PARTNER

A few couples were in contact in the morning while one administered medication to the other then.

> HENRY: I have glaucoma ... so she's very good about, we put the eye drops in right away in the morning, 'cause if we don't, you can forget it (chuckles), and I try to be so careful that the eye drops don't run out, so she'll always say, "Well, let's do the eye drops."

COORDINATING BY GETTING OUT OF BED AT DIFFERENT TIMES

Coordinating activities in the morning did not mean that the partners awoke and got out of bed at the same time. Often coordinating the morning routine meant that the partners got out of bed at different times. Especially if there was only one bathroom, one partner might stay in bed while the other got up to use it first.

> MICHELLE: You're usually up before I am.
>
> TONY: ...We really only have one bathroom, so it [prevents] arguing over (chuckling) who goes first.
>
> MICHELLE: He gets a half hour in the bathroom before I get up. And he moves into the kitchen and makes the coffee, and I get the bathroom.

The morning preparation for leaving home often took women in heterosexual couples longer than men, putting more time into hair, makeup, and dressing. So in some heterosexual couples the woman arose with considerably more lead time before she had to leave the house than did the man. They might interact near the end of the morning routine (what Karen, below, calls "a little bit of play time"), and they might leave the house at almost the same time, but to accomplish that the woman often arose earlier.

> KAREN: I get up first ... and my morning routine is the shower, the hair, the makeup. . . .
>
> RICHARD: I set my alarm for, I need to be to work at seven, so I set it for quarter after six, 'cause [my work] is real close. It's a five minute trip. And I don't do the makeup and all that stuff, so I can get dressed quite quickly.

COORDINATING WHEN CHILD CARE IS PART OF THE ROUTINE

Many couples had a wake up routine that included children. What the couple did in the morning was not simply about getting themselves going as individuals and about couple interaction. It was also about coordinating to get children out of bed, dressed, fed, and off to school or child care.

> SANDRA: We usually both get up about the same time. . . . One starts in the shower and the other one starts with the kids, and then we just flip flop, and the other goes helps the kids get going, and the other one takes a shower.

COFFEE IN THE MORNING ROUTINE

A substantial number of people said that part of their morning routine was that one of the partners was in charge of brewing the morning coffee [or perhaps tea] for both partners. Some people might wake up easily but be crabby and moody for hours (Dekker, Paley, Popkin, & Tepas, 1993), until their caffeine intake reached a high enough level. Thus, a morning person accustomed to drinking morning caffeine is not likely to be fully a morning person until he or she has loaded up on morning caffeine.

> CYNTHIA: I'm a night person and he's a morning person in getting up. But cheerful-wise and being in a good mood, he is not a morning person. He's extremely crabby in the morning. Where . . . I'm in a good mood from the time I get up. . . .
>
> TIM: Even with my workout in the morning it still takes me my pot of coffee, my workout; it takes a while to get going.

MORNING SNUGGLING, TALKING, AND OTHER INTIMACIES

Some couples had routines of relatively great contact in the morning. More of those couples mentioned snuggling than talking. Possibly, physical contact was emphasized because often they were not awake enough, and perhaps did not want to be awake enough, to talk.

> JANET: We cuddle . . . (CAROL: In the morning), when we're together and most days the radio goes on, unless it's like a Sunday or whenever that we both don't have to go to work. Most days the radio will go on and then, even if it's just for five or ten minutes, I'll cuddle again, I'll come over and put my head on her shoulder. . . . Once the radio goes on, I'm

not waking her up if I do that. (CAROL: No, no) And we don't talk much. Sometimes I get up and turn up the heat . . . go to the bathroom, and then I'll come back and cuddle, and that's a very nice time. (CAROL: Umhm).

MARIA: I usually have to get up earlier and go to work. So usually I set the alarm clock, whatever time I have to get up, but somehow we wake up earlier, and then we kind of just, it's a really nice time, don't you think? In the morning, like, I don't know, somewhere around five we seem to wake up and hold and just kind of, it's not real sleep, it's just kind of holding, and then around six the alarm goes off and I get up (VIC: yeah). And [he] will get up and make coffee and just go about our day.

MARIA: Yeah, I think the routine would be about a half hour before we get up. We have this little cuddle time everyday. . . . Either one of us will go over to the other (chuckles) (VIC: Yeah), and just hold. . . .

VIC: She just fits nicely right here (laughs), and I can stay in my sleep state, about a half doze and kind of maybe just a little bit awake, and it feels good.

One couple, Margaret and Josh, were typically unable to converse much in the evening, but in the morning they did. That was when they often interacted in ways that were common for other couples at night.

MARGARET: I just think it's real comforting, again, my comfort, security blanket, to reach over and there he is, and feels good, and muscles (JOSH: It's relaxing). Yeah, very relaxing. Stimulating.

JOSH: 'Cause we're running around during the day, and it's some quiet time for us.

MARGARET: Our days are pretty hectic. We have a big calendar. . . . We're involved in a lot of community . . . things (JOSH: Yeah) and church and so we're busy people. Morning, it seems like, is our best time (JOSH: time to talk, and talk about [our son]). Right.

JOSH: Talk about what's going on, what our day's going to be like.

MARGARET: 'Cause at night I go to sleep first.

JOSH: . . . Yeah, she tires earlier than I do, so that's the reason she goes to bed early, 'cause she gets tired first. And I'm still kind of wide awake. I like to watch the news.

One couple woke up early in the morning so that they could pray together.

JULIA: We're very strong Christians, so we get up early so we have time to pray, 'cause we're both showered by about five-thirty, (WILLIAM: five-twenty) quarter of six. And then we have until like six-fifteen (WILLIAM: ten), six-ten, to pray, so we have about twenty or twenty-five minutes (WILLIAM: to pray together).

A few couples exercised together in the morning. For example, Brad and Teresa went for a walk outside together on warm weather mornings and walked laps inside a shopping mall on cold winter mornings. Cheryl and Greg engaged in Tai Chi exercises together in the morning.

THE COUPLE SYSTEM

The couple system in the morning generally involves a lower level of contact than at night, which emphasizes how important the processes of getting to bed and being in bed together are in couple relationships. The morning couple routine is a coordinated one; there is definitely a patterned, interactive system in operation. But the low level of interaction in the typical morning routine makes obvious how central the bed and getting to sleep are in the relationship of most couples. Also, that there is so much more to say about what goes on at night shows how much delicacy there can be to getting to sleep and continuing to sleep, how vulnerable sleep is to disruption. If one thinks of a couple system as an achievement, for most couples the achievement is much greater around getting to bed and to sleep and then continuing to sleep than it is around waking up and getting going.

SIXTEEN

WHAT PEOPLE SAID they did on weekends when neither partner had to go work helps to illuminate the dominance, constraints, and frustrations of workday routines.

THINGS AREN'T SO DIFFERENT ON WEEKENDS

Many couples said that on weekends they went to bed at or close to the time they went to bed on weekdays. One can take that as a sign that the ordinary weekday routine works for a couple. But one can also take it as a sign that the circadian biological rhythm (the twenty-four hour cycle of activity, alertness, blood chemistry, body temperature, wakefulness, and sleep) does not stop working just because a person does not have to go to work the next day (see O'Connor, Mahowald, & Ettinger, 1994). When it comes to times for going to sleep, many people seemed to have been captured by the usual pattern of workday bedtime so that their body changed into time-to-go-to-bed mode as the usual bedtime approached.

Similarly, many people could not easily sleep much beyond their usual waking time, presumably because their circadian rhythm moved them into a wake-up phase at that time (Aldrich, 1999, p. 67).

> WILLIAM: Saturdays and Sundays are the days we normally get to sleep in until six. It's just . . . an arbitrary time. (JULIA: Yeah) 'Cause internal alarm clocks kick on (JULIA: Yeah). At five-thirty, six o'clock we go, "Time to wake up."
>
> JULIA: Yeah, we don't sleep late on the weekends.

One couple had experimented with staying in bed longer on weekends, but it had not worked. So the sleeping luxuries they allowed themselves on weekends were occasionally to stay up a bit later and not to use the alarm clock.

ME: How is your sleeping routine different on weekends?

JIM: It's not.

MADELINE: . . . We tend to get up at the same time.

JIM: Umhm. We might stay up a little later, sometimes. Usually weekends we're up at six-thirty, seven o'clock. . . . (MADELINE: Umhm) It's pretty much the same routine. We just don't set our alarm on the weekends (MADELINE: Umhm). We just kind of wake up, but it's always at seven (both chuckle).

MADELINE: . . . We actually tried a couple of times . . . to deliberately stay in bed longer, 'cause we'd say how we need to rest. We're gonna just try to relax and rest. It didn't last very long. . . . Don't want to waste time laying around.

A few couples were captured by a medication routine, so no matter what their personal circadian rhythms were and no matter how much they wanted to sleep later on weekends, they could not. The demands of taking, and perhaps administering, medication at a set time held them to the routine they had on weekdays.

I Wish He Could Sleep in More

In some couples, one partner might be more powerfully governed by circadian rhythm than the other. That could be why, on the weekend, one partner typically arose at the usual time, perhaps to the annoyance or mystification of the other.

CHARLES: Even on the weekends I still get up, well, this morning I was out the door by six-thirty. (LINDA: Yeah) I still wake up early. It doesn't matter if it's weekend, weekday, I wake up at the same time. Although on the weekend I maybe lay back down and go to sleep for another half hour. . . . She's always telling me, "Why are you getting up?" It's, "I'm awake." . . . Once I'm awake I cannot go back to sleep.

We Might Go to Sleep a Little Earlier

If the weekend is for self care, then it is only for play if that is good self care. For some people, good self care did not involve late night entertainment on a weekend but catching up on missed sleep. They might even go to bed earlier than they did on weekdays, though typically only a little bit earlier, which might have something to do with their circadian rhythms. Monica was one of the people who talked about going to bed earlier on Friday night because of accumulated exhaustion from the work week.

> MONICA: Friday night . . . I almost go to bed earlier than on a week-day night. I think sometimes because it's like after going through the whole week I'm (laughing) wiped out.

One heterosexual couple who also went to bed earlier on weekend nights did so partly because the husband worked late on weeknights and the wife forced herself to stay up late so that she could go to bed after he came home. On weekend nights they were free to go to bed at what was for them a more normal and comfortable time.

WE MIGHT GO TO SLEEP A LITTLE LATER

Without work or school the next morning, some couples stayed up later on Friday and Saturday nights. They used the time to watch television, go to a movie, visit with friends or relatives, or do something else that they could not do if they were going to work the next morning. However, quite a few of those couples found it difficult to stay up far past their regular bedtime.

> ME: How is your weekend sleep routine different from your weekday sleep routine?
> MARK: I'd say we usually go to bed later.
> PATRICIA: Go to bed later on Friday nights because our show is on on Friday night. . . . "Valleykissangel," Irish soap opera. . . . We have to watch it every Friday night. A lot of times I fall asleep within the first twenty minutes. I just can't stay awake.
> MARK: . . . On Saturday nights we usually go out and see a movie or something (PATRICIA: Umhm), stay up a little later, and I suppose we get up later, but not much.

SLEEPING LATE ON WEEKENDS

Despite circadian rhythms, there were some couples who used their weekend freedom to sleep in late. Sleeping in late on a weekend morning might not be, for those couples, only about catching up on missed sleep and unwinding. It might also be about contact with the partner.

LISA: Saturday morning, Sunday mornings are our special times to stay in bed as long as possible and just enjoy each other there. And that's been really nice.

In some couples, one partner slept in on weekends more than the other. One slept while the other arose to engage in sports, errands, home maintenance, parenting, reading, quiet reflection, or just fiddling about.

LIZ: On weekends, he has to be up because he takes our oldest to um, she has bowling on Saturdays and church on Sundays for her confirmation group, and I have to sleep. . . . (ANDY: I let her sleep to about eleven. . . .) That's my catch up day.

Sandra would use the extra time she had, because she awoke earlier on weekends than Ken, to remain in bed close to him, reading or reflecting.

SANDRA: I usually wake up at the same time, six-thirty, or between six and seven. And he will, if it's a day that he doesn't have to get up and it's not something that we have to do as a family, he'll sleep in. So sometimes I'll just lay there and I'll either have something to read or I'll be thinking about whatever the plans are, and then I oftentimes will stay in bed till he wakes up. . . . If he can, he'll try to catch a little bit of extra sleep . . . maybe till eight or so.

SEPARATE WEEKEND NAPS

Some people said that they took naps, particularly on weekends, when they were more likely to have freedom from the demands of the work week. They might need to catch up on sleep missed during the work week or on sleep missed on Friday night or Saturday night because they were up late. One woman whose husband's snoring undermined her sleep napped when she could, which was on weekends. For most couples in which one or both partners napped, weekend naps were taken alone, not with the partner.

GREG: We cherish the opportunity, especially on Sunday afternoons (CHERYL: Umhm) after church and maybe visiting the family, to nap for anywhere between half an hour and two hours. (CHERYL: Yeah) We usually pick different beds then.

Because many people defined a nap as individual, not a couple matter, a nap could give, not only needed sleep, but freedom to sleep away from whatever the partner did that disrupted one's nighttime sleeping.

THE COUPLE SYSTEM

One might imagine that there could be two couple bed sharing and sleep systems, one for weekdays and one for weekends. But for most couples there was relatively little variation from weekday to weekend. The weekday routine set patterns that became so ingrained that people deviated little from those patterns. Weekends were different; there is no doubt. But it seems that, basically, the same system operates day in and day out.

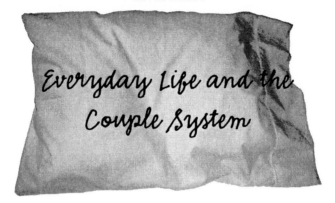

SEVENTEEN

Everyday Life and the Couple System

THIS BOOK PROVIDES an account of the centrality of bed sharing in the everyday life of couples. It makes clear that what goes on in couple bed sharing becomes routinized as it is shaped by personal and interpersonal processes and by the people, events, and aspects of technology that surround the couple. It shows that sharing a bed is an achievement that not infrequently is based on considerable struggle, inventiveness, compromise, and problem solving.

THE COUPLE SYSTEM

This book provides extensive documentation in support of the idea that if one wants to understand the sleep of an adult who shares a bed with another adult, one has to understand the couple system. For people who sleep with someone else, sleep is always a couple phenomenon. For people who share a bed, good sleeping is a couple achievement. If a person has sleep problems, the problems do not necessarily arise within that person; they may arise from the couple relationship. If a person develops a sleep problem, it often becomes a source of sleep difficulty for the partner as well.

Perhaps there is something perverse in thinking about the sleep of people who share a bed as a couple phenomenon. Perhaps by emphasizing the social nature of sleep, we lose a desired illusion of solitude, privacy, and individual coping with practical realities and demons of the night. Or perhaps the focus on the social nature of sleep misses the ways that, in the night, a person may confront existential aloneness. But I think there is a both/and nature to bed sharing. Yes, one can never fully leave behind the existential aloneness, the solitude, the privacy, and the individual confrontation with personal demons. And one can never fully leave behind the couple system either.

We should not underestimate the value of focusing on the individual in the treatment of sleep disorders. The insights and treatment approaches of medicine and psychology focused on the individual have been helpful to millions of people. But to the extent that medicine and psychology ignore the couple system, much of great importance is missed. We do not even have a vocabulary of concepts parallel to the concepts of individual sleep disorders to characterize the sleep problems that arise in and are part of the couple relationship. There is not, for example, a term to describe couple differences and disputes over thermostat settings and how many blankets to have on the bed. How much more successful might sleep medicine and sleep psychology be if they would work at understanding and treating the couple sleep system?

Most people who were interviewed reported that at some points in their bed sharing life there were sleep problems, in many cases problems that were serious and that went on for some time. Individual sleep can be quite fragile. It can be so fragile that a change in one partner's breathing can awaken the other. It can be so fragile that when one partner goes out of town, the other might take hours more than usual to fall asleep. It can be so fragile that many people I interviewed had great trouble sleeping because of a partner's snoring or tossing and turning. With individual sleep so fragile, it takes a finely tuned couple relationship to allow both partners good sleep night after night. Achieving such fine tuning requires considerable struggle, effort, negotiation, inventiveness, tolerance, and perhaps compromise.

In a relationship system the individuals are interconnected and phenomena emerge that cannot exist when people sleep alone. It is not only that one partner's process of going to bed, preferences regarding the sleep environment, patterns of falling asleep, sleep, and processes of awakening affect the other. Because of the interconnection, in a relationship system many things happen that only happen because the relationship exists—couple conversation, interpersonal conflict, and so on.

Sleeping with someone can be wonderfully rewarding and satisfying. It can be the center of one's universe, the place of greatest security and comfort. It also means that one cedes considerable power over one's sleeping to someone else, which can make for power battles and less than optimal sleep situations (Hislop & Arber, 2003a). And it can make for a lower level of satisfaction with the couple relationship (Strawbridge, Shema, & Roberts, 2004).

As is indicated throughout this book, the couple system is not isolated. It is linked to the larger systems that surround a couple. The couple bed can feel like an isolated eden to a couple, but it is linked to what has happened in the workplaces of the partners, what is going on in their families, the cost of heating fuel, the technology of heating and cooling, who else is in the house and what they might be doing, societal processes that lead to many people becoming overweight, whether the couple has health insurance to pay for the treatment of disorders that affect sleep, work schedules, the existence of television and what programs are shown when, the possibility of assault and burglary, the technology and medications that physicians supply, the technology of alarm clocks and clock radios, the technology of pagers, alarming news reports, and a million other things. The couple bed is not an isolated haven but richly interconnected with all of society. And the connections go both ways. A person who goes out into the world of relationships, work, and driving while sleep deprived can be less effective and more dangerous to others. A person whose bed sharing makes for chronically poor sleep can make demands on the health care system and can create substantial costs for health insurers. A person whose bed sharing leaves him or her feeling inadequately connected with the partner, with not enough quantity and quality of touching, talking, and satisfaction of various needs may go through the day preoccupied, dissatisfied, frustrated, and needy. Conversely, a person whose bed sharing goes very well each night is more likely to bring to each day a sense of energy and well being.

Individuals in heterosexual couples are not free from the larger societal forces that lead them to be gendered in the ways they are and that can lead to both satisfaction and frustration in bed sharing. The bedroom is not free from the burdens and inequities associated with gender in the larger society. In the heterosexual couples I interviewed, if there was a gender difference in who made the bed, it was the woman who made the bed. If there was a gender difference in who dealt with resident children or grandchildren during the night, the woman did more of that. Women, on the average, took more time to get to bed, and that was partly about having more household chores to complete and partly about having more appearance work to do on hair, skin, and so on before getting to bed. Women were more likely than men to have trouble falling asleep because of worry, review of what had gone on during the day, and planning for things coming up, and they were more likely to wake up in the middle of the night to do those things. One can take all that as being about women having a heavier load to deal with and having less spare time during the day to process matters. Women were, on the average, more inclined than men to talk at bedtime, to initiate talk, and to talk more. Perhaps that means that women more often than men have the primary responsibility for maintaining the couple connection and for seeing that the couple works together to do the tasks, chores, and plans of their lives. Perhaps the load that women carry is related to women being more likely than men to have nightmares that awakened them. And perhaps it also says something about the way that gender is constructed in the larger society that women were more likely than men to be fearful of night intruders.

What goes on in couple bed sharing reflects what goes on in the world of work. Work pressure and tension come to bed with a couple. So do work injuries. Work had a key role in determining when a couple would sleep and wake up. Couple bed sharing is also shaped substantially by the income and wealth that comes from work. Couples with greater income can buy bigger and better beds, bigger homes (and hence more separation at night from children and grandchildren), homes in a quieter and safer location, air conditioning, floors that do not squeak, and much else that might promote good couple sleeping.

What goes on in couple bed sharing no doubt reflects basic human processes. It is impossible to separate human biology from the sociocultural forces that shape, limit, define, and lead to what goes on in couple bed sharing. But one can certainly argue that biological processes are at work in the bed—for example, the human need for touch, circadian rhythms, menopause, and of course the basic need to sleep. To the extent that basic biological claims on humans are present in bed, they shape and limit what goes on in the couple bed sharing relationship.

This book is not a challenge to family systems theory, but it does offer a great deal of material to flesh out how couple systems are built, how they operate, and what influences them in the area of couple bed sharing. Systems theories are extremely useful for focusing attention and for highlighting what is systemic. They can not be very interesting, however, if they only offer broadly abstract principles. It is in the details of how those principles play out that insight and understanding are achieved and that we can be helped to problem solve and to carry out well-informed discovery processes. So the kind of research this book provides, which fleshes out the details, complexities, nuances, conflicts, and so on of a system operating in a particular domain, can be very helpful even if it adds no new principles to the general ideas of systems theory. Although it is not a challenge to systems theory, I believe that the contribution of this book to relationship systems thinking is to lay out basic phenomena of couple bed sharing and sleeping systems in ways that help people to see the complexity and processes of those systems, with all the patterns, constraints, stability maintenance, adaptive power, and so on of a system.

LEARNING

The couple system is a place of learning. To function together, people must learn. Each partner is, in pleasant and unpleasant ways, the other's teacher and a major part of the environment about which the other must learn. Each person must come to terms with how she or he affects the partner. So there is a never-ending circle of learning, with A learning from and about B, and vice versa, and each learning about the other's learning and learning from that, and then each learning about the other's new learning, and so on. One of many illustrations of that is to think about partner A learning that something about how she or he sleeps affects partner B's sleep adversely. Partner B may be learning to accommodate to the adversity, but, at the same time, partner A, out of consideration for partner B, may be changing something about how she or he sleeps, and those changes may have an adverse affect on the sleep of partner A (Hislop & Arber, 2003a). And the adverse affect on partner A's sleep sets up new demands for learning for both partners.

To complicate matters, the targets of learning are moving in the sense that people and their situations change, and so there are always new demands for learning. One would think that with learning being so much a focus of the field of psychology and in certain schools of therapy that there would be a substantial literature on how people learn to sleep as their situations change—for example, when they first begin to share a bed, when they change work shifts, when they have babies, and so on. But except for a literature on the treatment of insomnia through biofeedback or operant conditioning (e.g., Bootzin & Rider, 1997; Downey & Bennett, 1992; Hauri, 1981), I can find no such literature. Although this book offers people's testimony about their processes of learning to sleep as situations change, sleep learning is for the most part a field as yet to be explored.

SLEEP ROUTINES

A great deal of this book is an extended answer to the two questions: How do couples arrive at their bed sharing and sleep routines? What do they do when a routine is not working for them? Based on what is reported in this book, couples seem to arrive at their routines through individual and couple trial and error, through learning from what others have to say or from what they have read, through their previous experiences sharing a bed, and through their shared teaching/learning processes. Sleep routines can be so automated that some couples can arrive in bed at exactly the same minute every night, having followed a totally predictable path to bed, and following a totally predictable process once they are in bed. Despite the apparent ease of those routines, there may have been an enormous amount of learning and struggle to get to those routines, and the routines are fragile. It takes very little to disrupt them, and once they are disrupted, it may be much more difficult to get to bed, to fall asleep, to remain asleep, or to achieve restorative sleep. And the couple may enter a new and demanding round of learning and struggle in order to develop a new shared routine that works for them.

There is a large literature on how routines help infants and children (e.g., Kuhn & Weidinger, 2000; Wolfson, 1998) and the elderly (e.g., Johnson, 1988) to sleep. The sleep self-help literature, which focuses so much on the individual, also emphasizes routines (e.g., Dement & Vaughn, 1999, p. 425; Wiedman, 1999, pp. 113–116). This book shows that shared routines are vitally important when it comes to couple sleeping.

MEANINGS

This book is in many ways a contribution to the theory of meaning in relationship life. As they talked about their daily life, their routines, and their struggles related to sleeping, many people were articulate about how their life obtained meaning through their bed sharing routines, where they slept, with whom they slept, and how they slept. It seems that, at least for some people, there were many layers of meanings. For example, some people drew meaning from doing what they thought others did or expected them to do or from having a proper bed and bedroom. Most drew meaning from the intimacy of their relationship. Some drew meaning from the protection the partner afforded them or that they afforded the partner. Some drew meaning from having worked out how to overcome problems in order to sleep comfortably together. Some drew meaning from just doing things right by their own standards.

THE LIFE COURSE

Embedded in this book is a great deal on how couple sleeping changes over the life course of the two individuals. The book offers perspectives on youthful sexuality and sensuality and the entry of children into a couple's life. It traces what happens as bodies increase in size and as people change from being free of health-related sleep problems to having problems with snoring, sleep apnea, or other health issues that can undermine sleep. It addresses menopause. Individual sleeping is not a constant over the life cycle but changes and may even deteriorate as one ages (Bliwise, 1997).

Similarly, couple sleeping is not a constant over the couple relationship course. The couple must adapt to the individual changes. Plus the couple relationship has its own cycle, which affects couple sleeping, moving from early relationship sexuality to a more mature couple sexuality, moving (for many couples) from not having children to having them, or even to having grandchildren move in with them. The couple relationship may mature or deteriorate in interpersonal problem solving resources, which will affect how they deal with sleep difficulties. The relationship may move from a higher emphasis on touch and physical contact to a lower level. The relationship in bed will reflect the maturing of children and their possibly moving out. It will reflect the aging and death of older relatives. It will reflect the couple's relationship ups and downs and also the ups and downs of their work life and their income. It will reflect changes in the couple over the life course in economic resources for solving problems—for example, changes in being able to afford a larger bed or medical treatment for a sleep disorder. So the couple sleep relationship says a great deal about the individual and couple life course.

HYPOTHESES ABOUT SPECIFIC AREAS OF COUPLE LIFE

Most chapters of this book offer hypotheses that have potential for stimulating research and practical applications concerning particular areas of couple bed sharing. For example, there is discussion of how couples use humor to diffuse tensions over couple sleeping. There is discussion of possible factors underlying the move to a bigger bed or what underlies the move by some partners, when a couple has an angry bedtime encounter, to sleep elsewhere in the dwelling. The dozens of specific discussions in this book are, I hope, a contribution to future research on bed sharing and couple sleeping.

TEACHING WITH THIS BOOK

In teaching, I would use this book to stimulate students to think about the texture, complexity, challenges, and achievements of everyday life. Judging by what the people who were interviewed said, there is often considerable obliviousness about one's own everyday life. There is even more obliviousness about the everyday life of others. Obliviousness is not necessarily a bad thing. Life might be impossible to live if one were aware of and analytic about everything. But still, there is much to be gained from learning to see and ask questions about everyday life, to ask what the patterns are, what the struggles are, how much that goes on in one's everyday life is linked to what others in one's life do, and how one affects the everyday life of others. The social sciences and psychology often ask rather abstract questions about individual and social life. But asking questions about the concreteness of everyday life can reveal an awesome and fascinating universe of phenomena.

I hope this book also teaches that people have expertise in their own life. If we only observe and evaluate individuals and couples and do not ask them to say what has been going on in their lives and what they make of those things, we will miss important information about their lives and may come up with ways of analyzing their lives that are ignorant and simplistic and quite possibly wrong.

Good teaching in the social sciences and psychology might often have sub-versive elements, challenging assumptions and common sense. Perhaps the most subversive aspect of this book is that it challenges simplistic notions about love and romance in couple relationships. This book is about love and romance, but it is also filled with accounts and analyses of the many ways in which the dance of couple relationship does not come easily to people or is in some ways quite unsatisfying. From another angle, anyone who teaches courses on couple rela-tionships can attest to how students often think that couple conflict is a bad thing. Students have to learn that couple conflict is a normal part of maintain-ing a relationship in which people care for each other and are in the relation-ship for the long haul. In chapter after chapter, this book shows that conflict is part of sharing a bed and life together. It is a necessary part of dealing with indi-vidual differences, working out issues of comfort and fairness, and getting as much quality sleep as one can, given the constraints of the situation. Thus, one message of this book that I think is important to teach is that the journey of a single night's sleep and the journey of a couple relationship may often require disagreement, expressions of dissatisfaction, and the clash of two people who see things differently and need different things in order to function comfortably.

COUPLE THERAPY AND COUPLE SLEEPING

This book implies that couple sleeping can be an interesting and productive focus of couple therapy. Sleep is a window into a couple's life. Asking a client couple about their sleeping arrangements may be quite informative. For example, if they are sleeping apart, it might be helpful to know how that came about and how, if at all, they accomplish the talking, touching, and so on that is central to the relation-ship of many couples. If they sleep together, what issues have they had to work out and how, if at all, have they worked them out? If a couple who presents with seri-ous difficulties sleeps well together, that might say a lot about their resources for getting along. If a couple has serious difficulty in sleeping together, they might not be different from many other couples who are able to stay together and even achieve good sleep together, which might be reassuring for them to know. But they might be sleep deprived, which would make it much more difficult for them to solve any problems or to make good use of the therapy situation. And if a couple can be helped to move forward in addressing issues of sleep, they may learn aspects of getting along that will serve them well in all the other areas of their couple life.

THE NEXT RESEARCH ON COUPLE SLEEPING

A pioneering study like this one is like a surface survey in archeology. One walks around, observing what is on the surface, for example, pot shards and the remains of dwellings. A surface survey may tell a lot about who lived there and how they lived. But next one must dig. The digging tools for the next research on couple sleeping might include longitudinal studies that explore in much greater detail how the couple sleeping relationship develops and changes, the minutia and the big things that are part of achieving high quality couple bed sharing.

I do not doubt the truth of what people said to me, but I doubt that they remembered everything of importance or that in a two hour interview we could get to all that is important. So another place to dig would be all the things that people did not talk about. Related to this, I imagine that many people censored things or decided some things were not interesting or important enough to tell. I would want to know what those things were.

I think we also need observational studies of couple sleeping, partly to understand more about the relationship of what people say in an interview about their bed sharing to what actually goes on, partly to learn what might be worthwhile to ask that I never thought to ask and partly to understand better the links of people's narratives with what they do as they sleep. Observational sleep studies can be very intrusive (wires hooked up to people, sleeping in a strange bed, and so on), but I think it is possible to do much less intrusive studies of couple sleeping that still teach us a lot.

There are also a number of phenomena I did not explore that are worth pursuing. For example, the bed is a chemical environment. People bring chemicals with them, the residues of makeup, shampoos, detergents, soaps, perfumes, fabric softeners, tobacco, and so on. How or when do these chemicals become issues in couple bed sharing. I asked very little about couple sexual relationships as it relates to sleeping, and I am sure there is a lot there to be learned. And I never asked couples to talk systematically about how and when they process their shared sleeping. For example, do partners ever ask each other, "How did you sleep last night?" And if they do, what do they do with the answers to that question?

This book does not cover all that I learned. There were things I heard from some or maybe many people that I decided were not so central to the couple bed sharing system as I conceptualized it that they needed to be discussed here. For example, cats or dogs in the bedroom, sharp toe nails, whiskers, the location of bedside telephones. There may be much to learn about couple bed sharing from exploring topics like these.

I think almost everyone I interviewed could be said to come from the same culture, so this book offers almost nothing about cultural variations. However, there were hints in the chapter 7 discussion of differences in comfort with physical contact in bed that cultural differences in that area might be difficult to resolve. In fact, there are probably enormously interesting and important cultural variations in how and when couples share a bed and what it means to them. Understanding how different cultures do bed sharing and sleeping differently and understanding the special challenges faced by intercultural couples might be enormously illuminating. For example, in some cultures the couple bed is a family bed, and in some cultures many family members sleep in the same room. What does either of those characteristics of the sleeping situation mean to a couple and how does it affect their bed sharing and sleeping together? And if someone from a culture where bed sharing and sleep room sharing are the norm partners with someone who comes from a culture where the adult couple is alone in a bed and a sleeping room, how might the differences affect the couple bed sharing relationship?

From another angle, the question of what research to do next is a question of theory. My questions to couples were founded on a simple systems view. And I have organized the material people gave me with that view in mind. But there are many other ways to think theoretically about couple relationships or humans in general that might be enormously productive. Here, for example, are sketchy ideas about using three theories that could be very useful. One could use social construction theory (e.g., Wiley, 1994) to explore how couples construct what is a good bedroom environment, a good night's sleep, intimacy, and so on, and to explore how social construction processes in the larger society shape how a couple constructs these things. One could use dramaturgical theory (e.g., Goffman, 1959) to explore couple use of the bedroom as a back stage and also the ways that partners could be on stage with each other even when in bed together. Or one could use ideas about rights and obligations (e.g. Schwartz, 1970) to explore the ways that couples discuss issues of rights and obligations and how they deal with violations of implicit or explicit rights and obligations. Also, there may be theories that can emerge from what is in this book or what will come out of future work on couple sleeping that might lead to new and useful ways of thinking about and researching couple sleeping. For example, although there are places in this book where I mention, or the people quoted mention, the comparison of a previous bed sharing relationship with the current one, how to think about the connection of the old relationship and the new remains work to be done. Or, to take a very different kind of theoretical issue, I did not ask people for their own theories about bed sharing and sleeping. Even if only a few people had such theories, they might be worthwhile to use as analytic tools for thinking about the bed sharing of people in general or as ingredients for theorizing about how people come to theories to make sense of and guide their everyday life.

APPENDIX

Name, gender, age, years of schooling, occupation.

How long have the two of you been sleeping together?

What percentage of the nights do you sleep together?

Other household members—name, gender, age, years of schooling, occupation, relationship to respondent(s).

Pets?

Tell me about your sleeping arrangement. What kind of bed do you have? Do you have sides of the bed? If so, how did that get decided? What happens, in terms of side of the bed, when you two sleep at a hotel or somewhere else away from home? Do you have a phone in your room? If so, who is closest to it? Do you have an alarm clock? If so, who is closest to it? Reading lamps? A TV set? If a TV set, who, if anyone, controls the remote? Who is closest to the door? Who is closest to the bathroom?

Would you say the two of you have a going-to-sleep routine? If so, what is it? On weekdays? On weekends and holidays?

Do you have a waking up routine? On weekdays? On weekends and holidays?

Tell me about your sleeping together last night (or whenever the most recent night of sleeping together was).

Do you remember learning how to sleep with each other? How did you learn? What was difficult? Was there anything you had to help your partner learn in order for the two of you to sleep comfortably together? How has your sleeping together changed over the years?

Did you ever share a bed with someone growing up? If so, what was that like?
What did you learn?

Is either of you more of a night person or a morning person than the other? If
so, how does that affect your sleeping together? Do you ever have hassles with
each other about when to go to bed or when to wake up? If so, what are those
about? If not, how did you two work things out so that area of your sleep relationship became hassle-free?

Whose bed is it? Who picked the bed? Who picked the bedding?

Who makes the bed? If the bed is made and tucked in, does someone untuck
things before going to sleep? How do you work out how many covers to have
over you at night? How do you decide at what temperature to set the thermostat at night?

Do either of you ever unintentionally wake the other up during the night or
in the morning? If so, is that ever a problem?

Do you remember any conflicts with each other having to do with sleeping
together? Any having to do with watching TV in bed? Reading in bed? Eating in
bed? Setting the alarm clock? Whiskers? Odors? What to wear to bed? Cold feet?

When and how much physical contact do you have with each other when
you're both in bed? Are there ever disagreements about touching, holding, hugging, snuggling, rolling over against the other person?

Do you talk in bed? When? About what? Who talks more?

If you have others living in the house or pets or neighbors who can hear you,
how does that affect when and how you have sex together?

Does one of you fall asleep more easily than the other? If so, does that make
any problems for either of you?

Does one of you lie awake quite a bit at night? If so, does that make problems
for the other one?

Does either of you go to the washroom during the night? If so, does that make
any problems for either of you?

Is one of you a lighter sleeper than the other? Often when two people sleep
together one is more likely to wake up to tend to a child who is complaining,
to close windows when it starts raining, to notice suspicious sounds outside, etc.
Is that true of the two of you? If so, who is the person who wakes up more easily? Does the difference ever make trouble for either of you?

Are there any differences in your sleep together when the weather is very cold or very hot? Are there any differences when you have house guests sleeping in your house? How about when you are sharing a bed as guests at someone else's house?

Are there ever times when you don't share a bed? What makes that happen?

Does either of you take sleeping pills or kava kava or something else to make it easier to fall asleep? How do you think that affects your sleeping with each other?

Does either of you ever go to bed angry with the other? If so, what is being in bed together like then?

What happens when either of you is ill?

Have there ever been any relationship problems stemming from snoring, talking while asleep, nightmares, tossing in the sleep, vigorous leg movements, vigorous arm movements, sleep apnea, grinding the teeth during the sleep, insomnia, long toenails, what to wear in bed, eating in bed, pulling the covers away, covers tucked in or not, etc.?

Why do you sleep together even though, in some ways, it's easier to sleep apart?

Was there ever a time when something really heavy happened—for example, a death in a family, a serious illness, a car accident, loss of a job, hard things at work? If so, was sharing a bed with each other helpful at that time or not? Why or why not?

How do you think you would feel if you started sleeping in separate beds or even in separate rooms?

PART II: COUPLES' PSEUDONYMS, AGES, AND YEARS SLEEPING TOGETHER

(Listed alphabetically by the woman's name for heterosexual couples and by the name of the partner whose pseudonym begins earlier in the alphabet for lesbian couples).

Amy, 51. Karl, 50. Together 15 years.
Ana, 40. Carlos, 45. Together perhaps 17 years.
Angela, 27. Eric, 31. Together 2 years.
Barbara, 39. Hank, 38. Together 5 years.
Brenda, 51. Harvey, age unknown. Together 1/2 year.
Carol, 56. Janet, 57. (lesbian). Together 14 1/2 years.
Caroline, 22. Ben, 24. Together 3 1/2 years.
Cheryl, 57. Greg, 50. Together 22 years.

Christine, 31. George, 28. Together 4 years.

Cindy, 46. Ed, 48. Together 27 years.

Cynthia, 36. Tim, 34. Together 11 years.

Debbie, 51. Dot, 58. (lesbian). Together 13 years.

Debra, 56. Henry, 73. Together 28 years.

Diana, 36. Aaron, 47. Together 9 years.

Donna, 25. Jeff, 25. Together 2 years.

Emma, 21. Robert, 21. Together perhaps 1/2 year.

Grace, 69. Sam, 77. Together 51 years.

Hannah, 42. Jack, 47. Together 4 years.

Heather, 54. David, 58. Together 32 years.

Julia, 44. William, 47. Together 23 1/2 years.

Karen, 49. Richard, 60. Together 33 years.

Kate, age unknown. Mike, 53. Together 2 years.

Kathy, 23. Mitch, 26. Together 2 years.

Kristen, 31. Dan, 33. Together 2 years.

Laura, 73. Zack, 76. Together 47 years.

Linda, 42. Charles, 45. Together 21 years.

Lisa, 51. Walt, 57. Together 7 years.

Liz, 31. Andy, 35. Together 9 years.

Madeline, 36. Jim, 30. Together 6 years.

Margaret, 49. Josh, 48. Together 20 years.

Maria, 33. Vic, 36. Together 14 years.

Mary, 57. Matt, 59. Together 6 years.

Martha, 54. Al, 54. Together 33 years.

Michelle, 55. Tony, 60. Together 35 years.

Molly, 39. Thomas, 42. Together 19 years.

Monica, 45. Don, 44. Together 23 years.

Nancy, 43. Pam, 39. (lesbian). Together 9 years.

Natalie, 37. John, 52. Together 5 years.

Patricia, 33. Mark, 26. Together 3 years.

Rebecca, 27. Joe, 41. Together 2 1/2 years.

Sandra, 42. Ken, 42. Together 18 years.

Sarah, 28. Nick, 32. Together 3 1/2 years.

Shannon, 31. Steve, 30. Together 5 years.

Sharon, 44. Pete, 48. Together 26 years.

Susan, 42. Adam, 47. Together 16 years.

Teresa, 57. Brad, 58. Together 38 years.

REFERENCES

Adams, B. N., & Cromwell, R. E. (1978). Morning and night people in the family: A preliminary statement. *Family Coordinator, 27,* 1–13.

Akerstedt, T., Fredlund, P., Gillberg, M., & Jansson, B. (2002). Work load and work hours in relation to disturbed sleep and fatigue in a large representative sample. *Journal of Psychosomatic Research, 53,* 585–588.

Akerstedt, T., Knutsson, A., Westerholm, P., Theorell, T., Alfredsson, L., & Kecklund, G. (2002). Sleep disturbances, work stress and work hours: A cross-sectional study. *Journal of Psychosomatic Research, 53,* 741–748.

Aldous, J. (1996). *Family careers: Rethinking the developmental perspective.* Thousand Oaks, CA: Sage.

Aldrich, M. S. (1979). *Sleep medicine.* New York: Oxford University Press.

Almeida, D. M., McGonagle, K. A., Cate, R. C., Kessler, R. C., & Wethington, E. (2003). Psychosocial moderators of emotional reactivity to marital arguments: Results from a daily diary study. *Marriage and Family Review, 34*(1–2), 89–113.

Ancoli-Israel, S., & Roth, T. (1999). Characteristics of insomnia in the United States: Results of the 1991 National Sleep Foundation Survey. *Sleep, 22*(Suppl. 2), S347–S353.

Armstrong, M. W. J., Wallace, C. L., & Marais, J. (1999). The effect of surgery upon the quality of life in snoring patients and their partners: A between-subjects case-controlled trial. *Clinical Otolaryngology, 24,* 510–522.

Ashtyani, H., & Hutter, D. A. (2003). Collateral damage: The effects of obstructive sleep apnea on bed partners. *Chest, 124,* 942–947.

Aubert, V., & White, H. (1959a). Sleep: A sociological interpretation. I. *Acta Sociologica, 4*(2), 46–54.

Aubert, V., & White, H. (1959b). Sleep: A sociological interpretation. II. *Acta Sociologica, 4*(3), 1–16.

Avis, N. E., Stellato, R., Crawford, S., Bromberger, J., Ganz, P., Cain, V., & Kagawa-Singer, M. (2001). Is there a menopausal syndrome? Menopausal status and the symptoms across racial/ethnic groups. *Social Science and Medicine, 52,* 345–356.

Baker, A., Simpson, S., & Dawson, D. (1997). Sleep disruption and mood changes associated with menopause. *Journal of Psychosomatic Research, 43,* 359–369.

Barbe, P. J., Munoz, A., Findley, L., Anto, J. M., & Agusti, A. G. (1998). Automobile accidents in patients with sleep apnea syndrome: An epidemiological and mechanistic study. *American Journal of Respiratory and Critical Care Medicine, 158,* 18–22.

Beninati, W., Harris, C. D., Herold, D. L., & Shepard, J. W. (1999). The effect of snoring and obstructive sleep apnea on the sleep quality of bed partners. *Mayo Clinic Proceedings, 74,* 955–958.

Berger, A. A. (1997). *Bloom's morning: Coffee, comforters, and the secret meaning of everyday life.* Boulder, CO: Westview.

Berger, P. L., & Kellner, H. (1964). Marriage and the construction of reality. *Diogenes, 46,* 1–23.

Bianchi, S. M., Milkie, M. A., Sayer, L. D., & Robinson, J. P. (2000). Is anyone doing the housework? Trends in the gender division of household labor. *Social Forces, 79,* 191–228.

Bliwise, D. L. (1997). Sleep and aging. In M. R. Pressman & W. C. Orr (Eds.), *Understanding sleep: The evaluation and treatment of sleep disorders* (pp. 441–464). Washington, DC: American Psychological Association.

Bonekat, H. W., & Krumpe, P. E. (1990). Diagnosis of obstructive sleep apnea. *Clinical Reviews in Allergy, 8*(2–3), 197–213.

Bootzin, R. R., & Rider, S. P. (1997). Behavioral techniques and biofeedback for insomnia. In M. R. Pressman & W. C. Orr (Eds.), *Understanding sleep: The evaluation and treatment of sleep disorders* (pp. 315–338). Washington, DC: American Psychological Association.

Braudel, F. (1981). *The structures of everyday life: The limits of the possible.* New York: Harper & Row.

Breathe Right (2005). Effect of Breath Right nasal strips on snoring. Retrieved June 1, 2005 from http://www.breatheright.com/snoring/snoring.asp

Broughton, R. J. (1994). Parasomnias. In S. Chokroverty (Ed.), *Sleep disorders medicine: Basic science, technical considerations, and clinical aspects* (pp. 381–399). Boston: Butterworth-Heinemann.

Busch, A. (1999). *Geography of home: Writings on where we live.* New York: Princeton Architectural Press.

Butler, M. H., Gardner, B. C., & Bird, M. H. (1998). Not just a time-out: Change dynamics of prayer for religious couples in conflict situations. *Family Process, 37,* 451–475.

Cankar, K., & Finderle, Z. (2003). Gender differences in cutaneous vascular and autonomic nervous response to local cooling. *Clinical Autonomic Research, 13*(3), 214–220.

Cankar, K., Finderle, Z., & Strucl, M. (2000). Gender differences in cutaneous laser doppler flow response to local direct and contralateral cooling. *Journal of Vascular Research, 37*(3), 183–188.

Chiaramonte, J. A. (1992). And the war goes on. *Social Work, 37*, 469–470.

Chokroverty, S. (1994). An approach to a patient with sleep complaints. In S. Chokroverty (Ed.), *Sleep disorders medicine: Basic science, technical considerations, and clinical aspects* (pp. 181–186). Boston: Butterworth-Heinemann.

Coltrane, S., & Adams, M. (2003). The social construction of the divorce "problem": Morality, child victims, and the politics of gender. *Family Relations, 52*, 363–372.

Cromwell, R. E., Keeney, B. P., & Adams, B. N. (1976). Temporal patterning in the family. *Family Process, 13*, 343–348.

Daly, K. (2003). Family theory versus the theories families live by. *Journal of Marriage and Family, 65*, 771–784.

Dancey, D. R., Hanly, P. J., Soong, C., Lee, B., Shepard, J. Jr., & Hoffstein, V. (2003). Gender differences in sleep apnea: The role of neck circumference. *Chest, 123*, 1544–1550.

DeFrancisco, V. L. (1991). The sounds of silence: How men silence women in marital relations. *Discourse and Society, 2*, 413–423.

Dekker, D. K., Paley, M. J., Popkin, S. M., & Tepas, D. I. (1993). Locomotive engineers and their spouses: Coffee consumption, mood, and sleep reports. *Ergonomics, 36*, 233–238.

Dement, W. C., & Vaughn, C. (1999). *The promise of sleep.* New York: Dell.

Douglas, J. D. (1980). Introduction to the sociologies of everyday life. In J. D. Douglas, P. A. Adler, P. Adler, A. Fontana, C. R. Freeman, & J. A. Kotarba (Eds.), *Introduction to the sociologies of everyday life* (pp. 1–19). Boston: Allyn & Bacon.

Downey, R., III, & Bennett, M. H. (1992). Training subjective insomniacs to accurately perceive sleep onset. *Sleep, 15*, 58–63.

Dunkel, S. (1977). *Sleeping positions: The night language of the body.* New York: Morrow.

Eich, E. (1990). Learning during sleep. In R. R. Bootzin, J. F. Kihlstrom, & D. L. Schachter (Eds.), *Sleep and cognition* (pp. 88–108). Washington, DC: American Psychological Association.

Engleman, H. M., Hirst, W. S., & Douglas, N. J. (1997). Under reporting of sleepiness and driving impairment in patients with sleep apnoea/hypopnoea syndrome. *Journal of Sleep Research, 6*, 272–275.

Ewan, C., Lowy, E., & Reid, J. (1991). "Falling out of culture": The effects of repetition strain injury on sufferers' roles and identity. *Sociology of Health and Illness, 13*, 168–192.

Fanslow, C. A. (1990). Touch and the elderly. In K. E. Barnard & T. B. Brazelton (Eds.), *Touch: The foundation of experience* (pp. 541–557). Madison, CT: International Universities Press.

Fietze, I., & Diefenbach, K. (2003). Healthy sleepers are rare: Problems and success rates in establishing a control group for sleep studies. *Neuropsychopharmacology, 28,* 558–561.

Frisoni, G. B., de Leo, D., Bernardini, M., Dello Buono, M., Rozzini, R., & Trabucchi, M. (1993). Night sleep symptoms in an elderly population and their relation with age, gender, and education. *Clinical Gerontologist, 13,* 51–68.

Gander, P. H., Marshall, N. S., Harris, R. B., & Reid, P. (2005). Sleep, sleepiness and motor vehicle accidents: A national survey. *Australian and New Zealand Journal of Public Health, 29,* 16–21.

Gantz, W. (2001). Conflicts and resolution strategies associated with television in marital life. In J. Bryant & J. A. Bryant (Eds.), *Television and the American family,* 2nd ed. (pp. 289–316). Mahwah, NJ: LEA.

Gleichmann, P. R. (1980). Einige soziale Wandlungen des Schlafens. *Zeitschrift fur Soziologie, 9* (3), 236–250.

Goffman, E. (1959). *The presentation of self in everyday life.* New York: Doubleday Anchor.

Gottlieb, N. H., & Green, L. W. (1984). Life events, social network, life-style, and health: An analysis of the 1979 National Survey of Personal Health Practices and Consequences. *Health Education Quarterly, 11,* 91–105.

Haermae, M., Tenkanen, L., Sjoeblom, T., Alikoski, T., & Heinsalmi, P. (1998). Combined effects of shift work and life-style on the prevalence of insomnia, sleep deprivation and daytime sleepiness. *Scandinavian Journal of Work, Environment and Health, 24,* 300–307.

Hauri, P. (1981). Treating psycho-physiologic insomnia with bio-feedback. *Archives of General Psychiatry, 38,* 752–758.

Hislop, J., & Arber, S. (2003a). Sleepers awake! Nature of sleep disruption among midlife women. *Sociology, 37,* 695–711.

Hislop, J., & Arber, S. (2003b). Understanding women's sleep management: Beyond medicalization-healthicization? *Sociology of Health and Illness, 25,* 815–837.

Horstmann, S., Hess, C. W., Bassetti, C., Gugger, M., & Mathis, J. (2000). Sleepiness-related accidents in sleep apnea patients. *Sleep, 23,* 383–389.

Hur, Y.-M., Bouchard, T. J. Jr., & Lykken, D. T. (1998). Genetic and environmental influence on morningness-eveningness. *Personality and Individual Differences, 25,* 917–925.

Imbernon, E., Warret, G., Roitg, C., Chastang, J.-F., & Goldberg, M. (1993). Effects on health and social well-being of on-call shifts. *Journal of Occupational Medicine, 35,* 1131–1137.

Janson, C., Lindberg, E., Gislason, T., Elmasry, A., & Boman, G. (2001). Insomnia in men: A ten-year prospective population based study. *Sleep, 24,* 425–430.

Johnson, J. E. (1988). Bedtime routines: Do they influence the sleep of elderly women? *Journal of Applied Gerontology, 7,* 97–110.

Katz, F. E. (1999). *Immediacy: How our world confronts us and how we confront our world.* Raleigh, NC: Pentland.

Keogh, E., & Herdenfeldt, M. (2002). Gender, coping and the perception of pain. *Pain, 97*(3), 195–201.

Kuhn, B. R., & Weidinger, D. (2000). Interventions for infant and toddler sleep disturbance: A review. *Child and Family Behavior Therapy, 22*(2), 33–50.

Kunstler, J. H. (1993). *The geography of nowhere: The rise and decline of America's man-made landscape.* New York: Simon & Schuster.

Lange, A., Waterman, D., & Kerkhof, G. (1998). Sleep-wake patterns of partners. *Perceptual and Motor Skills, 86,* 1141–1142.

Larson, J. H., Crane, D. R., & Smith, C. W. (1991). Morning and night couples: The effect of wake and sleep patterns on marital adjustment. *Journal of Marital and Family Therapy, 17,* 53–65.

Leach, M. S., & Braithwaite, D. O. (1996). A binding tie: Supportive communication of family kinkeepers. *Journal of Applied Communication Research, 24,* 200–216.

Lee, K. A. (1992). Self-reported sleep disturbances in employed women. *Sleep, 15,* 493–498.

Lefebvre, H. (1971). *Everyday life in the modern world.* New York: Harper Torchbooks.

Li, R. H.Y., Wing, Y. K., Ho, S. C., & Fong, S.Y.Y. (2002). Gender differences in insomnia: A study in the Hong Kong Chinese population. *Journal of Psychosomatic Research, 53,* 601–609.

Lugaresi, E., Cirignotta, F., & Montagna, P. (1989). Snoring: Pathogenic, clinical and therapeutic aspects. In M. H. Kryger, T. Roth, & W. C. Dement, (Eds.), *Principles and practice of sleep medicine* (pp. 494–500). Philadelphia: Saunders.

Lye, D. N. (1996). Adult child-parent relationships. *Annual Review of Sociology, 22,* 79–102.

Maddock, J. W. (1993). Ecological dialectics: An approach to family theory construction. *Family Science Review, 6,* 137–161.

McArdle, N., Kingshott, R., Engleman, H. M., Mackay, T. W., & Douglas, N. J. (2001). Partners of patients with sleep apnoea/hypopnoea syndrome: Effect of CPAP treatment on sleep quality and quality of life. *Thorax, 56,* 513–518.

McFadyen, T. A., Espie, C. A., McArdle, N., Douglas, N. J., & Engleman, H. M. (2001). Controlled, prospective trial of psychosocial function before and after continuous positive airway pressure therapy. *European Respiratory Journal, 18,* 996–1002.

Melbin, M. (1987). *Night as frontier: Colonizing the world after dark.* New York: Free Press.

Michaelson, P. G., & Mair, E. A. (2004). Popular snore aids: Do they work? *Otolaryngology: Head and Neck Surgery, 130,* 649–658.

Middelkoop, J. A. M., Smilde-van den Doel, D. A., Neven, A. K., Kamphuisen, H. A. C., & Springer, C. P. (1996). Subjective sleep characteristics of 1,485 males and females aged 50–93: Effects of sex and age, and factors related to self-evaluated quality of sleep. *Journals of Gerontology: Series A: Biological Sciences and Medical Sciences, 51A,* M108–M115.

Minuchin, S. (1974). *Families and family therapy.* Cambridge, MA: Harvard University Press.

Mitropoulos, D., Anastasiou, I., Giannopoulou, C., Nikolopoulos, P., Alamanis, C., Zervas, A., & Dimopoulos, C. (2002). Symptomatic benign prostate hyperplasia: Impact on partners' quality of life. *European Urology, 41*(3), 240–244.

Montserrat, J. M., Ferrer, M., Hernandez, L., Farre, R., Vilagut, G., Navajas, D., Badia, J. R., Carrasco, E., DePablo, J., & Ballester, E. (2001). Effectiveness of CPAP treatment in daytime function in sleep apnea syndrome: A randomized controlled study with an optimized placebo. *American Journal of Respiratory and Critical Care Medicine, 164,* 608–613.

MSN.Encarta (2005). Women in the U.S. labor force. Retrieved June 1, 2005 from http://encarta.msn.com/media_46154506/Women_in_the_U_S_Labor_Force.html

Nakata, A., Ikeda, T., Takahashi, M., Haratani, T., Fujioka, Y., Fukui, S., Swanson, N. G., Hojou, M., & Araki, S. (2005). Sleep-related risk of occupational injuries in Japanese small and medium-scale enterprises. *Industrial Health, 43,* 89–97.

National Center for Health Statistics (2005). Prevalence of overweight and obesity among adults in the United States. Retrieved June 1, 2005 from http://www.cdc.gov/nchs/products/pubs/pubd/hestats/3and4/overweight.htm

National Center on Sleep Disorder Research (2000). *Restless legs syndrome: Detection and management in primary care.* Bethesda, MD: National Heart, Lung, and Blood Institute.

National Sleep Foundation (2002). *2002 "Sleep in America" Poll.* Washington, DC: National Sleep Foundation.

National Sleep Foundation (2005). Sleep apnea. Retrieved June 1, 2005 from http://www.sleepfoundation.org

Neubauer, P. R. (2003). *Understanding sleeplessness: Perspectives on insomnia.* Baltimore: Johns Hopkins University Press.

Neylan, T. C., Marmar, C. R., Metzler, T. J., Weiss, D. S., Zatzick, D. F., Delucchi, K. L., Wu, R. M., & Schoenfeld, F. B. (1998). Sleep disturbances in the Vietnam generation: Findings from a nationally representative sample of male Vietnam veterans. *American Journal of Psychiatry, 155,* 929–933.

O'Connor, K. A., Mahowald, M. W., & Ettinger, M. G. (1994). Circadian rhythm disorders. In S. Chokroverty (Ed.), *Sleep disorders medicine: Basic science, technical considerations, and clinical aspects* (pp. 369–379). Boston: Butterworth-Heinemann.

Ohayon, M. M., & Zulley, J. (2001). Correlates of global sleep dissatisfaction in the German population. *Sleep, 24,* 780–787.

Parish, J. M., & Lyng, P. J. (2003). Quality of life in bed partners of patients with obstructive sleep apnea or hypopnea after treatment with continuous positive airway pressure. *Chest, 124,* 942–947.

Pew Research Center for the People and the Press (2005). *Embargoed.* Washington, DC: Pew Research Center for the People and the Press. Retrieved June 1, 2005 from http://people-press.org/reports/pdf/241.pdf

Regestein, Q. R., & Monk, T. H. (1991). Is the poor sleep of shift workers a disorder? *American Journal of Psychiatry, 148,* 1487–1493.

Richardson, F. C., Fowers, B. J., & Guignon, C. B. (1999). *Re-envisioning psychology: Moral dimensions of theory and practice.* San Francisco: Jossey-Bass.

Riedel, B. W. (2000). Sleep hygiene. In K. L. Lichstein & C. M. Morin (Eds.), *Treatment of late life insomnia* (pp. 125–146). Thousand Oaks, CA: Sage.

Robinson, J. P., & Godbey, G. (1997). *Time for life: The surprising ways Americans use their time.* University Park, PA: Pennsylvania State University Press.

Roehrs, T., Hollebeek, E., Drake, C., & Roth, T. (2002). Substance use for insomnia in metropolitan Detroit. *Journal of Psychosomatic Research, 53,* 571–576.

Rosenblatt, P. C. (1974). Behavior in public places: Comparisons of couples accompanied and unaccompanied by children. *Journal of Marriage and the Family, 36,* 750–755.

Rosenblatt, P. C. (1994). *Metaphors of family systems theory: Toward new constructions.* New York: Guilford.

Rosenblatt, P. C. (2000). *Help your marriage survive the death of a child.* Philadelphia: Temple University Press.

Rosenblatt, P. C., & Cleaves, W. T. (1981). Family behavior in public places: Interaction patterns within and across generations. *Merrill-Palmer Quarterly, 27,* 257–269.

Rosenblatt, P. C., & Cunningham, M. R. (1976). Television watching and family tension. *Journal of Marriage and the Family, 38,* 105–111.

Rosenblatt, P. C., & Titus, S. L. (1976). Together and apart in the family. *Humanitas, 12,* 367–379.

Rosenblatt, P. C., & Wright, S. E. (1984). Shadow realities in close relationships. *American Journal of Family Therapy, 12* (2), 45–54.

Rosenthal, C. J. (1985). Kinkeeping in the familial division of labor. *Journal of Marriage and the Family, 47,* 965–974.

Rubin, L. B. (1976). *Worlds of pain: Life in the working class family.* New York: Basic Books.

Sandywell, B. (2004). The myth of everyday life: Toward a heterology of the ordinary. *Cultural Studies, 18,* 160–180.

Schmaling, K. B., & Afari, N. (2000). Couples coping with respiratory illness. In K. B. Schmaling & T. G. Sher (Eds.), *The psychology of couples and illness: Theory, research, and practice* (pp. 71–104). Washington, DC: American Psychological Association.

Schwartz, B. (1970). Notes on the sociology of sleep. *Sociological Quarterly, 11,* 485–499.

Scott, S., Ah-See, K., Richardson, H., & Wilson, J. A. (2003). A comparison of physician and patient perception of the problems of habitual snoring. *Clinical Otolaryngology and Allied Sciences, 28,* 18–21.

Shariq, K. (2005). Sleep centers in the U.S. reach 2,515 in 2004. *Sleep, 28,* 145–146.

Shiomi, T., Arita, A. T., Sasanabe, R., Banno, K., Yamakawa, H., Hasegawa, R., Ozeki, K., Okada, M., & Ito, A. (2002). Falling asleep while driving and automobile accidents among patients with obstructive sleep apnea-hypopnea syndrome. *Psychiatry and Clinical Neuroscience, 56,* 333–334.

Shvartzman, P., Borkan, J. M., Stoliar, L., Peleg, A., Nakar, S., Nir, G., & Tabenkin, H. (2002). Second-hand prostatism: Effects of prostatic symptoms on spouses' quality of life, daily routines and family relationships. *Family Practice, 18,* 610–613.

Sin, D. D., Mayers, I., Man, G. C., & Pawluk, L. (2002). Long-term compliance rates to continuous positive airway pressure in obstructive sleep apnea: A population-based study. *Chest, 121,* 430–435.

Smith, A. P., Maben, A., & Brockman, P. (1993). The effects of caffeine and evening meals on sleep and performance, mood and cardiovascular functioning the following day. *Journal of Psychopharmacology, 7,* 203–206.

Smith, D. E. (1987). *The everyday world as problematic: A feminist sociology.* Boston: North-eastern University Press.

Smith, L., & Folkard, S. (1993). The perceptions and feelings of shiftworkers' partners. *Ergonomics, 36,* 299–305.

Sproule, B. A., Busto, U. E., Buckle, C., Herrmann, N., & Bowles, S. (1999). The use of non-prescription sleep products in the elderly. *International Journal of Geriatric Psychiatry, 14,* 851–857.

Strauss, A., & Corbin, J. (1998). *Basics of qualitative research,* 2nd ed. Newbury Park, CA: Sage.

Strawbridge, W. J., Shema, S. J., & Roberts, R. E. (2004). Impact of spouses' sleep problems on partners. *Sleep, 27,* 527–531.

Strazdins, L., & Broom, D. H. (2004). Acts of love (and work): Gender imbalance in emotional work and women's psychological distress. *Journal of Family Issues, 25,* 365–378.

Taylor, B. (1993). Unconsciousness and society: The sociology of sleep. *International Journal of Politics, Culture and Society, 6,* 463–471.

Tichenor, V. J. (1999). Status and income as gendered resources: The case of marital power. *Journal of Marriage and the Family, 61,* 638–650.

Ulfberg, J., Carter, N., Talback, M., & Edling, C. (1996). Excessive daytime sleepiness at work and subjective work performance in the general population and among heavy snorers and patients with obstructive sleep apnea. *Chest, 110,* 659–663.

Ulfberg, J., Carter, N., Talback, M., & Edling, C. (2000). Adverse health effects among women living with heavy snorers. *Health Care for Women International, 21*(2), 81–90.

Victor, L. D. (1999). Obstructive sleep apnea. *American Family Physician, 60,* 2279–2286.

Voda, A. M. (1982). Menopausal hot flash. In A. M. Voda, M. Dinnerstein, & S. R. O'Donnell (Eds.), *Changing perspectives on menopause* (pp. 136–159). Austin: University of Texas Press.

Walker, A. J. (1996). Couples watching television: Gender, power, and the remote control. *Journal of Marriage and the Family, 58,* 813–823.

Walsh, J. K., Harman, P. G., & Kowall, J. P. (1994). Insomnia. In S. Chokroverty (Ed.), *Sleep disorders medicine: Basic science, technical considerations, and clinical aspects* (pp. 219–239). Boston: Butterworth-Heinemann.

Ware, J. C., McBrayer, R. H., & Scott, J. A. (2000). Influence of sex and age on duration and frequency of sleep apnea events. *Chest, 123,* 165–170.

Ware, J. C., & Morin, C. M. (1997). Sleep in depression and anxiety. In M. R. Pressman & W. C. Orr (Eds.), *Understanding sleep: The evaluation and treatment of sleep disorders* (pp. 483–503). Washington, DC: American Psychological Association.

Weigert, A. J. (1981). *Sociology of everyday life.* New York: Longman.

Wellman, J. J., Bohannon, M., & Vogel, G. W. (1999). Influence of lateral motion transfer on sleep. *Perceptual and Motor Skills, 89,* 209–217.

Whiting, J. W. M. (1964). Effects of climate on certain cultural practices. In W. H. Goodenough (Ed.), *Explorations in cultural anthropology: Essays in honor of George Peter Murdock* (pp. 511–544). New York: McGraw-Hill.

Whiting, J. W. M., & Whiting, B. B. (1975). Aloofness and intimacy of husbands and wives: A cross-cultural study. *Ethos, 3,* 183–207.

Wiedman, J. (1999). *Desperately seeking snoozin': The insomnia cure from awake to zzzzz.* Memphis, TN: Towering Pines Press.

Wiley, N. F. (1994). Marriage and the construction of reality. In G. Handel & G. G. Whitchurch (Eds.), *The psychosocial interior of the family,* 4th ed. (pp. 37–51). New York: Aldine de Gruyter.

Williams, S. J. (2001). Dormant issues? Towards a sociology of sleep. In S. Cunningham-Burley & K. Backett-Milburn (Eds.), *Exploring the body* (pp. 137–160). New York: Palgrave.

Williams, S. J. (2002). Sleep and health: Sociological reflections on the dormant society. *Health, 6,* 173–200.

Wilmer, H.A. (1996).The healing nightmare:War dreams ofVietnam veterans. In D. Barrett (Ed.), *Trauma and dreams* (pp. 85–99). Cambridge, MA: Harvard University Press.

Wilson, K., Stoohs, R. A., Mulrooney, T. F., Johnson, L. J., Guilleminault, C., & Huang, Z. (1999).The snoring spectrum:Acoustic assessment of snoring sound intensity in 1,139 individuals undergoing polysomnography. *Chest, 115,* 762–770.

Wolfson, A. R. (1998). Working with parents on developing efficacious sleep/wake habits for infants and young children. In J. M. Briesmeister & C. E. Shaefer (Eds.), *Handbook of parent training: Parents as co-therapists for children's behavior problems,* 2nd ed. (pp. 347–383). New York: Wiley.

Yeung, W. J., Sandberg, J. F., Davis-Kean, P. E., & Hofferth, S. L. (2001). Children's time with fathers in intact families. *Journal of Marriage and the Family, 63,* 136–154.

NAME INDEX

Adams, B. N., 42, 44
Adams, M., 175
Afari, N., 148
Ah-See, K., 3
Akerstedt, T., 113, 123, 126, 168
Aldous, J., 14
Aldrich, M. S., 3, 113, 136, 137, 154, 155, 183
Almeida, D. M., 103
Ancoli-Israel, S., 113
Arber, S., 5, 22, 113, 114, 153, 170, 174, 190, 193
Armstrong, M. W. J., 3, 147, 153
Ashtyani, H., 154
Aubert, V., 4, 14, 15, 59
Avis, N. E., 71

Baker, A., 114
Barbe, P. J., 155
Beninati, W., 3, 154
Bennett, M. H., 193
Berger, A. A., 1, 2, 3, 23
Berger, P. L., 11
Bianchi, S. M., 28, 29, 79
Bird, M. H., 63
Bliwise, D. L., 194
Bohannon, M., 134
Bonekat, H. W., 3, 154
Bootzin, R. R., 193
Bouchard, T. J., Jr., 41
Braithwaite, D. O., 79

Braudel, F., 1, 3
Breathe Right, 152
Brockman, P., 119
Broom, D. H., 79
Broughton, R. J., 139, 140
Busch, A., 26
Butler, M. H., 63

Cankar, K., 65
Carter, N., 3, 147, 155
Chiaramonte, J. A., 141
Chokroverty, S., 3
Cirignotta, F., 148, 149, 151
Cleaves, W. T., 81
Coltrane, S., 175
Corbin, J., 6
Crane, D. R., 42
Cromwell, R. E., 42, 44
Cunningham, M. R., 54

Daly, K., 4
Dancey, D. R., 154
Davis-Kean, P. E., 79
Dawson, D., 114
DeFrancisco, V. L., 79
Dekker, D. K., 119, 180
Dement, W. C., 194
Diefenbach, K., 6
Douglas, J. D., 2, 3
Douglas, N. J., 155, 156
Downey, R., 193

Drake, C., 120
Dunkel, S., 2

Edling, C., 3, 147, 155
Eich, E., 21
Engleman, H. M., 155, 156
Ettinger, M. G., 183
Ewan, C., 105

Fanslow, C. A., 81
Fietze, I., 6
Finderle, Z., 65
Folkard, S., 123
Fong, S.Y.Y., 113, 119
Fowers, B. J., 8
Fredlund, P., 113, 123
Frisoni, G. B., 113

Gander, P. H., 113
Gantz, W., 53, 54
Gardner, B. C., 63
Gillberg, M., 113, 123
Gleichmann, P. R., 4
Godbey, G., 9, 51
Goffman, E., 8, 29, 198
Gottlieb, N. H., 114
Green, L.W., 114
Guignon, C. B., 8

Haermae, M., 119, 123
Harman, P. G., 4
Harris, C. D., 3, 154
Harris, R. B., 113
Hauri, P., 193
Herdenfeldt, M., 65
Herold, D. L., 3, 154
Hirst, W. S., 155, 156
Hislop, J., 5, 22, 113, 114, 153, 170, 174,
     190, 193
Ho, S. C., 113, 119
Hofferth, S. L., 79
Hollebeek, E., 120
Horstmann, S., 155, 159

Hur, Y.-M., 41
Hutter, D. A., 154

Imbernon, E., 125

Janson, C., 119
Jansson, B., 113, 123
Johnson, J. E., 194

Katz, F. E., 159
Keeney, B. P., 42
Kellner, H., 11
Keogh, E., 65
Kerkhof, G., 42
Knutsson, A., 123, 126, 168
Kowall, J. P., 4
Krumpe, P. E., 3, 154
Kuhn, B. R., 194
Kunstler, J. H., 51

Lange, A., 42
Larson, J. H., 42
Leach, M. S., 79
Lee, K. A., 123
Lefebvre, H., 2
Li, R. H.Y., 113, 119
Lowy, E., 105
Lugaresi, E., 148, 149, 151
Lye, D. N., 79
Lykken, D.T., 41
Lyng, P. J., 3, 158, 159

Maben, A., 119
Maddock, J.W., 8
Mahowald, M.W., 183
Mair, E. A., 152
Man, G. C., 158
Marais, J., 3, 147, 153
Marshall, N. S., 113
Mayers, I., 158
McArdle, N., 159
McBrayer, R. H., 159
McFadyen, T. A., 159

Melbin, M., 123
Michaelson, P. G., 152
Middelkoop, J. A. M., 113
Milkie, M. A., 28, 29, 79
Minuchin, S., 8
Mitropoulos, D., 3
Monk, T. H., 123
Montagna, P., 148, 149, 151
Montserrat, J. M., 158
Morin, C. M., 113
MSN.Encarta, 11

Nakata, A., 113
National Center for Health Statistics, 26
National Center on Sleep Disorder
    Research, 136
National Sleep Foundation, 148, 154
Neubauer, P. R., 113, 114
Neylan, T. C., 141

O'Connor, K. A., 183
Ohayon, M. M., 113

Paley, M. J., 119, 180
Parish, J. M., 3, 158, 159
Pawluk, L., 158
Pew Research Center for the People and
    the Press, 11
Popkin, S. M., 119, 180

Regestein, Q. R., 123
Reid, J., 105
Reid, P., 113
Richardson, F. C., 8
Richardson, H., 3
Rider, S. P., 193
Riedel, B. W., 119
Roberts, R. E., 190
Robinson, J. P., 9, 28, 29, 51, 79
Roehrs, T., 120
Rosenblatt, P. C., 8, 11, 14, 39, 42, 54,
    81
Rosenthal, C. J., 79

Roth, T., 113, 120
Rubin, L. B., 29, 103

Sandberg, J. F., 79
Sandywell, B., 1
Sayer, L. D., 28, 29, 79
Schmaling, K. B., 148
Schwartz, B., 4, 14, 198
Scott, J. A., 154
Scott, S., 3
Shariq, K., 157
Shema, S. J., 190
Shepard, J. W., 3, 154
Shiomi, T., 155
Shvartzman, P., 3, 132
Simpson, S., 114
Sin, D. D., 158
Smith, A. P., 119
Smith, C. W., 42
Smith, D. E., 3
Smith, L., 123
Sproule, B. A., 120
Strauss, A., 6
Strawbridge, W. J., 190
Strazdins, L., 79
Strucl, M., 65

Talback, M., 3, 147, 155
Taylor, B., 5
Tepas, D. I., 119, 180
Tichenor, V. J., 80
Titus, S. L., 39, 42

Ulfberg, J., 3, 147, 155

Vaughn, C., 194
Victor, L. D., 154
Voda, A. M., 71
Vogel, G. W., 134

Walker, A. J., 63
Wallace, C. L., 3, 147, 153
Walsh, J. K., 3

Ware, J. C., 113, 154
Waterman, D., 42
Weidinger, D., 194
Weigert, A. J., 2
Wellman, J. J., 134
White, H., 4, 14, 15, 59
Whiting, B. B., 35, 65
Whiting, J. W. M., 35, 65
Wiedman, J., 194
Wiley, N. F., 11, 198

Williams, S. J., 5
Wilmer, H. A., 141
Wilson, J. A., 3
Wilson, K., 147, 148
Wing, Y. K., 113, 119
Wolfson, A. R., 194
Wright, S. E., 11

Yeung, W. J., 79

Zulley, J., 113

SUBJECT INDEX

age, 5, 7, 26, 145–146, 194–195,
    201–202. *See also* menopause
alcohol, 100, 119, 136–137, 149
anger, 93–104, 151
apnea, 106, 147, 153–159

backstage regions of couple life, 8, 19,
    198
bathroom, 19, 22, 33, 131–133, 177, 179
bed, 25–36, 60–61, 134–135
    clothing, 45–47, 66, 69, 70, 167
    making, 29–30, 74–75, 125
    sides, 31–35, 165–166
    size, 25–26, 137
    territory, 15, 17, 26–28
    uses, 30–31
bedding, 15, 66, 71–75, 133–134
    choice of, 28–31
    tucking in, 30, 73
bedroom
    doors, 32–33, 34, 62
    windows, 67–68, 118
bedtime, 37–48, 123–125, 128
    bedtime security check of house,
        38–39
    partners going to bed at different
        times, 39–45, 58–59, 72–73,
        82–83, 123–125, 150
blankets. *See* bedding
body size, 30, 74, 85–86, 148–149, 163,
    191

caffeine, 41, 119, 177, 180
children, 34, 46–47, 60–62, 78–79, 124,
    127–130, 140–141, 168, 170, 180
    grandchildren, 124, 129–130, 140
cold bodies, hands, or feet. *See* feet
colds, 109, 149–150
couple
    names, ages, years together, 201–202
    system, 1, 3–4, 8, 9–11, 13–23, 35–36,
        47–48, 62–64, 75, 92, 104, 112,
        121, 130, 146, 159, 175, 182, 187,
        189–195
    time together, 9–11. *See also* together-
        ness and apartness
covers. *See* bedding
culture, 83, 170, 197

data analysis, 6–7
death, 2, 88–89
depression, 90–92, 108
diabetes, 107–108
dreams, 2, 138. *See also* nightmares

empty nest, 62
everyday life, 1–3, 189–198

family background, 83–84
family development theory, 14
family systems theory, 11, 14, 192. *See
    also* couple system
family theory, 4

feet, 30, 66, 68–70
first sleeping together, 14–23, 40, 42–43, 57
flu, 109

gender, 5, 11, 28–31, 33–34, 38–39, 50–51, 59, 65–67, 71, 79–81, 85, 86, 89–90, 95, 99, 102–104, 113–114, 162–165, 191
grandparents, 15
grief, 88–89, 90
grinding teeth, 139–140
grounded theory, 6–7

health, 34, 105–112, 132, 147–159, 179, 182. *See also* illness, injury
heart disease, 107, 143–144, 156–157
heavy sleepers, 116–118

illness, 106–109, 132, 179. *See also* health
injury, 13–14, 109–112
    injury by partner, 134, 135, 138
insomnia. *See* sleeplessness
intimacy, 74, 170–173

kissing. *See* touching

learning to sleep together, 13–23, 192–193
learning while asleep, 21
lesbian couples, 5, 81, 96, 130
light sleepers, 116–118

meaning, 2–3, 74, 194
menopause, 65, 71, 114
migraines, 106–107
morning people and night people, 41–45

napping, 31, 186
nightmares, 128–129, 140–146, 161–162

observing a bed partner sleep, 8–9, 148, 154
on call, 125, 191

pillows. *See* bedding
prayer, 2, 49–51, 181–182
previous bed-sharing relationships, 7, 15–16, 52
protection from danger, 33, 161–165, 191

reading in bed, 55–57
religion, 2, 49–51
research methods, 5–8, 199–202
restless legs, 136–137
retirement, 39
roles, 4, 5, 14
rules, 4–5, 14, 15, 97–101
routines, 1, 2, 20, 22–23, 29, 37–47, 49, 77–92, 127, 157, 165, 166, 167, 174, 177–182, 193–194

safety. *See* protection from danger
season, 68, 71
sex, 2, 40, 42, 52, 57–62, 82, 86, 102
shift work, 123–125
siblings, 15–16, 32
sleep
    apnea, 106, 147, 153–159
    couple versus individual perspective, 1, 3–5, 58, 189–190
    learning to sleep together, 13–23
    learning while asleep, 21
    medications, 119–121
    self-help books about, 4
    sleeping apart, 58, 93–94, 135, 153, 161–175
    walking, 138–139
sleeplessness, 113–121, 145
snoring, 118, 141, 147–154
snuggling. *See* touching
sweat, 71, 86
systems theory, 8, 198. *See also* couple system, family systems theory

talking, 11, 53–54, 101, 165, 177–182
    in bed, 53–54, 77–81, 90–92, 96, 97, 115, 142–145, 151–152
    in sleep, 137–139, 142

teaching one's partner what one needs
and wants, 17–18, 85–86
television, 11, 22, 51–55, 146, 168, 177, 191
temperature, 35, 48, 65–75, 118
thermostat, 66–67, 118, 125
togetherness and apartness, 9–11, 39–40,
178. *See also* couple time together
tossing and turning, 118, 133–136
touching, 15, 41, 77, 81–92, 93, 180

wakefulness. *See* sleeplessness
waking up in the morning, 4–5, 34, 98,
116, 177–182
war veterans, 141–142, 144
weather. *See* seasons
weekends, 124, 183–187
weight. *See* body size
work, 11, 110–112, 114, 115, 123–127,
165, 190, 191, 192